2006 Edition
Tourism Market Trends

Middle East

D1404609

World Tourism Organization
Capitán Haya 42, 28020 Madrid, Spain
Tel: (+34) 915678100; Fax: (+34) 915713733
E-mail: omt@unwto.org
Web: www.unwto.org

Copyright © 2007 World Tourism Organization
Calle Capitán Haya, 42
28020 Madrid, Spain

Tourism Market Trends: Middle-East
ISBN-13: 978-92-844-1220-4

Published and printed by the World Tourism Organization, Madrid, Spain
First printing in July 2007
All rights reserved

World Tourism Organization
Calle Capitán Haya, 42
28020 Madrid, Spain
Tel.: (+34) 915 678 100
Fax: (+34) 915 713 733
Website: www.unwto.org
Email: omt@unwto.org

Foreword

This report has been prepared by the World Tourism Organization's (UNWTO's) Market Trends, Trade and Competitiveness Section. Chapters I and II, Highlights and Quantitative Analysis of Tourism Performance, were drafted by members of The Travel Business Partnership, led by UNWTO Consultant Nancy Cockerell. UNWTO's Regional Representation for the Middle East also made a valuable contribution, as did the organization's Panel of Experts from the Middle East, which monitors tourism trends and developments on a regular basis for the three times yearly *UNWTO World Tourism Barometer*.

Except where otherwise indicated, the data presented was gathered by the UNWTO Secretariat from the official institutions of the respective countries and territories. Quantitative data has been supplied by National Tourism Administrations (NTAs), National Tourism Organizations (NTOs), statistical offices, national banks and international organizations.

UNWTO wishes to express its sincere gratitude to all those who have participated in the elaboration of this report for their valuable cooperation, in particular to the organizations and individuals involved from the different countries and territories. It welcomes the active involvement of all countries, as well as their comments and suggestions on the design and contents of this series.

Explanation of symbols and conventions used

*	=	provisional figure or data
..	=	figure or data not (yet) available
0	=	rounded figure where the original figure is lower than 0.5 (-0 when rounding a negative figure)
0.0	=	rounded figure where the original figure is lower than 0.05 (-0.0 when rounding a negative figure)

|	≐	change of series
(000)	=	thousand
mn	=	million (1,000,000)
bn	=	billion (1,000,000,000)

Due to rounding, some totals may not correspond exactly with the sum of the separate figures.

Table of Contents

The *Tourism Market Trends, 2006 Edition* series

Tourism Market Trends is one of UNWTO's regular series of reports, the objective of which is to present international tourism trends worldwide, as well as in each region, subregion and individual destination country. The full series, which was launched in 2001, comprises six volumes. The first, *World Overview & Tourism Topics*, provides an overview of global tourism trends, and the five regional volumes highlight international tourism trends in each of the UNWTO world regions – Africa, the Americas, Asia and the Pacific, Europe and the Middle East (including North Africa).

Some changes have been made to the structure of the *Tourism Market Trends* series. Each regional volume now includes the following:

- Section I, Highlights, provides a summary of key trends and developments in tourism in the region, stressing the main factors influencing trends in 2005.

- Section II, Quantitative Analysis of Tourism Performance, includes a more in-depth assessment of trends in the region and its subregions, in terms of international tourist arrivals and international tourism receipts, as well as a breakdown of inbound tourism by region of origin, transport mode and purpose of visit. Statistical trends in outbound tourism are also presented, including data on international tourism expenditure, volume of trips abroad and outbound flows by region of origin/destination.

- Section III, Statistical Trends by Destination Country, comprises detailed statistical results for the individual countries and/or territories of the region. For each country the following information is included (to the extent that data is available):

    - A summary table including the following data series:

        - International arrivals: different categories of inbound tourism;
        - Tourism accommodation: room capacity and number of nights (for inbound and domestic tourism);
        - Trips abroad (outbound tourism);
        - International tourism receipts and expenditure;
        - Various economic and general indicators.

    - Detailed tables on arrivals and nights broken down by country of origin/source market.

- Each of the six volumes concludes with an annex comprising detailed tables containing the latest yearly data on international tourist arrivals and international tourism receipts (in US dollars and in euros) for all countries worldwide for which data is available. Information is also provided on methodologies, concepts and definitions, as well as on sources of the data and other information.

Care should be taken in interpreting the data presented in these reports. In particular, the following should be noted:

- In accordance with the nature of the data provided by the countries and territories, the focus is on inbound tourism. Outbound tourism trends are largely derived from the same inbound-oriented data except for countries that monitor outbound departures.

- The main focus of the analysis, and corresponding tables, is on medium-term rather than on short-term trends and developments. For short-term trends, please refer to the *UNWTO World Tourism Barometer*, which is published three times a year (in January,

June and October). Each issue contains three regular sections: an overview of short-term tourism data from destination and generating countries and air transport; the results of the latest survey among the UNWTO Panel of Tourism Experts, providing an evaluation of and prospects for short-term tourism performance; and selected economic data relevant for tourism. (For further information, refer to the annex or to UNWTO's website at <www.unwto.org/facts/menu.html>).

- The reports generally reflect the data collected by the UNWTO Secretariat for the current edition. However, data is often still provisional and may be updated or revised by the reporting countries at a later stage without further notice. When making references to the data contained in the reports, it is therefore advisable to ensure that the statistics quoted are the most up to date available

- For the world and (sub)regional aggregates (totals, subtotals), estimates are included to make allowance for those countries and territories that do not yet have final full-year data, or which have estimated full-year results. The data presented for the individual countries, however, reflects what has been reported for each country and does not include estimates made by the UNWTO Secretariat.

- The UNWTO Secretariat is aware of the limitations of tourism data. Despite considerable progress made in recent years, statistics are rarely uniform since definitions and data collection methodologies tend to differ from one country to another. This means that the international comparability of statistical data still leaves a lot to be desired.

I

Highlights:
Middle East & North Africa

I   Highlights: Middle East and North Africa Summary of Key Trends and Developments

I.1   The Region in the Context of World Tourism

Terrorism, natural disasters, health scares, oil price rises, exchange rate fluctuations and economic and political uncertainties – these were just some of the issues facing the tourism industry in 2005. Yet international tourist arrivals worldwide beat all expectations, reaching 802 million and, at the same time, achieving an all-time record. The estimated increase reflects a staggering 40 million additional arrivals – of which more than 16 million in Europe, 11 million in Asia and the Pacific, 7.5 million in the Americas, 3 million in Africa and 2 million in the Middle East.

The 2005 total of 802 million arrivals represents an increase of more than 5% worldwide – a consolidation of the bumper growth achieved in 2004 (+10%). Although world tourism growth was much more moderate in 2005, it was still more than one percentage point above the long-term average annual growth rate of 4%.

Results by region show that Europe recorded the weakest growth in percentage terms (+4%) although, as already stated, this translated into a higher volume of arrivals. Africa registered the strongest arrivals growth (+9%), ahead of Asia and the Pacific (+8%), the Middle East (+6%) and the Americas (+6%).

Worldwide, international tourism receipts totalled some US$ 676 billion in 2005, up US$ 47 billion in absolute terms. Most regions and subregions shared in the increase. Europe gained an additional US$ 20 billion, raising receipts to just US$ 349 billion – 52% of the world total. The Americas improved results by US$ 12 billion to US$ 145 billion – a 21% share – and Asia and the Pacific added US$ 11 billion, taking the regional total to US$ 134 billion, or a 20% share.

Estimates based on available data for the respective regions point to an increase of US$ 3 billion to US$ 22 billion for Africa and a rise of US$ 1 billion to US$ 26 billion for the Middle East, representing 3% and 4% of the world total respectively.

Inbound leaders

No country in the Middle East and North Africa ranked among the world's top ten tourism destinations in 2005. Egypt and Saudi Arabia both ranked among the top 30, however, with arrivals of over 8 million each. These two are followed by the United Arab Emirates (UAE), Tunisia, Morocco, Bahrain, Syria and Jordan. However, in terms of receipts, Lebanon is ranked second only to Egypt, followed by Saudi Arabia.

Outbound leaders

In terms of international tourism expenditure, the UAE is the most important outbound market in the Middle East and North Africa. Its spending of over US$ 5 billion a year places it in 26th position worldwide, followed closely by Kuwait, Saudi Arabia and Lebanon.

I.2 Overall Performance

International Tourist Arrivals and Tourism Receipts

Middle East

From 1990-2005 the Middle East generally led the world's regions in terms of growth in inbound tourism, with an average increase in arrivals of over 10% a year, outperforming even Asia and the Pacific (+7%). Its share of world arrivals increased from 2.2% in 1990 to 3.6% in 2000 and 4.7% in 2005.

Arrivals increased by 23% in 2004 and 6% in 2005 to over 38 million. International tourism receipts as expressed in local currencies at costant prices in the region increased by 25% in 2004 to US$ 26 billion. These were very substantial increases in view of the serious political conflicts, including the wars in Iraq and Israel/Palestine, and the threats of terrorist attacks that afflicted the region.

The growth of the region's tourism in recent years can largely be attributed to the efforts of many of the governments in the region to diversify their (largely) oil-based economies into tourism. Improved product development, enhanced funding for tourism and an increase in marketing and promotions have all facilitated the task and helped to secure good returns on investment.

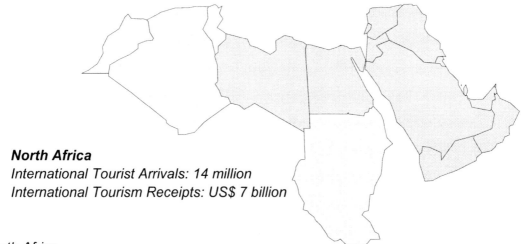

Middle East
International Tourist Arrivals: 38 million
International Tourism Receipts: US$ 26 billion

North Africa
International Tourist Arrivals: 14 million
International Tourism Receipts: US$ 7 billion

North Africa

Due its proximity and interrelation, North Africa is frequently linked to the Middle East and is perceived as part of the wider Middle East/North Africa area. Like the Middle East, North Africa also made substantial progress in 2004-2005. Arrivals increased by 15% in 2004 and 9% in 2005 to 14 million – a welcome improvement on the very modest increases obtained in the 1990s (averaging only 2% a year). International tourism receipts rose by 13% in 2004 and by 15% in 2005 (in local currencies, constant prices) to US$ 7 billion, reflecting the continued success of Tunisia and Morocco in establishing themselves as tourism destinations.

Generating Markets

International arrivals in Middle East destinations are fairly evenly balanced between those originating within the region and those coming from further afield. This is unusual among the world's regions: usually, intraregional arrivals greatly outnumber interregional arrivals.

Of the 38 million arrivals in Middle East destinations in 2005, 46% came from countries within the region, 48% from other regions, and 6% were of unspecified origin. A notable complement of the increased tension since 2001 has been the interest generated within the Middle East in travel to local destinations – an interest supported by the increased spending power associated with rising international oil prices. In spite of those tensions, however, interregional arrivals – and even arrivals from the Americas – continued to grow from 2000-2005 (+6% a year on average).

Overall, intraregional arrivals in the Middle East increased by an average of 12% a year from 2000-2005, while interregional arrivals increased by 8% annually. In 2005, intraregional arrivals rose 12%, but arrivals from other regions slipped by 1%. Those from Africa and from Asia and the Pacific were down 10-11%, but those from Europe and the Americas continued to grow.

The pattern in North Africa does not fit conveniently into the conventional breakdown. Only 10% of arrivals come from Africa and only 20% from Africa and the Middle East. But most of Europe is no further from North Africa than the rest of Africa and the Middle East, and Europe accounts for nearly 50% of all arrivals in North Africa. Arrivals from Europe in North Africa continued to grow rapidly in 2000-2005, but there was also remarkable growth in arrivals from the Middle East and from neighbouring countries.

I.3   Main Factors Influencing Tourism in 2005

Geopolitical situation

2005 was yet another year marred by regional conflicts and the threat, and sometimes sadly the reality, of terrorist attacks. Although generally, worldwide, tourists seem to have learnt to live with the risks, there is a perception that the threats are more serious in the Middle East. Such fears are by no means universal, but it would be idle to deny that they have been a factor in discouraging or diverting some tourists. This has been both an advantage and a disadvantage to the local tourism industries. Some nationals from the region, for instance, have felt happier to choose destinations within the region, while some tourists from the Americas, Europe and Asia Pacific have stayed away.

As for the reality of the conflicts and terrorist attacks, the situations in Iraq and Palestine not only keep them virtually closed to tourists, but make things very difficult for the tourism industries in neighbouring countries. Elsewhere, there were isolated terrorist incidents in Egypt, Lebanon, Jordan and Turkey, but the effects of these attacks on tourist flows have generally been limited and short-lived. Generally, the situation across most of North Africa is much more relaxed than it was even ten years ago, and the Gulf Cooperation Council (GCC) countries – ie the countries of the Arabian Peninsula – have remained largely immune to the strife further north.

Economic situation

The world was very prosperous in 2004-2005, with real GDP growing faster than at any time in nearly a quarter of a century. According to the International Monetary Fund (IMF), world GDP grew in real terms by 4.8% in 2005, almost as fast as in 2004, and is set to turn in another positive performance in 2006. Real GDP increased by about 6% a year in the GCC countries and 5% a year in North Africa in 2004-2005.

This growth has been associated with very high international prices for hydrocarbons (oil prices averaged about US$60 per barrel in 2005, or three times their level in 2003). This has brought great prosperity to almost all the countries of the Middle East and North Africa – the few that are not major oil or gas producers themselves are still sharing in the prosperity. Over and above the increase in real GDP, the increases in oil revenues are financing large increases in investments – including investments in local tourism industries, notably in Egypt and the UAE – and in consumer spending (including spending on international tourism).

Exchange rates

Most currencies in the region are tied, or loosely linked, to the US dollar. And the US dollar fell sharply against the euro in 2004 and remained weak in 2005. This has helped the local tourism industries to remain price-competitive, in spite of the inflationary pressures induced by boom conditions in their economies.

More precisely, 2005 saw a gradual (re)appreciation of the US dollar against major currencies from its low at the end of 2004. While the dollar bought only 75 euro cents in December 2004, in December 2005 it bought 84 euro cents. However, with the downward trend during 2004 and the upward trend in 2005, the average rate for the full years 2004 and 2005 was the same in both years (US$1.00 = 0.80 euros).

Air transport

One very important factor in the growth of tourism in the Arabian Peninsula and North Africa has been the opening up of air transport regulatory regimes (e.g. in Egypt, Morocco and Lebanon), investments in airports (e.g. in Egypt and throughout the GCC countries), the rapid growth of existing airlines and the launch of new ones – both traditional flag carriers and low-cost carriers (LCCs).

Some of the GCC countries' national carriers are among the world's fastest growing airlines. They include Dubai's Emirates, Abu Dhabi's new Etihad Airways, Bahrain-based Gulf Air, and Qatar's Qatar Airways. New LCCs launched in the Middle East in 2004 and 2005 include Air Arabia (UAE), Al-Jazeera Airways (Kuwait) and MenaJet (Lebanon).

II

Quantitative Analysis of Tourism Performance

II Quantitative Analysis of Tourism Performance

II.1 Tourism Trends in the Middle East

II.1.1 Inbound Tourism

International tourist arrivals

In 2005, international tourist arrivals in the Middle East increased by 6%, or just one percentage point above the world average. This was unusual: for the last 15 years, arrivals in the Middle East have been consistently rising much faster (by an average of 9-10% a year) than those worldwide (which increased by just 3-4% a year). However, too much should not be read into the slower growth in 2005, since it followed an exceptional 23% increase in 2004, and since the individual destinations in such a turbulent region reported widely varying results in 2004 and 2005. Total arrivals in the region (38 million) represented 5% of the world total, up from 4% in 2000 and 2% in 1990.

In spite of the enduring impact of 9/11, of the tensions between Palestine and Israel, and of the ongoing conflict in Iraq, the overall growth of tourism in the region was not seriously affected during the difficult and catastrophe-strewn years for world tourism between 2000 and 2004, when world arrivals grew by an average of less than 3% a year. Arrivals in the Middle East continued to grow by more than 10% a year. Therefore, while the industry worldwide was continuing to 'catch up' in 2005, the growth in the Middle East represented an increase on base figures which were already strong.

Middle East: Inbound tourism

International Tourist Arrivals (million)

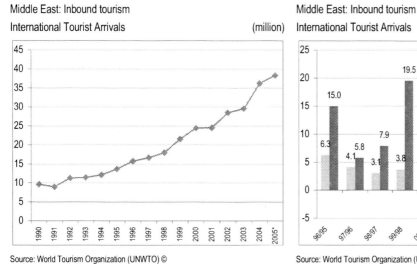

Source: World Tourism Organization (UNWTO) ©

Middle East: Inbound tourism

International Tourist Arrivals (change over previous year, %)

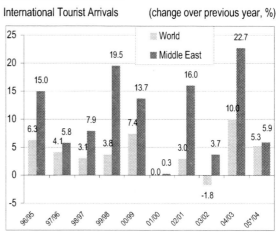

Source: World Tourism Organization (UNWTO) ©

International Tourist Arrivals by (Sub)region

| | International Tourist Arrivals | | | | | | | | Market share | | Growth rate | | Average annual growth (%) | |
| | | | | | | | | (million) | (%) | | | (%) | | |
	1990	1995	2000	2001	2002	2003	2004	2005*	2000	2005*	04/03	05*/04	90-00	00-05*
World	438.4	538.5	684.7	684.4	704.7	692.2	761.4	801.6	100	100	10.0	5.3	4.6	3.2
Middle East	*9.6*	*13.7*	*24.5*	*24.5*	*28.4*	*29.5*	*36.2*	*38.4*	*3.6*	*4.8*	*22.7*	*5.9*	*9.8*	*9.4*

Source: World Tourism Organization (UNWTO) ©   (Data as collected by UNWTO for TMT 2006 Edition)

Travel to the Middle East is fairly heavily concentrated in three major destinations which represent nearly two thirds of all arrivals in the region: Egypt, Saudi Arabia and the United Arab Emirates (UAE), the two firstl of which receive about 8 million tourists a year while the UAE reports a volume of 6 million in 2003. Other destinations receiving 3 million arrivals a year or more include Bahrain, the Syrian Arab Republic and Jordan. Lebanon and Oman (2004 data) attract more than 1 million each.

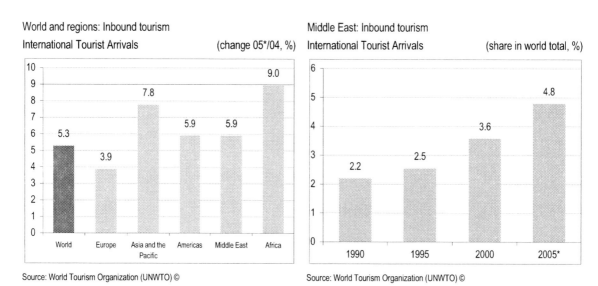

World and regions: Inbound tourism
International Tourist Arrivals   (change 05*/04, %)

Middle East: Inbound tourism
International Tourist Arrivals   (share in world total, %)

Source: World Tourism Organization (UNWTO) ©   Source: World Tourism Organization (UNWTO) ©

In 2004, most destinations in the region recorded large increases in tourist arrivals, in the range of +5% to +77%. In 2005, those that have so far posted their results – and there are several that have not – all reported much smaller increases (with the one exception of Palestine, whose numbers are still tiny). However, the circumstances and results of the individual markets vary so widely that generalizations are not very meaningful.

Egypt overtook Saudi Arabia to become the most important destination in the Middle East in 2005, thanks to an increase of 6%. This followed a 36% rise in 2004, which was so far above the average in recent years of around 10% that a further 6% increase in 2005 can scarcely be regarded as disappointing. The attractiveness of Egypt as a leisure destination for both Westerners (primarily Europeans) and Arabs has not seriously been jeopardized by the terrorist attacks in Sinai in October 2004 and July 2005, although there was a one third decline in arrivals from Israel in 2005. There were also some large variations in arrivals from other individual markets, including a 53% increase from the UK and a 19% decline from Italy – which meant that the UK overtook Italy to become Egypt's second most important market, behind Germany. Egypt continued to benefit, like other sun & sea destinations, from the strength of the euro and sterling – although the Egyptian pound rose against the US dollar, the euro and sterling in 2005.

International Tourist Arrivals by Country of Destination

	Series	International Tourist Arrivals (1000)						Market share in the region (%)			Change (%)		Average annual growth (%)	
		1990	1995	2000	2003	2004	2005*	1990	2000	2005*	04/03	05*/04	90-00	00-05*
Middle East		*9,630*	*13,704*	*24,451*	*29,509*	*36,220*	*38,358*	*100*	*100*	*100*	*22.7*	*5.9*	*9.8*	*9.4*
Bahrain	TF	1,376	1,396	2,420	2,955	3,514	3,914	14.3	9.9	10.2	18.9	11.4	5.8	10.1
Egypt	TF	2,411	2,871	5,116	5,746	7,795	8,244	25.0	20.9	21.5	35.7	5.8	7.8	10.0
Iraq	VF	748	61	78	..	..	..	7.8	0.3				-20.2	
Jordan	TF	572	1,075	1,580	2,353	2,853	2,987	5.9	6.5	7.8	21.2	4.7	10.7	13.6
Kuwait	THS	15	72	78	94	91	..	0.2	0.3		-3.2		17.9	
Lebanon	TF	..	450	742	1,016	1,278	1,140		3.0	3.0	25.9	-10.9		9.0
Libyan Arab Jamahiriya	TF	96	56	174	142	149	..	1.0	0.7		4.9		6.1	
Oman	THS/TF	149	279	571	1,039	1,195	..	1.5	2.3		15.0		14.4	
Palestine	THS	..	..	310	37	56	88		1.3	0.2	51.4	57.1		-22.3
Qatar	TF	136	309	378	557	732	913	1.4	1.5	2.4	31.5	24.6	10.8	19.3
Saudi Arabia	TF	2,209	3,325	6,585	7,332	8,599	8,037	22.9	26.9	21.0	17.3	-6.5	11.5	4.1
Syrian Arab Republic	TCE/TF	562	815	1,685	2,085	3,033	3,368	5.8	6.9	8.8	45.5	11.0	11.6	14.9
Untd Arab Emirates	THS	973	2,315	3,907	5,871	..	..	10.1	16.0				14.9	
Yemen	THS	52	61	73	155	274	336	0.5	0.3	0.9	77.0	22.8	3.5	35.7

Source: World Tourism Organization (UNWTO) ©   (Data as collected by UNWTO for TMT 2006 Edition)

Saudi Arabia, usually the most important destination in the Middle East, registered 8 million arrivals in 2005, 6.5% fewer than in 2004. Most of these, of course, were Muslim pilgrims visiting the holy shrines in Makkah and Madinah. Saudi Arabia also reported a decline in international tourism receipts, of 20% to US$ 5.2 billion.

Unfortunately recent arrivals figures are not available for the United Arab Emirates (UAE) which, according to anecdotal information and hotel statistics for the main cities – Dubai and Abu Dhabi – is one of the most dynamic destination in the region. Dubai, which lacks significant petroleum resources of its own, is emerging as an extraordinarily successful leisure, business and MICE destination, with a wide range of extravagantly conceived and generously financed attractions and resorts, including vast new shopping malls and theme parks designed to attract all types of visitors, including couples and families. Abu Dhabi, whose economy is more directly based on its vast oil reserves, has nevertheless been keen to diversify into tourism in recent years, and is making the appropriate heavy investments. This is illustrated by its US$ 6.8 billion planned investment in its new airport and its support for Etihad Airways as a flag carrier in competition with Dubai-based Emirates.

Dubai's eclectic appeal is reflected in the fact that about a third of its tourists come from the Middle East, a third from Europe and a third from the rest of the world. (Most other significant destinations in the region depend heavily on visitors from either the Middle East or Europe.) Bahrain, which like Dubai is an important local trading centre and entrepôt, depends much more heavily on its role as an offshore leisure and business destination for Saudi Arabia, which provides over 60% of its 4 million tourist. Tourist (overnight visitor) arrivals in Bahrain were up 19% in 2004 and 11% in 2005 to 3.9 million.

Qatar's tourism industry may be growing as fast or even faster than the UAE's. The gas-rich emirate has raised its profile as a venue for Arab culture, business and society by its sponsorship of the news channel, Al Jazeera and its sister channel, Al Jazeera English, which is the world's first English-language news channel headquartered in the Middle East. Like Abu Dhabi, Qatar is investing generously in its airport, its airline (Qatar Airways) and tourist accommodation and facilities. Arrivals were up 32% in 2004 and 25% in 2005 to 0.9 million. International tourism receipts in US dollars were up even more sharply – by 35% and 53% in the two years.

Arrivals in Kuwait remain on a much lower level – at less than 100,000 a year – perhaps because it is so close to Iraq – and figures for 2005 are not available. Oman, meanwhile, has made quiet progress as an important leisure destination in recent years, but figures for 2005 are not available and those for earlier years are obscured by changes in methodology. However, arrivals are now running at well over 1 million a year, and hotels reported very large increases in arrivals from the UK, Germany and some other countries in 2004 and 2005.

Further north, the tourism industries are blighted by their proximity to the conflicts in Iraq and Palestine. Nevertheless, arrivals in Syria were up 46% in 2004 and 11% in 2005 to 3.4 million, and those in Jordan were up 21% and 5% to 3.0 million. Both countries have significant historical and cultural attractions to lure visitors from Europe and further afield. Jordan reports large increases in both intraregional (largely Arab) and interregional (largely European) arrivals. Syria depends much more heavily on intraregional arrivals – three quarters of arrivals in 2005 came from within the region, and two thirds of the remainder came from Turkey and Iran. Political and commercial relations with both countries have improved greatly in recent years.

Lebanon suffered an 11% decline in arrivals in 2005, after a 26% increase in 2004. Arrivals are running at a little over 1 million a year, but with its attractive coastline, its range of historical and cultural resources, and its huge diaspora bridging the Muslim and Christian divide, it has the potential to be a much more important destination.

The political rapprochement of Libyan Arab Jamahiriya (Libya) with Europe and the USA also gives scope for an increase in tourism activity, but on a much smaller scale. However, in 2003-2004 arrivals remained at a very low level – at around 150,000 a year – and figures for 2005 are still not available.

International tourism receipts

In 2005, the Middle East earned US$ 26 billion from international tourism, an increase of US$ 1 billion over the previous year. It is important to note that financial trends are always difficult to interpret correctly, as the figures are usually expressed in current US dollars and are subject to fluctuations in the exchange rate between the dollar and local currencies, as well as in local inflation rates. Expressed in (weighted) local currencies and at constant prices (i.e. taking account of inflation), international tourism receipts for the Middle East actually declined by 2% in 2005, but this followed exceptional increases of 25% in 2004 and 28% in 2003.

In the longer term, the Middle East's share of world receipts has been rising as dramatically as its share of international arrivals: it rose from less than 2% in 1990 to nearly 4% in 2005.

International Tourism Receipts, Middle East

	International Tourism Receipts							Change current prices (%)				Change constant prices (%)			
							(billion)								
	1990	1995	2000	2002	2003	2004	2005*	02/01	03/02	04/03	05*/04	02/01	03/02	04/03	05*/04
Local currencies								7.5	30.2	29.7	2.2	6.0	27.5	25.3	-1.8
US$	4.3	9.7	15.2	16.2	19.7	25.2	26.3	4.3	21.6	27.9	4.0	2.6	18.9	24.5	0.6
Euro	3.4	7.4	16.5	17.2	17.5	20.3	21.1	-1.2	1.7	16.3	4.0	-3.5	-0.4	13.9	1.8

Source: World Tourism Organization (UNWTO) ©   (Data as collected in UNWTO database November 2006)

Middle East: Inbound tourism
International Tourism Receipts   (US$ billion)

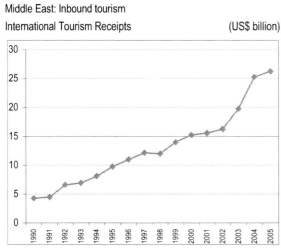

Source: World Tourism Organization (UNWTO) ©

Middle East: Inbound tourism
International Tourism Receipts   (share in world total, %)

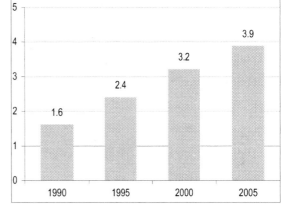

Source: World Tourism Organization (UNWTO) ©

World and regions: Inbound tourism
Receipts per Arrival, 2005   (US$)

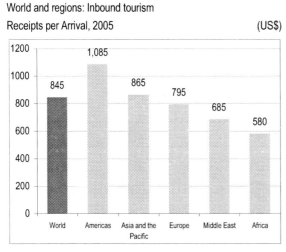

Source: World Tourism Organization (UNWTO) ©

World and regions: Inbound tourism   (change 05/04, %,
International Tourism Receipts   local currencies, constant prices)

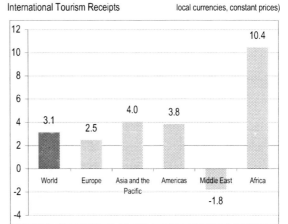

Source: World Tourism Organization (UNWTO) ©

Receipts per arrival in the Middle East averaged only US$ 685 in 2005 – rather lower than the US$ 845 for the world as a whole, and lower than in any other region of the world except Africa. They ranged widely in individual destinations, from US$ 4,765 in Lebanon, US$ 1,940 in Kuwait and US$ 1,465 in Libya to US$ 345 in Oman, US$ 245 in UAE and US$ 235 in Bahrain. These figures illustrate the difficulty of interpreting tourism statistics without a thorough examination of the definitions and methodologies used by the statistical agencies in different countries, and an understanding of the nature of the tourism industries they describe. By way of example, Lebanon and the UAE are both countries receiving large numbers of same-day traders and visitors in transit, but the former reports receipts per tourist arrival of US$ 4,765 and the latter US$ 245.

International Tourism Receipts by (Sub)region

| | Change | | | | | US$ | | | US$ | | | euro | Market |
| | Local currencies, constant prices (%) | | | | | (billion) | | Receipts per arrival | | (billion) | | Receipts per arrival | share (%) |
	01/00	02/01	03/02	04/03	05*/04	2004	2005*	2005*	2004	2005*	2005*	2005*
World	-1.9	-0.5	-1.4	9.8	3.1	629.0	675.7	845	505.7	543.1	680	100
Middle East	4.8	6.0	27.5	25.3	-1.8	25.2	26.3	685	20.3	21.1	550	3.9
Africa	17.1	5.3	23.9	5.9	10.4	18.9	21.6	580	15.2	17.4	465	3.2
North Africa	21.3	-5.6	-2.3	13.4	15.0	6.1	7.0	505	4.9	5.6	405	1.0

Source: World Tourism Organization (UNWTO) ©   (Data as collected in UNWTO database November 2006)

As is the case with tourist arrivals, earnings are fairly heavily concentrated in a few destinations in the region. Three countries account for two thirds of the total. Egypt slipped briefly behind Saudi Arabia as the biggest earner in the region in 2004, but regained first position with a 12% increase, in US dollar terms, to US$ 6.9 billion in 2005. However, estimated receipts in Saudi Arabia fell back by 20% to US$ 5.2 billion. This decline allowed Lebanon, with the very high reported receipts per arrival mentioned above, to move up into second place with US$ 5.4 billion, although this was very much the same as in 2004. With its very modest receipts per arrival, the UAE earns only US$ 2.2 billion, much the same as Syria.

International Tourism Receipts by Country of Destination

	International Tourism Receipts (US$, million)						Market share in the region (%)			Change (%)		Receipts per arrival[1]	Receipts per capita[1]
	1990	1995	2000	2003	2004	2005*	1990	2000	2005*	04/03	05*/04		US$
Middle East	*4,279*	*9,744*	*15,242*	*19,740*	*25,239*	*26,254*	*100*	*100*	*100*	*27.9*	*4.0*	*685*	*133*
Bahrain	135	247	573	720	864	920	3.2	3.8	3.5	20.0	6.5	235	1,337
Egypt	1,100	2,684	4,345	4,584	6,125	6,851	25.7	28.5	26.1	33.6	11.8	830	88
Iraq	173	18	2	..	..	..	4.1	0.0					
Jordan	512	660	723	1,062	1,330	1,441	12.0	4.7	5.5	25.2	8.3	480	250
Kuwait	132	121	98	117	176	164	3.1	0.6	0.6	50.2	-6.8	1,940	70
Lebanon	..	..	..	6,374	5,411	5,432			20.7	-15.1	0.4	4,765	1,420
Libyan Arab Jamahiriya	6	2	75	205	218	250	0.1	0.5	1.0	6.3	14.7	1,465	43
Oman	69	..	221	385	414	481	1.6	1.5	1.8	7.4	16.4	345	160
Palestine	..	255	283	107	56	..		1.9		-47.7		1,000	15
Qatar	..	..	128	369	498	760		0.8	2.9	35.0	52.8	835	881
Saudi Arabia	..	..	..	3,413	6,486	5,177			19.7	90.0	-20.2	645	196
Syrian Arab Republic	320	1,258	1,082	773	1,800	2,175	7.5	7.1	8.3	132.9	20.8	645	118
Untd Arab Emirates	315	632	1,063	1,439	1,594	2,200	7.4	7.0	8.4	10.8	38.0	245	858
Yemen	20	50	73	139	213	262	0.5	0.5	1.0	53.2	23.0	780	13

Source: World Tourism Organization (UNWTO) ©   (Data as collected by UNWTO for TMT 2006 Edition)

[1] Last year with data available

Inbound tourism by region of origin

In the Middle East as a whole, intraregional and interregional arrivals are roughly evenly balanced. The Middle East shares this feature of its international tourism with Africa; in all other regions of the world, intraregional arrivals greatly outnumber interregional arrivals.

More precisely, 46% of international arrivals in Middle East destinations come from countries within the region, 27% come from Europe, 14% from Asia and the Pacific – mostly from neighbouring countries such as Iran, India and Pakistan – 3% from the Americas and 3.5% from Africa. The origin of 6% of arrivals is not specified.

During the decade 1990-2000, interregional tourist arrivals developed at a somewhat faster pace than those from within the region, but this pattern was reversed in 2000-2005. Arrivals from within the region increased by 22% in 2004 and by 12% in 2005. Those from other regions increased by 25% in 2004 but fell slightly in 2005. There were increases in arrivals from the Americas and Europe in 2005, building on the strong results of 2004, but arrivals from Africa and Asia and the Pacific declined by over 10% in 2005.

Middle East
Inbound Tourism by Region of Origin (including estimates for countries with missing data)

	International Tourist Arrivals (1000)					Market share (%)			Change (%)			Average annual growth (%)	
	1990	1995	2000	2004	2005*	1990	2000	2005*	03/02	04/03	05*/04	'95-'00	'00-'05*
Middle East	**9,630**	**13,704**	**24,451**	**36,220**	**38,358**	**100**	**100**	**100**	**3.7**	**22.7**	**5.9**	**12.3**	**9.4**
From:													
Middle East	*5,071*	*6,130*	*10,142*	*15,858*	*17,725*	*52.7*	*41.5*	*46.2*	*-2.3*	*22.0*	*11.8*	*10.6*	*11.8*
Other regions	*4,412*	*6,851*	*12,549*	*18,497*	*18,289*	*45.8*	*51.3*	*47.7*	*7.4*	*25.3*	*-1.1*	*12.9*	*7.8*
Africa	665	574	1,099	1,522	1,359	6.9	4.5	3.5	-4.2	23.5	-10.7	13.9	4.3
Americas	284	529	871	1,072	1,172	2.9	3.6	3.1	9.8	22.0	9.3	10.5	6.1
Asia and the Pacific	1,626	2,235	4,094	6,085	5,460	16.9	16.7	14.2	6.6	13.0	-10.3	12.9	5.9
Europe	1,837	3,514	6,485	9,818	10,298	19.1	26.5	26.8	10.0	35.1	4.9	13.0	9.7
Origin not specified	*146*	*723*	*1,760*	*1,865*	*2,344*	*1.5*	*7.2*	*6.1*	*24.1*	*7.1*	*25.7*		

Source: World Tourism Organization (UNWTO) ©   (Data as collected by UNWTO for TMT 2006 Edition)

Middle East: Inbound tourism by region of origin
International Tourist Arrivals, 2005*   (share, %)

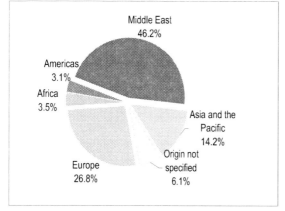

Source: World Tourism Organization (UNWTO) ©

Middle East: Inbound tourism by region of origin
International Tourist Arrivals   (share, %)

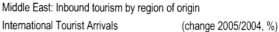
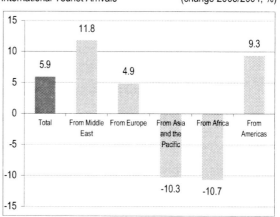

Source: World Tourism Organization (UNWTO) ©

Middle East: Inbound tourism by region of origin
International Tourist Arrivals, 2005*   (million)

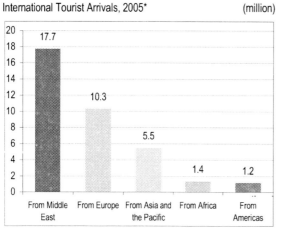

Source: World Tourism Organization (UNWTO) ©

Middle East: Inbound tourism by region of origin
International Tourist Arrivals   (change 2005/2004, %)

Source: World Tourism Organization (UNWTO) ©

World and regions: Inbound tourism by region of origin
International Tourist Arrivals, 2005*   (share, %)

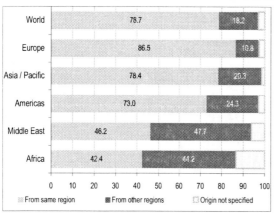

Source: World Tourism Organization (UNWTO) ©

World regions: Inbound tourism by region of origin
International Tourist Arrivals, 2005*   (million)

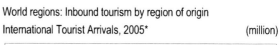
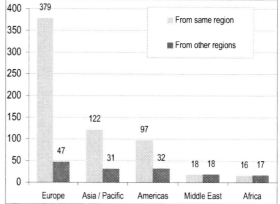

Source: World Tourism Organization (UNWTO) ©

Inbound tourism by means of transport

Data for the last ten years shows that land and air transport are by far the preferred means of transport for international tourists travelling to the Middle East. In 2005, an equal share of international tourist arrivals in the region came by land and air (18 million each, or 47% of the total). Water/sea transport accounted for 2.2 million arrivals – just 6% of the total.

The shares of air and land transport have not changed much since 1990 (although air transport has grown very slightly faster than land transport over this period), but that of water transport has fallen from 8% in 1990 to 6% in 2005. However, in 2005, arrivals by water increased by 18%, while air and land managed increases of only 5%.

Middle East: Inbound tourism by mode of transport
International Tourist Arrivals   (share, %)

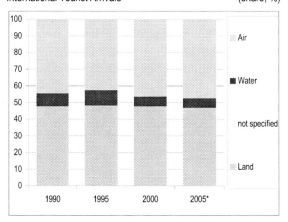

Source: World Tourism Organization (UNWTO) ©

World and subregions: Inbound tourism by mode of transport
International Tourist Arrivals, 2005*   (share, %)

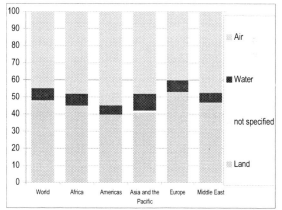

Source: World Tourism Organization (UNWTO) ©

Middle East
Arrivals by mode of transport (including estimates for countries with missing data)

	International Tourist Arrivals						Share			Change		Average annual growth (%)	
						(million)		(%)		(%)			
	1990	1995	2000	2003	2004	2005*	1990	2000	2005*	04/03	05*/04	90-00	00-05*
Total	9.6	13.7	24.5	29.5	36.2	38.4	100	100	100	22.7	5.9	9.8	9.4
Air	4.3	5.8	11.3	13.8	17.3	18.2	44.4	46.3	47.4	24.7	5.4	10.2	9.9
Land	4.6	6.6	11.7	14.2	17.1	18.0	47.8	47.7	46.9	20.6	5.0	9.7	9.0
Water	0.7	1.2	1.5	1.5	1.8	2.2	7.8	6.0	5.7	24.6	18.4	6.9	8.3

Source: World Tourism Organization (UNWTO) ©   (Data as collected by UNWTO for TMT 2006 Edition)

Inbound tourism by purpose of visit

Care must be taken in interpreting data on purpose of trip, since many trips involve more than one purpose and the purpose tourists give as their "main reason" for travel is influenced by factors which vary in different destinations. For instance, it is well known that travellers often claim to be travelling for leisure rather than business as the visa or entry requirements tend to be less strict, or are perceived to be less strict.

Leisure, recreation and holidays appear to be the most common purpose of travel to Middle East destinations in 2005, with a 54% market share (21 million arrivals). The relative importance of this motive has remained steady since 1990, and arrivals held up well in 2005, increasing by 6%. The second most important category was travel to visit friends and relatives (VFR), or for religion, health or other purposes – currently accounting for 34% of arrivals. This category lost a little share from 2000-2003, but gained a little in 2005, with an increase in numbers of 10%. Travel for business and professional purposes represented 12% of arrivals in 2005, up from 7.5% in 1990 and 9% in 2000, but the numbers fell back by 5.5% in 2005.

Middle East: Inbound tourism by purpose of visit
International Tourist Arrivals (share, %)

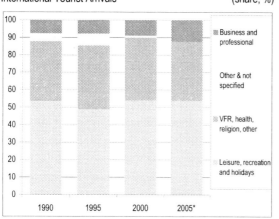

Source: World Tourism Organization (UNWTO) ©

World and subregions: Inbound tourism by purpose of visit
International Tourist Arrivals, 2005* (share, %)

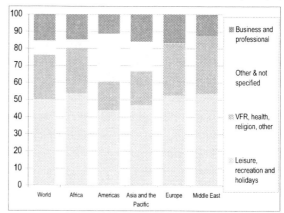

Source: World Tourism Organization (UNWTO) ©

Middle East

Arrivals by purpose of visit (including estimates for countries with missing data)

| | International Tourist Arrivals | | | | | | Share | | | Change | | Average annual growth (%) | |
| | | | | | (million) | | (%) | | | (%) | | | |
	1990	1995	2000	2003	2004	2005*	1990	2000	2005*	04/03	05*/04	90-00	00-05*
Total	9.6	13.7	24.5	29.5	36.2	38.4	100	100	100	22.7	5.9	9.8	9.4
Leisure, recreation and holidays	5.2	6.7	13.2	15.8	19.4	20.6	53.6	54.0	53.8	23.1	6.3	9.9	9.3
Business and professional	0.7	1.1	2.2	4.1	5.0	4.7	7.5	8.9	12.3	20.1	-5.5	11.5	16.8
VFR, health, religion, other	3.3	5.0	8.8	9.6	11.8	13.0	34.4	36.0	33.9	23.3	10.1	10.2	8.2
Not specified	0.4	0.9	0.3	0.0	0.0	0.0	4.5	1.2	0.0				

Source: World Tourism Organization (UNWTO) ©   (Data as collected by UNWTO for TMT 2006 Edition)

II.1.2 Outbound Tourism

Outbound tourism by (sub) region of destination

In 2005, the Middle East generated 23 million international tourist arrivals worldwide, or 11% more than in 2004. As in most world regions, the majority of arrivals originating from the Middle East were to destinations within the region itself (78%), while 22% were for destinations in other regions. In recent years, outbound to the Middle East has generally been increasing slightly faster than that to other regions, and this trend was sustained in 2004-2005.

Middle East: Outbound tourism by region of destination
International Tourist Arrivals, 2005*   (share, %)

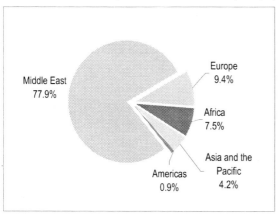

Source: World Tourism Organization (UNWTO) ©

Middle East: Outbound tourism by region of destination
International Tourist Arrivals   (share, %)

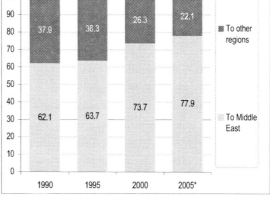

Source: World Tourism Organization (UNWTO) ©

In 2005, Europe accounted for 9% of worldwide arrivals out of Middle East countries, and 42% of interregional arrivals out of the Middle East. Southern/Mediterranean Europe took the lion's share of arrivals in Europe – a share that grew rapidly from 2000-2005. Arrivals in Central and Eastern Europe also grew over the period, but remained very much smaller in absolute volume. Those in Northern and Western Europe were still slightly lower than they were in 2000, but arrivals in Western Europe rose by 11% in 2005.

Africa is the second most important destination region for Middle East travellers outside their region, with 1.7 million arrivals from the Middle East in 2005. More than 90% of this traffic was to North Africa (and roughly a quarter corresponded to travel from Libya, which UNWTO defines as part of the Middle East, to its neighbour Tunisia).

Asia and the Pacific accounted for 4% of arrivals from the Middle East, a share which has been approximately stable since 1990. Nearly half of these were in South-East Asia and nearly a third in South Asia. Much smaller numbers go to North-East Asia and Oceania. However, North-East Asia has been generating the fastest growth among all destination subregions, with increases of 55% in 2004 and 30% in 2005.

The Americas represented 1% of total arrivals out of the Middle East. Relations between some Middle East countries and the continent's principal destination, the USA, have of course been problematic since 2001 and arrivals from the Middle East in North America in 2005 were still 8% down on their 2000 level. However, arrivals in other American subregions besides the Northern destinations were also down 5%.

Middle East

Outbound Tourism by (sub)region of destination (including estimates for countries with missing data)

	International Tourist Arrivals (1000)					Market share (%)			Growth rate (%)		Average annual growth (%)	
	1990	1995	2000	2004	2005*	1990	2000	2005*	04/03	05*/04	90-00	00-05*
Total	8,168	9,621	13,760	20,458	22,739	100	100	100	21.0	11.1	5.4	10.6
To:												
Middle East	*5,071*	*6,130*	*10,142*	*15,858*	*17,725*	*62.1*	*73.7*	*77.9*	*22.0*	*11.8*	*7.2*	*11.8*
Interregional	*3,097*	*3,491*	*3,619*	*4,600*	*5,014*	*37.9*	*26.3*	*22.1*	*17.7*	*9.0*	*1.6*	*6.7*
Europe	1,578	2,007	1,772	1,844	2,139	19.3	12.9	9.4	19.0	16.0	1.2	3.8
Northern Europe	455	638	415	372	374	5.6	3.0	1.6	11.2	0.5	-0.9	-2.0
Western Europe	294	443	609	532	591	3.6	4.4	2.6	11.2	11.1	7.6	-0.6
Central/Eastern Europe	123	118	118	152	164	1.5	0.9	0.7	11.2	7.6	-0.4	6.7
Southern Europe	706	809	630	787	1,010	8.6	4.6	4.4	31.4	28.3	-1.1	9.9
Africa	989	806	910	1,713	1,705	12.1	6.6	7.5	9.1	-0.5	-0.8	13.4
North Africa	968	741	814	1,579	1,560	11.9	5.9	6.9	8.3	-1.2	-1.7	13.9
Other Africa	21	65	96	134	145	0.3	0.7	0.6	19.7	8.3	16.4	8.6
Asia and the Pacific	366	464	626	847	961	4.5	4.5	4.2	35.2	13.4	5.5	9.0
North-East Asia	34	53	81	124	161	0.4	0.6	0.7	55.2	30.2	9.0	14.6
South-East Asia	167	197	281	408	466	2.0	2.0	2.0	49.3	14.2	5.3	10.6
Oceania	11	22	37	47	54	0.1	0.3	0.2	24.0	13.5	13.0	7.6
South Asia	154	191	226	268	280	1.9	1.6	1.2	13.9	4.5	3.9	4.4
Americas	163	214	311	196	209	2.0	2.3	0.9	21.8	6.6	6.7	-7.6
North America	157	206	294	185	196	1.9	2.1	0.9	23.3	5.9	6.5	-7.8
Other Americas	6	8	17	11	13	0.1	0.1	0.1	0.3	17.9	11.0	-5.1

Source: World Tourism Organization (UNWTO) ©   (Data as collected by UNWTO for TMT 2006 Edition)

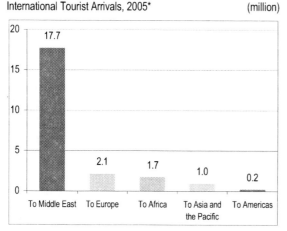

Middle East: Outbound tourism by region of destination
International Tourist Arrivals, 2005*   (million)

Source: World Tourism Organization (UNWTO) ©

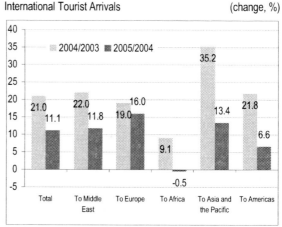

Middle East: Outbound tourism by region of destination
International Tourist Arrivals   (change, %)

Source: World Tourism Organization (UNWTO) ©

World and regions: Outbound tourism by region of destination
International Tourist Arrivals, 2005*   (share, %)

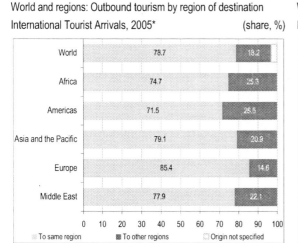

Source: World Tourism Organization (UNWTO) ©

World regions: Outbound tourism by region of destination
International Tourist Arrivals, 2005*   (million)

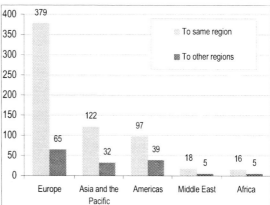

Source: World Tourism Organization (UNWTO) ©

International tourism expenditure

In 2005, tourists and same-day visitors from the Middle East spent an estimated US$ 23 billion on international tourism (including estimates for countries with missing data). This corresponded to an average expenditure of US$ 116 per resident of the Middle East (travellers and non-travellers), US$ 11 above the world average (US$ 105). However, the total still represented just over 3% of worldwide expenditure on foreign travel.

World and regions: Outbound tourism
International Tourism Expenditure, 2005*   (share, %)

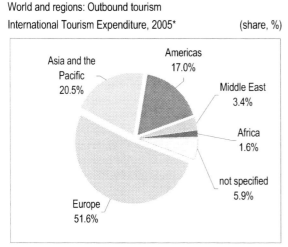

Source: World Tourism Organization (UNWTO) ©

World and regions: Outbound tourism
International Tourism Expenditure, 2005*   (US$ per capita)

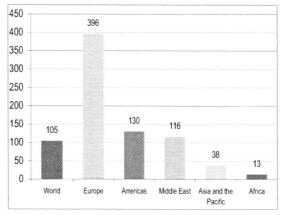

Source: World Tourism Organization (UNWTO) ©

About 70% of all expenditure generated in the Middle East was concentrated in four source markets – the UAE (with US$ 5.3 billion), Kuwait (US$ 4.3 billion), Saudi Arabia (US$ 3.8 billion) and Lebanon (US$ 2.9 billion). Among these four, the UAE and Kuwait have been generating the fastest growth. Saudi Arabia has been falling down the ranking, and expenditure decreased by 11% in 2005.

There are two other significant markets in the region. Residents of Egypt spent US$ 1.6 billion in 2005, 30% more than in 2004, while Qatar recorded spending of US$ 1.8 billion, up from US$ 691 million in 2004 – a remarkable 155% increase. And that US$ 691 million was already 125% higher than spending in 2000.

It is significant to note that spending per capita in three countries in the Middle East – the UAE, Qatar and Kuwait – is around US$ 2,000 per capita. Spending by Lebanon is around a third of that level, but nowhere else in the Middle East does it much exceed US$ 200 per person per year. In Egypt, Syria and Yemen it is only US$ 10 - 30 per person per year.

International Tourism Expenditure by Generating Country

	International Tourism Expenditure (US$, million)						Market share in the region (%)			Change (%)		Population (million)	per capita[1]
	1990	1995	2000	2003	2004	2005*	1990	2000	2005*	04/03	05*/04	2005	US$
Middle East	*10,152*	*14,692*	*17,575*	*19,321*	*20,925*	*22,962*	*100*	*100*	*100*	*8.3*	*9.7*	*198*	*116*
Bahrain	94	122	224	372	387	414	0.9	1.3	1.8	4.0	7.0	0.7	601
Egypt	129	1,278	1,072	1,321	1,257	1,629	1.3	6.1	7.1	-4.8	29.6	77.5	21
Iraq	247	117	9	..	..	..	2.4	0.1				26.1	1
Jordan	336	425	350	452	524	585	3.3	2.0	2.5	15.9	11.6	5.8	102
Kuwait	1,837	2,248	2,494	3,349	3,702	4,277	18.1	14.2	18.6	10.5	15.5	2.3	1,831
Lebanon	..	..	..	2,943	3,170	2,878			12.5	7.7	-9.2	3.8	752
Libyan Arab Jamahiriya	424	76	397	557	603	680	4.2	2.3	3.0	8.3	12.8	5.8	118
Oman	47	47	471	577	616	645	0.5	2.7	2.8	6.8	4.6	3.0	215
Palestine	..	162	309	317	286	..		1.8		-9.8		3.8	79
Qatar	..	..	307	471	691	1,759		1.7	7.7	46.8	154.6	0.9	2,038
Saudi Arabia	..	..	..	4,160	4,256	3,775			16.4	2.3	-11.3	26.4	143
Syrian Arab Republic	249	498	669	741	804	550	2.5	3.8	2.4	8.5	-31.6	18.4	30
Untd Arab Emirates	..	..	3,017	3,956	4,472	5,255		17.2	22.9	13.0	17.5	2.6	2,050
Yemen	64	76	70	77	126	167	0.6	0.4	0.7	63.6	32.5	20.7	8

Source: World Tourism Organization (UNWTO) ©   (Data as collected by UNWTO for TMT 2006 Edition)

[1] Last year with data available

Trips Abroad

Data on outbound trips in 2005 is still lacking for all but four countries in the Middle East and it is often not clear whether the reported figures refer only to tourists or to visitors in general. Egypt and Saudi Arabia each reported 5 million trips abroad, and Syria rather fewer. Jordan recorded 1.5 million and, for 2004, Kuwait registered 1.9 million.

Outbound Tourism, trips abroad (trips can either refer to overnight visits only, or also include same-day visits)

						(1000)	per 100 popu-	Change (%)		Average (%)	
	1990	1995	2000	2003	2004	2005*	lation[1]	04/03	05*/04	'90-'00	'00-'05*
Middle East											
Egypt	2,012	2,683	2,964	3,644	5,210	5,307	7	43.0	1.9	4.0	12.4
Iraq	239	..	..	..	..	..					
Jordan	1,143	1,128	1,625	1,229	1,420	1,523	26	15.5	7.3	3.6	-1.3
Kuwait	..	878	1,236	1,774	1,928	..	85	8.7			
Libyan Arab Jamahiriya	425	484	..	..	..	..					
Oman	..	..	..	..	..	..					
Saudi Arabia	..	..	..	4,104	4,235	5,009	19	3.2	18.3		
Syrian Arab Republic	1,041	1,746	3,863	3,997	4,309	4,564	25	7.8	5.9	14.0	3.4

Source: World Tourism Organization (UNWTO) ©   (Data as collected by UNWTO for TMT 2006 Edition)

[1] values correspond to most recent year with data available

World Tourism Organization ©

II.2 Tourism Trends in North Africa

Inbound Tourism

International tourist arrivals

The North African subregion consists of just four countries – Morocco and Tunisia, which are well-established sun & beach destinations for European and Middle Eastern tourists; Algeria, which has ambitions along the same lines; and Sudan. Arrivals in the subregion as a whole have been rising steadily since the mid-1990s, and they rose by a further 15% in 2004 and 9% in 2005, to 13.9 million (37% of the African total).

Morocco and Tunisia achieved growth of 6-7% in arrivals in 2005, building on their strong increases of 15-17% in 2004. In the case of Morocco, this is attributable to the positive returns generated by enhanced promotions and marketing, as well as by the increased public and private sector investments in tourism infrastructure, hotels, attractions and other facilities.

The pattern in Algeria was the reverse, with increases of 6% in 2004 and 17% in 2005. All three countries benefited from the high value of the euro, which sustained their price competitiveness. Morocco and Tunisia reported large increases in arrivals from most of their major European markets in 2005.

Conditions were also favourable for investments: all three countries are politically more stable and peaceful than they were in the 1990s, and all three are benefiting from the high international prices of oil and gas, which are generating funds for investment in infrastructure and in tourism facilities. These same conditions are also encouraging inbound and outbound business travel.

But the outstanding story in 2005 was the fourfold increase in arrivals in Sudan – albeit from a very small base (they reached 246,000 in 2005). Following the peace negotiated with the rebels in the south in 2004, investments in the oilfields have been stepped up and a very ambitious construction programme has got underway in the capital, financed by the promise of those oil revenues. However, the political situation in the Sudan remains fragile, not least because of the terrible events in the Darfur region.

International Tourist Arrivals by Country of Destination

	Series	International Tourist Arrivals (1000)						Market share in the region (%)			Change (%)		Average annual growth (%)	
		1990	1995	2000	2003	2004	2005*	1990	2000	2005*	04/03	05*/04	90-00	00-05*
North Africa		**8,398**	**7,271**	**10,240**	**11,094**	**12,769**	**13,911**	**55.3**	**36.7**	**37.3**	**15.1**	**8.9**	**2.0**	**6.3**
Algeria	VF	1,137	520	866	1,166	1,234	1,443	7.5	3.1	3.9	5.8	17.0	-2.7	10.8
Morocco	TF	4,024	2,602	4,278	4,761	5,477	5,843	26.5	15.3	15.7	15.0	6.7	0.6	6.4
Sudan	TF	33	29	38	52	61	246	0.2	0.1	0.7	15.8	305.8	1.4	45.3
Tunisia	TF	3,204	4,120	5,058	5,114	5,998	6,378	21.1	18.1	17.1	17.3	6.3	4.7	4.7

Source: World Tourism Organization (UNWTO) ©   (Data as collected by UNWTO for TMT 2006 Edition)

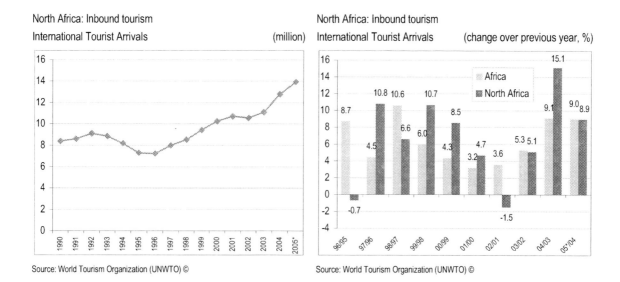

North Africa: Inbound tourism
International Tourist Arrivals   (million)

North Africa: Inbound tourism
International Tourist Arrivals   (change over previous year, %)

Source: World Tourism Organization (UNWTO) ©

Source: World Tourism Organization (UNWTO) ©

It should be pointed out that, in 2005, 69% of arrivals in Algeria and 48% of those in Morocco were by nationals resident abroad. Tunisia measures arrivals by nationality, but its own nationals are not included in the total arrivals count. Nearly 45% of arrivals in Sudan in 2005 came from Asia – presumably mainly from China, which is heavily committed to the investments in the country.

International tourism receipts

International tourism receipts in North African destinations reached US$ 7.0 billion in 2005, ranking North Africa second in terms of receipts of all African subregions after Southern Africa. This represented a growth of 15% expressed in local currencies at constant prices.

Morocco, with US$ 4.6 billion in 2005, accounts for 66% of North African tourism receipts, and Tunisia, with US$ 2.1 billion, for 30%. That leaves just 4% of the total for Algeria and Sudan.

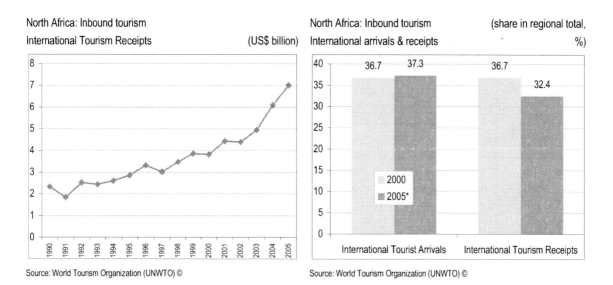

North Africa: Inbound tourism
International Tourism Receipts   (US$ billion)

North Africa: Inbound tourism   (share in regional total,
International arrivals & receipts   %)

Source: World Tourism Organization (UNWTO) ©

Source: World Tourism Organization (UNWTO) ©

World Tourism Organization ©

Receipts per tourist arrival in North Africa averaged US$ 505 in 2005, but this disguises wide variations: US$ 790 for Morocco (with its more sophisticated tourism offer, attracting higher yield tourists), US$ 335 for Tunisia, US$ 365 for Sudan and just US$ 130 for Algeria (with its high proportion of VFR visitors).

International Tourism Receipts by Country of Destination

	International Tourism Receipts (US$, million)						Market share in the region (%)			Change (%)		Receipts per arrival[1]	Receipts per capita[1]
	1990	1995	2000	2003	2004	2005*	1990	2000	2005*	04/03	05*/04		US$
North Africa	**2,333**	**2,867**	**3,822**	**4,938**	**6,093**	**7,018**	**36.4**	**36.7**	**32.4**	**23.4**	**15.2**	**505**	**61**
Algeria	105	33	96	112	179	184	1.6	0.9	0.9	59.4	3.1	130	6
Morocco	1,259	1,296	2,039	3,225	3,924	4,621	19.7	19.6	21.4	21.6	17.8	790	141
Sudan	21	8	5	18	21	89	0.3	0.0	0.4	16.7	324.4	365	2
Tunisia	948	1,530	1,682	1,582	1,970	2,124	14.8	16.2	9.8	24.5	7.8	335	211

Source: World Tourism Organization (UNWTO) ©   (Data as collected by UNWTO for TMT 2006 Edition)

[1] Last year with data available

II.3   Tourism Trends in Mediterranean Destinations

International tourist arrivals in Mediterranean-bordering destinations – the world's leading tourism destination region – increased by 3% in 2004, accelerating further in 2005 to 260 million (+5%). This important region, comprising 25 countries, attracts almost one third of total international tourist arrivals worldwide. Over the past decade, emerging destinations in the East Mediterranean and North Africa have gained share – last year's solid performance is attributable in no small part to Turkey, for example – but the mature destinations of France, Spain and Italy still dominate arrivals, accounting together for slightly less than two thirds of the Mediterranean's total arrivals count.

Mediterranean tourism results 2005

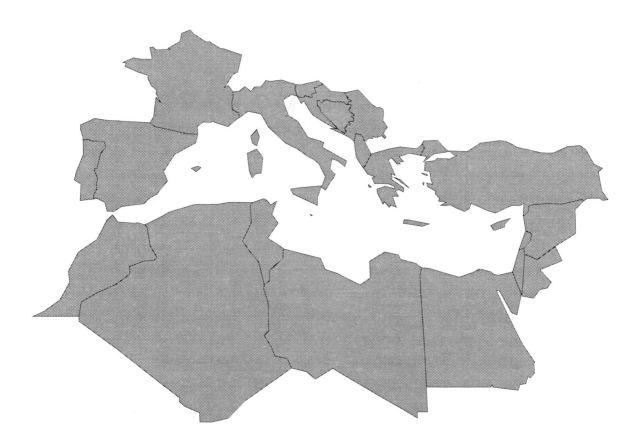

> • *International Tourist Arrivals:*   *260 million*
> • *International Tourism Receipts:*   *165 billion euros / US$ 205 billion*

International Tourist Arrivals

The top five destinations in the Mediterranean, in terms of arrivals in 2005, were unchanged from the previous year – France, Spain, Italy, Turkey and Greece, in order of arrivals volume. Of the top three, Italy recorded a 2% decline and France managed only a 1% rise. But Spain achieved 7% growth, largely as a result of the boom in demand for low-cost airline (LCC) flights to the destination. The availability of LCCs has stimulated demand for short city breaks, contributing to a healthy diversification of Spain's market mix. It has also helped the country reduce its dependence on mass-market, low- yield "Sun & Beach" tourism.

Turkey was one of the region's best performers in terms of arrivals growth, up 21% on 2004's level. And, following a disappointing 2004, when the country's capital Athens hosted the summer Olympic Games, Greece recorded an arrivals increase of 7%, highlighting the fact that many would-be visitors stayed away during the actual Games. Like Greece, Portugal – in sixth position in the Mediterranean ranking – had also failed to maximize the expected growth potential of a major event in 2004, the Euro Footbal Cup.

In 2005, there were strong performances from Israel (+26%), Syria (+11%), Croatia, and Morocco (both +7%), as well as from a number of smaller destinations such as Serbia & Montenegro and Bosnia & Herzegovina. Lebanon was the only country to record a double-digit decline (-11%), this was due to the civil unrest and violence that started with the assassination of Lebanon's Prime Minister, Rafiq Hariri, on 14 February 2005. By contrast, slight decreases were only observed in two destinations: Italy (-1.5%) and Portugal (-0.3%).

Cyprus staged a recovery (+5%) following a disappointing 2004, thanks to concerted efforts to improve standards and ensure greater value for money. But both government and the industry believe the destination has suffered from two important factors: having to impose visa restrictions on growth markets such as Russia (following its entry into membership of the EU), and the lack of LCCs serving the destination. Israel had a second consecutive year of very healthy growth (+26%), hopefully reflecting a major step on the path to full recovery. But it is still early days, especially given the overall uncertainties in the region

European destinations in the Mediterranean region have generally benefited from LCCs and most say they cannot afford not to have them, because it makes them look much less attractive to potential holidaymakers. Some North African destinations, notably Morocco, are looking to attract LCCs to boost inbound tourism demand. But other Mediterranean destinations, like Malta, fear that the LCCs may use them simply as a hub, diverting tourists who might have stayed in the country to destinations further afield.

Following its outbreak in Turkey and apparent spread to the Aegean coast, there are understandably concerns about the spread of avian flu within bird populations, and the risk that the H5N1 virus might mutate, resulting in a possible human flu pandemic. While all evidence so far suggests that the new cases provide no indication that the virus can spread easily from human to human, UNWTO member countries have been developing contingency plans, under the leadership of the UNWTO Secretariat and the World Health Organization, to ensure they are ready for all eventualities.

Mediterranean: Inbound tourism
International Tourist Arrivals   (million)

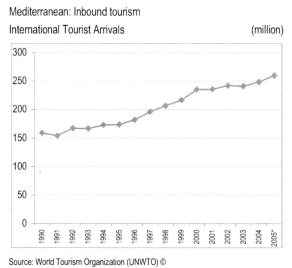

Source: World Tourism Organization (UNWTO) ©

Mediterranean: Inbound tourism
International Tourist Arrivals   (change over previous year, %)

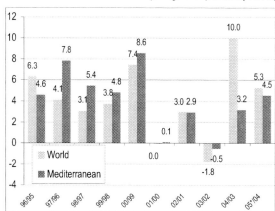

Source: World Tourism Organization (UNWTO) ©

International Tourist Arrivals by Country of Destination

	Series	International Tourist Arrivals (1000)						Market share in the region (%)			Change (%)		Average annual growth (%)	
		1990	1995	2000	2003	2004	2005*	1990	2000	2005*	04/03	05*/04	90-00	00-05*
Mediterranean		158,879	173,933	235,356	241,132	248,755	259,996	100	100	100	3.2	4.5	4.0	2.0
Portugal	TF	8,020	9,511	12,097	11,707	10,639	10,612	5.0	5.1	4.1	-9.1	-0.3	4.2	-2.6
Spain	TF	34,085	34,920	47,898	50,854	52,430	55,916	21.5	20.4	21.5	3.1	6.6	3.5	3.1
France	TF	52,497	60,033	77,190	75,048	75,121	75,910	33.0	32.8	29.2	0.1	1.1	3.9	-0.3
Monaco	THS	245	233	300	235	250	286	0.2	0.1	0.1	6.6	14.2	2.0	-1.0
Italy	TF	26,679	31,052	41,181	39,604	37,071	36,513	16.8	17.5	14.0	-6.4	-1.5	4.4	-2.4
Malta	TF	872	1,116	1,216	1,118	1,156	1,171	0.5	0.5	0.5	3.4	1.3	3.4	-0.8
Yugoslav SFR	TF	7,880	..	..	..	..	..	5.0						
Slovenia	TC	..	732	1,090	1,373	1,499	1,555		0.5	0.6	9.2	3.7		7.4
Croatia	TCE	..	1,485	5,831	7,409	7,912	8,467		2.5	3.3	6.8	7.0		7.7
Bosnia & Herzg	TCE	..	..	171	165	190	217		0.1	0.1	15.0	14.2		4.9
Serbia & Montenegro	TCE	..	228	239	481	580	725		0.1	0.3	20.5	25.0		24.8
Albania	THS	30	40	32	41	42	46	0.0	0.0	0.0	2.4	9.5	0.6	7.5
Greece	TF	8,873	10,130	13,096	13,969	13,313	14,276	5.6	5.6	5.5	-4.7	7.2	4.0	1.7
Turkey	TF	4,799	7,083	9,586	13,341	16,826	20,273	3.0	4.1	7.8	26.1	20.5	7.2	16.2
Cyprus	TF	1,561	2,100	2,686	2,303	2,349	2,470	1.0	1.1	1.0	2.0	5.2	5.6	-1.7
Syrian Arab Republic	TCE/TF	562	815	1,685	2,085	3,033	3,368	0.4	0.7	1.3	45.5	11.0	11.6	14.9
Lebanon	TF	..	450	742	1,016	1,278	1,140		0.3	0.4	25.9	-10.9		9.0
Israel	TF	1,063	2,215	2,417	1,063	1,506	1,903	0.7	1.0	0.7	41.6	26.4	8.6	-4.7
Palestine	THS	..	..	310	37	56	88		0.1	0.0	51.4	57.1		-22.3
Jordan	TF	572	1,075	1,580	2,353	2,853	2,987	0.4	0.7	1.1	21.2	4.7	10.7	13.6
Egypt	TF	2,411	2,871	5,116	5,746	7,795	8,244	1.5	2.2	3.2	35.7	5.8	7.8	10.0
Libyan Arab Jamahiriya	TF	96	56	174	142	149	..	0.1	0.1		4.9		6.1	
Tunisia	TF	3,204	4,120	5,058	5,114	5,998	6,378	2.0	2.1	2.5	17.3	6.3	4.7	4.7
Algeria	VF	1,137	520	866	1,166	1,234	1,443	0.7	0.4	0.6	5.8	17.0	-2.7	10.8
Morocco	TF	4,024	2,602	4,278	4,761	5,477	5,843	2.5	1.8	2.2	15.0	6.7	0.6	6.4

Source: World Tourism Organization (UNWTO) ©   (Data as collected by UNWTO for TMT 2006 Edition)

International tourism receipts

International tourism receipts also showed good growth, increasing by 5.5% in both euro and US dollar terms, at current prices but only by 1.8% in local currencies, constant prices. Among the three leading destinations, Spain and France recorded an increase in receipts, but Italy's slipped slightly. However, the strongest growth was seen in countries in the Eastern Mediterranean and North Africa, including Albania, Cyprus, Israel, Libya, Morocco and Syria.

The euro is the official currency of five of the major tourism destinations in the Mediterranean – Spain (with receipts of 39 billion euros), France (34 billion euros), Italy (28 billion euros), Greece (11 billion euros) and Portugal (6 billion euros), accounting together for 72% of international tourism receipts generated in the region. The appreciation of the euro against the US dollar in 2004 (and therefore against many currencies in the Middle East and North Africa, which are either pegged to the US dollar or loosely associated with it) did not continue in 2005, but the high exchange rate of the euro sustained the price competitiveness of the Middle Eastern and North African destinations vis-à-vis their eurozone competitors.

International Tourism Receipts, Mediterranean

	International Tourism Receipts (billion)							Change current prices (%)				Change constant prices (%)			
	1990	1995	2000	2002	2003	2004	2005*	02/01	03/02	04/03	05*/04	02/01	03/02	04/03	05*/04
Local currencies								1.2	3.6	5.9	4.7	-1.0	1.4	3.0	1.8
US$	76.2	114.9	138.0	143.2	169.7	194.6	205.3	5.1	18.5	14.7	5.5	3.5	15.9	11.7	2.0
Euro	59.8	87.9	149.4	151.4	150.0	156.4	165.0	-0.4	-0.9	4.3	5.5	-2.7	-3.0	2.1	3.2

Source: World Tourism Organization (UNWTO) ©   (Data as collected in UNWTO database November 2006)

Receipts per tourist arrival in the Mediterranean region averaged 635 euros in 2005, slightly below the European average of 640 euros and some 8% below the world average of 680 euros. However, this figure should only be used as a rough indicator since international tourism receipts not only account for expenditure by overnight visitors, but also for that of same-day visitors. The effect of the latter is in particular significant for many of the European destinations where cross-border traffic over land is substantial.

Mediterranean: Inbound tourism

International Tourism Receipts   (euro billion)

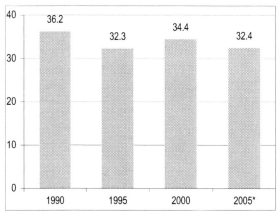

Source: World Tourism Organization (UNWTO) ©

Mediterranean: Inbound tourism

Receipts per Arrival, 2005   (euro)

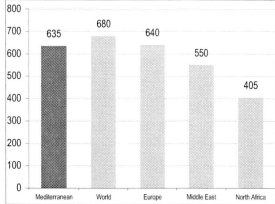

Source: World Tourism Organization (UNWTO) ©

Mediterranean: Inbound tourism

International Tourist Arrivals   (share in world total, %)

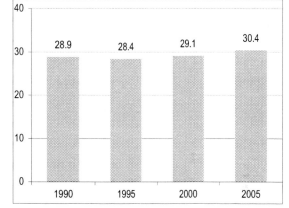

Source: World Tourism Organization (UNWTO) ©

Mediterranean: Inbound tourism

International Tourism Receipts   (share in world total, %)

Source: World Tourism Organization (UNWTO) ©

International Tourism Receipts by Country of Destination

	International Tourism Receipts (euro, million)						Market share in the region (%)			Change (%)		Receipts per arrival[1]	Receipts per capita[1]
	1990	1995	2000	2003	2004	2005*	1990	2000	2005*	04/03	05*/04		euro
Mediterranean	**59,799**	**87,855**	**149,446**	**150,004**	**156,439**	**165,040**	**100**	**100**	**100**	**4.3**	**5.5**	**635**	**349**
Portugal	2,792	3,693	5,677	5,849	6,195	6,199	4.7	3.8	3.8	5.9	0.1	585	587
Spain	14,515	19,306	32,446	35,047	36,376	38,558	24.3	21.7	23.4	3.8	6.0	690	956
France	15,850	21,056	33,301	32,349	32,833	33,981	26.5	22.3	20.6	1.5	3.5	450	560
Italy	12,924	21,965	29,767	27,623	28,665	28,453	21.6	19.9	17.2	3.8	-0.7	780	490
Malta	389	500	639	638	622	610	0.7	0.4	0.4	-2.5	-1.9	520	1,530
Yugoslav SFR	2,178	..	..	..	..	..	3.6						
Slovenia	..	827	1,045	1,184	1,310	1,447		0.7	0.9	10.6	10.5	930	720
Croatia	..	1,031	3,012	5,573	5,506	5,999		2.0	3.6	-1.2	9.0	710	1,334
Bosnia & Herzg	..	..	252	332	388	413		0.2	0.3	16.8	6.4	1,900	93
Serbia & Montenegro	..	32	32	178	..	..		0.0				370	16
Albania	3	50	421	461	585	692	0.0	0.3	0.4	26.7	18.3	15,035	194
Greece	2,032	3,161	9,981	9,495	10,348	11,037	3.4	6.7	6.7	9.0	6.7	775	1,035
Turkey	2,533	3,790	8,268	11,672	12,773	14,590	4.2	5.5	8.8	9.4	14.2	720	209
Cyprus	988	1,375	2,102	1,848	1,811	1,874	1.7	1.4	1.1	-2.0	3.5	760	2,402
Syrian Arab Republic	251	962	1,171	683	1,447	1,748	0.4	0.8	1.1	111.8	20.8	520	95
Lebanon	..	..	..	5,635	4,350	4,366			2.6	-22.8	0.4	3,830	1,141
Israel	1,097	2,288	4,426	1,821	1,914	2,293	1.8	3.0	1.4	5.1	19.8	1,205	365
Palestine	..	195	306	95	45	..		0.2		-52.4		805	12
Jordan	402	505	783	939	1,069	1,158	0.7	0.5	0.7	13.9	8.3	390	201
Egypt	864	2,052	4,704	4,052	4,924	5,506	1.4	3.1	3.3	21.5	11.8	670	71
Libyan Arab Jamahiriya	5	2	81	181	175	201	0.0	0.1	0.1	-3.3	14.7	1,175	35
Tunisia	744	1,170	1,821	1,399	1,584	1,707	1.2	1.2	1.0	13.2	7.8	270	169
Algeria	82	25	104	99	144	148	0.1	0.1	0.1	44.9	3.1	100	5
Morocco	989	991	2,208	2,851	3,154	3,714	1.7	1.5	2.3	10.6	17.8	635	114

Source: World Tourism Organization (UNWTO) ©

(Data as collected by UNWTO for TMT 2006 Edition)

III

Statistical Trends by Destination Country

III.1	Middle East	

III.1.1	Bahrain	Middle East

Profile

Bahrain

Capital	Manama
Year of entry in UNWTO	2001
Area (10 km²)	71
Population (2005, 1000)	688
Gross Domestic Product (GDP) (2005, US$ million)	13,515
GDP per capita (2005, US$)	18,403
GDP growth (real, %)	

Middle East   '-> 2004: 5.4;   2005: 6.9;   2006*: 7.1;   2007*: 6.3

	2003	2004	2005*	2004/2003	2005*/2004
International Arrivals					
Visitors (1000)	4,844	5,667	6,313	17.0	11.4
Tourists (overnight visitors) (1000)	2,955	3,514	3,914	18.9	11.4
- per 100 of inhabitants	443	518	569		
Same-day visitors (1000)	1,889	2,153	2,399	14.0	11.4
Tourism accommodation					
Number of rooms	7,880	..	..		
Nights spent in hotels and similar establishments (1000)					
by non-residents (inbound tourism)	1,290	2,290	2,224	77.5	-2.9
Receipts and Expenditure for International Tourism					
International Tourism Receipts (US$ million)	720	864	920	20.0	6.5
- per Tourist Arrival (US$)	244	246	235	0.9	-4.4
- per Visitor Arrival (US$)	149	152	146	2.6	-4.4
- per capita (US$)	1,079	1,275	1,337		
International Fare Receipts (US$ million)	486	640	683	31.7	6.7
International Tourism Expenditure (US$ million)	372	387	414	4.0	7.0
- per capita (US$)	558	571	601		
International Fare Expenditure (US$ million)	120	141	160	17.5	13.5
Δ International Tourism Balance (US$ million)	348	477	506		
Δ International Fare Balance (US$ million)	366	499	523		

Source: World Tourism Organization (UNWTO)   (Data as collected by UNWTO for TMT 2006 Edition)

See annex for methodological notes and reference of external sources used.

International Tourism by Origin

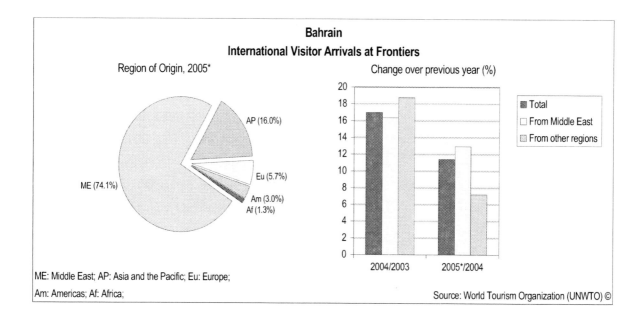

Bahrain
International Visitor Arrivals at Frontiers

Region of Origin, 2005*

AP (16.0%)
Eu (5.7%)
Am (3.0%)
Af (1.3%)
ME (74.1%)

Change over previous year (%)

- Total
- From Middle East
- From other regions

2004/2003   2005*/2004

ME: Middle East; AP: Asia and the Pacific; Eu: Europe;
Am: Americas; Af: Africa;

Source: World Tourism Organization (UNWTO) ©

World Tourism Organization ©

Bahrain
International Visitor Arrivals at Frontiers (by nationality)

	1995	2000	2003	2004	2005*	Market share (%) 2000	Market share (%) 2005*	Growth rate (%) 04/03	Growth rate (%) 05*/04	Average per year (%) 2000-2005*
Total	2,310,828	3,868,738	4,844,497	5,667,331	6,313,232	100	100	17.0	11.4	10.3
From Middle East	*1,781,522*	*3,060,206*	*3,558,805*	*4,140,624*	*4,676,446*	*79.1*	*74.1*	*16.3*	*12.9*	*8.9*
Saudi Arabia	1,538,161	2,617,406	2,963,641	3,415,008	3,864,624	67.7	61.2	15.2	13.2	8.1
Kuwait	88,686	170,734	180,711	213,821	239,532	4.4	3.8	18.3	12.0	7.0
Qatar	48,753	82,923	86,680	103,172	132,546	2.1	2.1	19.0	28.5	9.8
Jordan	13,677	33,997	74,362	90,365	95,732	0.9	1.5	21.5	5.9	23.0
Egypt	23,365	33,060	60,651	79,913	88,040	0.9	1.4	31.8	10.2	21.6
Lebanon	8,039	25,330	52,285	68,549	70,018	0.7	1.1	31.1	2.1	22.6
Syrian Arab Republic	8,718	16,953	35,178	42,670	45,236	0.4	0.7	21.3	6.0	21.7
Untd Arab Emirates	20,822	33,222	37,328	41,953	44,296	0.9	0.7	12.4	5.6	5.9
Yemen	..	14,964	29,422	35,248	38,905	0.4	0.6	19.8	10.4	21.1
Oman	21,633	20,740	25,593	29,089	32,482	0.5	0.5	13.7	11.7	9.4
Palestine	2,313	9,052	8,897	13,666	14,489	0.2	0.2	53.6	6.0	9.9
Iraq	370	1,478	3,600	6,506	9,804	0.0	0.2	80.7	50.7	46.0
Libyan Arab Jamahiriya	..	347	457	664	742	0.0	0.0	45.3	11.7	16.4
Other Middle East	6,985	..	..	..	..					
From other regions	*529,149*	*808,532*	*1,285,692*	*1,526,707*	*1,636,786*	*20.9*	*25.9*	*18.7*	*7.2*	*15.1*
India	118,641	213,509	350,996	418,767	466,849	5.5	7.4	19.3	11.5	16.9
United Kingdom	103,509	132,836	159,888	191,003	210,103	3.4	3.3	19.5	10.0	9.6
Philippines	39,556	49,982	109,730	134,369	143,641	1.3	2.3	22.5	6.9	23.5
Pakistan	33,999	56,473	107,723	124,522	138,049	1.5	2.2	15.6	10.9	19.6
United States	67,557	96,948	149,569	149,321	137,323	2.5	2.2	-0.2	-8.0	7.2
Bangladesh	10,979	29,726	43,171	47,975	51,679	0.8	0.8	11.1	7.7	11.7
Canada	10,268	21,559	37,307	45,008	44,829	0.6	0.7	20.6	-0.4	15.8
Australia	8,025	14,170	19,990	28,293	33,906	0.4	0.5	41.5	19.8	19.1
Indonesia	..	15,308	30,379	34,776	29,648	0.4	0.5	14.5	-14.7	14.1
Sudan	4,558	11,999	20,646	25,397	28,084	0.3	0.4	23.0	10.6	18.5
Germany	7,973	11,360	14,251	24,930	26,498	0.3	0.4	74.9	6.3	18.5
Thailand	1,878	2,346	13,194	18,270	23,528	0.1	0.4	38.5	28.8	58.6
Sri Lanka	41,148	17,974	21,594	23,061	23,042	0.5	0.4	6.8	-0.1	5.1
South Africa	..	5,151	15,340	22,513	22,386	0.1	0.4	46.8	-0.6	34.2
Iran	1,974	2,632	16,161	20,304	21,934	0.1	0.3	25.6	8.0	52.8
France	5,626	10,959	16,979	21,277	21,819	0.3	0.3	25.3	2.5	14.8
Nepal	2,326	11,404	21,104	12,977	17,974	0.3	0.3	-38.5	38.5	9.5
Japan	8,995	11,509	12,430	12,749	14,158	0.3	0.2	2.6	11.1	4.2
Turkey	..	12,722	12,209	14,305	14,140	0.3	0.2	17.2	-1.2	2.1
Ireland	5,599	9,317	10,714	13,314	13,297	0.2	0.2	24.3	-0.1	7.4
Netherlands	4,655	7,638	9,158	13,262	13,279	0.2	0.2	44.8	0.1	11.7
Italy	3,177	5,920	7,886	10,837	11,395	0.2	0.2	37.4	5.1	14.0
Morocco	..	7,175	9,162	11,992	10,995	0.2	0.2	30.9	-8.3	8.9
Malaysia	584	1,340	4,670	8,071	9,132	0.0	0.1	72.8	13.1	46.8
China	..	2,383	6,051	7,669	8,699	0.1	0.1	26.7	13.4	29.6
Other interregional	48,122	46,192	65,390	91,745	100,399	1.2	1.6	40.3	9.4	16.8
Other World/Not specified	*157*	*..*	*..*	*..*	*..*					

Source: World Tourism Organization (UNWTO) ©   (Data as collected by UNWTO for TMT 2006 Edition)

III.1.2   Egypt   Middle East

Promotional: www.visitegypt.gov.eg ; www.touregypt.net ; www.festival.com.eg

Profile

Egypt

Capital	Cairo
Year of entry in UNWTO	1975
Area (1000 km²)	1,001
Population (2005, million)	77.5
Gross Domestic Product (GDP) (2005, US$ million)	89,477
GDP per capita (2005, US$)	1,265
GDP growth (real, %)	

Middle East

'-> 2004: 4.1;   2005: 4.9;   2006*: 5.6;   2007*: 5.6

	2003	2004	2005*	2004/2003	2005*/2004
International Arrivals					
Visitors (1000)	6,044	8,104	8,608	34.1	6.2
Tourists (overnight visitors) (1000)	5,746	7,795	8,244	35.7	5.8
- per 100 of inhabitants	8	10	11		
Same-day visitors (1000)	298	309	363	3.7	17.5
Tourism accommodation					
Number of rooms	136,510	148,039	170,776	8.4	15.4
Nights spent in hotels and similar establishments (1000)	57,912				
by non-residents (inbound tourism)	53,130	81,668	85,172	53.7	4.3
by residents (domestic tourism)	4,782	..	..		
Outbound Tourism					
Trips abroad (1000)	3,644	5,210	5,307	43.0	1.9
- per 100 of inhabitants	5	7	7		
Receipts and Expenditure for International Tourism					
International Tourism Receipts (US$ million)	4,584	6,125	6,851	33.6	11.8
- per Tourist Arrival (US$)	798	786	831	-1.5	5.8
- per Visitor Arrival (US$)	758	756	796	-0.3	5.3
- per capita (US$)	61	80	88		
International Fare Receipts (US$ million)	120	203	355	69.2	74.9
International Tourism Expenditure (US$ million)	1,321	1,257	1,629	-4.8	29.6
- per trip (US$)	363	241	307	-33.4	27.2
- per capita (US$)	18	17	21		
International Fare Expenditure (US$ million)	144	286	303	98.6	5.9
Δ International Tourism Balance (US$ million)	3,263	4,868	5,222		
Δ International Fare Balance (US$ million)	-24	-83	52		

Source: World Tourism Organization (UNWTO)   (Data as collected by UNWTO for TMT 2006 Edition)

See annex for methodological notes and reference of external sources used.

International Tourism by Origin

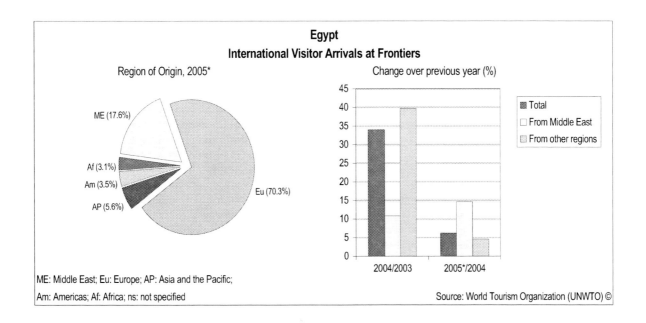

Egypt
International Visitor Arrivals at Frontiers

Region of Origin, 2005*

ME (17.6%)
Af (3.1%)
Am (3.5%)
AP (5.6%)
Eu (70.3%)

Change over previous year (%)

Total
From Middle East
From other regions

2004/2003   2005*/2004

ME: Middle East; Eu: Europe; AP: Asia and the Pacific;
Am: Americas; Af: Africa; ns: not specified

Source: World Tourism Organization (UNWTO) ©

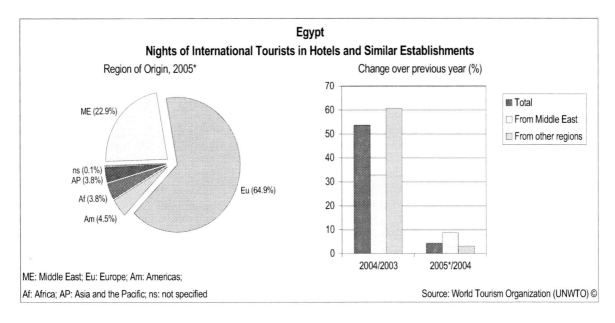

Egypt
Nights of International Tourists in Hotels and Similar Establishments

Region of Origin, 2005*

ME (22.9%)
ns (0.1%)
AP (3.8%)
Af (3.8%)
Am (4.5%)
Eu (64.9%)

Change over previous year (%)

Total
From Middle East
From other regions

2004/2003   2005*/2004

ME: Middle East; Eu: Europe; Am: Americas;
Af: Africa; AP: Asia and the Pacific; ns: not specified

Source: World Tourism Organization (UNWTO) ©

Egypt
International Visitor Arrivals at Frontiers (by nationality)

	1995	2000	2003	2004	2005*	Market share (%)		Growth rate (%)		Average per year (%)
						2000	2005*	04/03	05*/04	2000-2005*
Total	3,133,461	5,506,179	6,044,160	8,103,609	8,607,807	100	100	34.1	6.2	9.3
From Middle East	741,581	889,886	1,188,994	1,317,883	1,511,285	16.2	17.6	10.8	14.7	11.2
Libyan Arab Jamahiriya	156,882	152,528	305,393	344,490	376,378	2.8	4.4	12.8	9.3	19.8
Saudi Arabia	179,463	240,198	269,120	309,606	361,108	4.4	4.2	15.0	16.6	8.5
Palestine	99,272	149,821	187,785	172,166	217,365	2.7	2.5	-8.3	26.3	7.7
Jordan	49,126	78,481	98,716	118,108	125,673	1.4	1.5	19.6	6.4	9.9
Kuwait	70,752	63,984	79,235	89,825	99,363	1.2	1.2	13.4	10.6	9.2
Syrian Arab Republic	72,622	67,407	81,267	86,484	93,010	1.2	1.1	6.4	7.5	6.7
Yemen	31,344	34,456	46,145	58,484	64,383	0.6	0.7	26.7	10.1	13.3
Lebanon	23,227	37,078	41,729	45,087	47,903	0.7	0.6	8.0	6.2	5.3
Iraq	2,570	10,636	7,205	19,975	44,324	0.2	0.5	177.2	121.9	33.0
Untd Arab Emirates	24,863	25,571	31,984	31,790	34,958	0.5	0.4	-0.6	10.0	6.5
Qatar	12,124	10,378	12,806	15,035	17,642	0.2	0.2	17.4	17.3	11.2
Bahrain	12,640	11,050	15,425	14,883	14,851	0.2	0.2	-3.5	-0.2	6.1
Oman	6,696	8,298	12,184	11,950	14,327	0.2	0.2	-1.9	19.9	11.5
From other regions	2,389,845	4,613,719	4,852,348	6,781,154	7,092,764	83.8	82.4	39.7	4.6	9.0
Germany	319,312	786,336	693,445	993,178	979,631	14.3	11.4	43.2	-1.4	4.5
United Kingdom	284,611	358,781	357,248	546,892	837,950	6.5	9.7	53.1	53.2	18.5
Italy	257,272	752,166	795,903	1,010,444	823,199	13.7	9.6	27.0	-18.5	1.8
Russian Federation	110,108	..	497,465	785,419	777,665		9.0	57.9	-1.0	
France	122,224	379,888	310,791	465,174	495,164	6.9	5.8	49.7	6.4	5.4
Israel	295,933	326,524	309,994	389,897	256,346	5.9	3.0	25.8	-34.3	-4.7
Netherlands	39,048	142,074	131,537	188,504	205,877	2.6	2.4	43.3	9.2	7.7
United States	154,851	235,301	125,778	169,658	195,821	4.3	2.3	34.9	15.4	-3.6
Former Czechoslovakia	10,700	27,023	96,840	198,286	176,357	0.5	2.0	104.8	-11.1	45.5
Belgium	44,672	106,633	94,634	136,906	154,414	1.9	1.8	44.7	12.8	7.7
Poland	16,782	57,496	120,158	145,414	153,729	1.0	1.8	21.0	5.7	21.7
Spain	23,484	103,275	102,113	155,782	147,344	1.9	1.7	52.6	-5.4	7.4
Austria	34,396	99,652	105,173	150,698	137,135	1.8	1.6	43.3	-9.0	6.6
Switzerland	72,181	104,138	95,614	132,886	130,757	1.9	1.5	39.0	-1.6	4.7
Sweden	19,395	70,040	49,686	88,965	122,401	1.3	1.4	79.1	37.6	11.8
Sudan	46,063	52,697	70,021	102,585	113,777	1.0	1.3	46.5	10.9	16.6
Denmark	19,897	51,321	46,491	68,437	92,132	0.9	1.1	47.2	34.6	12.4
Japan	69,253	86,131	60,860	70,597	74,446	1.6	0.9	16.0	5.5	-2.9
Korea, Republic of	27,572	40,282	27,096	38,624	68,912	0.7	0.8	42.5	78.4	11.3
India	17,922	34,277	34,941	45,313	54,141	0.6	0.6	29.7	19.5	9.6
Canada	26,093	46,514	36,056	48,259	52,152	0.8	0.6	33.8	8.1	2.3
Norway	11,033	30,112	25,126	42,989	51,529	0.5	0.6	71.1	19.9	11.3
Hungary	13,718	15,098	36,513	51,775	49,389	0.3	0.6	41.8	-4.6	26.7
Finland	5,701	25,005	27,524	39,936	47,807	0.5	0.6	45.1	19.7	13.8
Australia	24,468	38,787	26,079	38,523	45,744	0.7	0.5	47.7	18.7	3.4
Other interregional	323,156	644,168	575,262	676,013	848,945	11.7	9.9	17.5	25.6	5.7
Other World/Not specified	2,035	2,574	2,818	4,572	3,758	0.0	0.0	62.2	-17.8	7.9

Source: World Tourism Organization (UNWTO) ©　　　　　　　　　　　　(Data as collected by UNWTO for TMT 2006 Edition)

Egypt
Nights of International Tourists in Hotels and Similar Establishments (by nationality)

	1995	2000	2003	2004	2005*	Market share (%) 2000	Market share (%) 2005*	Growth rate (%) 04/03	Growth rate (%) 05*/04	Average per year (%) 2000-2005*
Total	20,451,364	32,787,881	53,129,907	81,667,918	85,171,917	100	100	53.7	4.3	21.0
From Middle East	*5,789,150*	*4,849,825*	*13,495,221*	*17,928,497*	*19,486,816*	*14.8*	*22.9*	*32.9*	*8.7*	*32.1*
Saudi Arabia	1,846,796	1,726,630	3,532,114	5,014,559	5,353,870	5.3	6.3	42.0	6.8	25.4
Libyan Arab Jamahiriya	799,277	314,947	3,566,009	4,401,213	4,537,073	1.0	5.3	23.4	3.1	70.5
Palestine	328,757	457,324	1,703,241	1,907,097	2,182,823	1.4	2.6	12.0	14.5	36.7
Kuwait	730,766	536,745	1,048,435	1,385,414	1,498,350	1.6	1.8	32.1	8.2	22.8
Yemen	437,861	401,423	724,538	1,207,888	1,336,186	1.2	1.6	66.7	10.6	27.2
Jordan	367,637	359,415	857,381	1,171,889	1,239,064	1.1	1.5	36.7	5.7	28.1
Syrian Arab Republic	413,663	290,071	628,169	858,685	919,897	0.9	1.1	36.7	7.1	26.0
Iraq	20,319	23,493	65,333	252,772	608,245	0.1	0.7	286.9	140.6	91.7
Untd Arab Emirates	308,272	266,989	455,256	572,401	576,010	0.8	0.7	25.7	0.6	16.6
Lebanon	168,843	204,616	354,475	429,173	432,930	0.6	0.5	21.1	0.9	16.2
Qatar	132,278	112,656	173,836	238,430	280,417	0.3	0.3	37.2	17.6	20.0
Oman	81,782	69,017	170,548	225,888	264,655	0.2	0.3	32.4	17.2	30.8
Bahrain	152,899	86,499	215,886	263,088	257,296	0.3	0.3	21.9	-2.2	24.4
From other regions	*14,638,378*	*27,924,952*	*39,603,327*	*63,674,721*	*65,628,658*	*85.2*	*77.1*	*60.8*	*3.1*	*18.6*
Germany	2,472,277	5,687,305	6,310,407	10,921,832	10,352,593	17.3	12.2	73.1	-5.2	12.7
Russian Federation	543,670	..	4,054,784	7,521,465	8,569,480		10.1	85.5	13.9	
United Kingdom	1,595,151	1,965,722	2,793,473	4,854,127	7,495,989	6.0	8.8	73.8	54.4	30.7
Italy	1,929,932	5,436,280	6,442,011	8,547,755	6,582,930	16.6	7.7	32.7	-23.0	3.9
France	895,678	2,710,350	2,763,301	4,380,786	4,577,583	8.3	5.4	58.5	4.5	11.1
United States	1,025,121	1,463,973	1,590,263	2,458,703	2,676,285	4.5	3.1	54.6	8.8	12.8
Netherlands	248,566	967,196	1,242,608	1,913,390	2,114,398	2.9	2.5	54.0	10.5	16.9
Sudan	550,706	489,270	1,053,349	1,694,715	2,033,291	1.5	2.4	60.9	20.0	33.0
Former Czechoslovakia	77,590	149,804	916,664	1,924,327	1,595,189	0.5	1.9	109.9	-17.1	60.5
Belgium	286,440	720,674	826,479	1,395,212	1,507,295	2.2	1.8	68.8	8.0	15.9
Poland	91,371	226,398	1,147,142	1,442,053	1,446,176	0.7	1.7	25.7	0.3	44.9
Austria	213,499	609,283	933,102	1,563,129	1,391,870	1.9	1.6	67.5	-11.0	18.0
Spain	191,311	850,449	1,008,868	1,423,183	1,344,425	2.6	1.6	41.1	-5.5	9.6
Switzerland	506,158	727,095	797,265	1,304,050	1,218,051	2.2	1.4	63.6	-6.6	10.9
Sweden	98,102	373,170	381,571	854,107	1,157,870	1.1	1.4	123.8	35.6	25.4
Israel	796,677	1,222,028	1,307,079	1,781,840	1,133,583	3.7	1.3	36.3	-36.4	-1.5
Denmark	127,283	316,056	348,103	653,569	878,637	1.0	1.0	87.8	34.4	22.7
Canada	174,013	255,867	407,337	662,433	732,531	0.8	0.9	62.6	10.6	23.4
Australia	178,677	274,552	274,004	560,667	619,947	0.8	0.7	104.6	10.6	17.7
Norway	50,007	140,691	182,931	385,700	518,259	0.4	0.6	110.8	34.4	29.8
Yugoslav SFR	..	20,635	493,058	..	..	0.1				
Japan	356,677	404,609	355,316	486,921	493,030	1.2	0.6	37.0	1.3	4.0
Hungary	84,315	69,431	266,027	449,589	405,562	0.2	0.5	69.0	-9.8	42.3
Finland	31,171	116,210	170,952	386,743	400,973	0.4	0.5	126.2	3.7	28.1
India	92,179	127,815	220,689	328,601	389,493	0.4	0.5	48.9	18.5	25.0
Other interregional	2,021,807	2,600,089	3,316,544	5,779,824	5,993,218	7.9	7.0	74.3	3.7	18.2
Other World/Not specified	*23,836*	*13,104*	*31,359*	*64,700*	*56,443*	*0.0*	*0.1*	*106.3*	*-12.8*	*33.9*

Source: World Tourism Organization (UNWTO) ©   (Data as collected by UNWTO for TMT 2006 Edition)

III.1.3   Iraq Middle East

Profile

Iraq

Middle East

Capital	Baghdad
Year of entry in UNWTO	1975
Area (1000 km²)	438
Population (2005, million)	26.1

Source: World Tourism Organization (UNWTO)   (Data as collected by UNWTO for TMT 2006 Edition)

See annex for methodological notes and reference of external sources used.

International Tourism by Origin

Iraq
International Visitor Arrivals at Frontiers (by nationality)

	1995	2000	2002	2003	2004	Market share (%) 2000	Market share (%) 2004	Growth rate (%) 03/02	Growth rate (%) 04/03	Average per year (%) 2000-2004
Total	60,540	78,457	..	..	..	100				
From Middle East	*39,910*	*56*	*..*	*..*	*..*	*0.1*				
Yemen	4,114	..	..	..	..					
Saudi Arabia	3,240	..	..	..	..					
Bahrain	934	..	..	..	..					
Syrian Arab Republic	573	..	..	..	..					
Egypt	550	..	..	..	..					
Kuwait	119	..	..	..	..					
Libyan Arab Jamahiriya	148	31	..	..	..	0.0				
Untd Arab Emirates	66	16	..	..	..	0.0				
Lebanon	3,913	8	..	..	..	0.0				
Jordan	26,253	1	..	..	..	0.0				
From other regions	*18,865*	*78,401*	*..*	*..*	*..*	*99.9*				
Iran	..	69,155	..	..	..	88.1				
India	4,015	3,092	..	..	..	3.9				
Pakistan	7,034	2,985	..	..	..	3.8				
Afghanistan	..	1,041	..	..	..	1.3				
Tunisia	250	..	..	..	..					
All Southern Africa	222	..	..	..	..					
Bulgaria	154	..	..	..	..					
Romania	113	..	..	..	..					
Azerbaijan	..	15	..	..	..	0.0				
Germany	431	367	..	..	..	0.5				
Czech Rep	91	..	..	..	..					
Poland	90	..	..	..	..					
United Kingdom	463	302	..	..	..	0.4				
Turkey	469	405	..	..	..	0.5				
Tanzania	..	112	..	..	..	0.1				
Serbia & Montenegro	67	..	..	..	..					
France	336	73	..	..	..	0.1				
Greece	54	..	..	..	..					
Korea, Republic of	54	32	..	..	..	0.0				
Italy	249	110	..	..	..	0.1				
South Africa	..	87	..	..	..	0.1				
Bangladesh	..	65	..	..	..	0.1				
Indonesia	..	6	..	..	..	0.0				
Austria	..	54	..	..	..	0.1				
Brazil	22	..	..	..	..					
Other interregional	4,751	500	..	..	..	0.6				
Other World/Not specified	*1,765*	*..*	*..*	*..*	*..*					

Source: World Tourism Organization (UNWTO) ©   (Data as collected by UNWTO for TMT 2006 Edition)

III.1.4   Jordan   Middle East

Promotional: www.tourism.jo ; www.see-jordan.com
Institutional/corporate: www.tourism.jo
Research and data: http://hotels.mota.gov.jo ; www.tourism.jo

Profile

Jordan

Capital	Amman
Year of entry in UNWTO	1975
Area (1000 km²)	89
Population (2005, million)	5.8
Gross Domestic Product (GDP) (2005, US$ million)	12,712
GDP per capita (2005, US$)	2,317

GDP growth (real, %)

Middle East

'-> 2004: 8.4;   2005: 7.2;   2006*: 6.0;   2007*: 5.0

	2003	2004	2005*	2004/2003	2005*/2004
International Arrivals					
Visitors (1000)	4,600	5,587	5,817	21.5	4.1
Tourists (overnight visitors) (1000)	2,353	2,853	2,987	21.2	4.7
- per 100 of inhabitants	43	51	52		
Same-day visitors (1000)	2,247	2,734	2,831	21.7	3.5
Cruise passengers (1000)	3	9	26	200.0	188.9
Tourism accommodation					
Number of rooms	19,698	19,945	20,827	1.3	4.4
Nights spent in hotels and similar establishments (1000)	3,816	5,032	5,552	31.9	10.3
by non-residents (inbound tourism)	2,842	3,980	4,488	40.0	12.8
by residents (domestic tourism)	974	1,052	1,064	8.0	1.1
Outbound Tourism					
Trips abroad (1000)	1,229	1,420	1,523	15.5	7.3
- per 100 of inhabitants	23	25	26		
Receipts and Expenditure for International Tourism					
International Tourism Receipts (US$ million)	1,062	1,330	1,441	25.2	8.3
- per Tourist Arrival (US$)	451	466	482	3.3	3.5
- per Visitor Arrival (US$)	231	238	248	3.1	4.1
- per capita (US$)	194	237	250		
International Fare Receipts (US$ million)	204	291	318	42.6	9.3
International Tourism Expenditure (US$ million)	452	524	585	15.9	11.6
- per trip (US$)	368	369	384	0.3	4.1
- per capita (US$)	83	93	102		
International Fare Expenditure (US$ million)	51	61	68	19.6	11.5
Δ International Tourism Balance (US$ million)	610	806	856		
Δ International Fare Balance (US$ million)	153	230	250		

Source: World Tourism Organization (UNWTO)   (Data as collected by UNWTO for TMT 2006 Edition)

See annex for methodological notes and reference of external sources used.

International Tourism by Origin

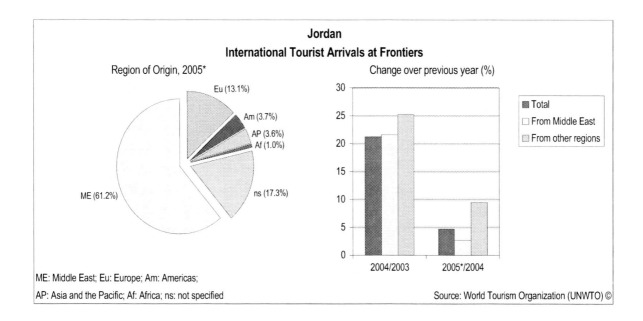

Jordan
International Tourist Arrivals at Frontiers

Region of Origin, 2005*

Change over previous year (%)

ME: Middle East; Eu: Europe; Am: Americas;
AP: Asia and the Pacific; Af: Africa; ns: not specified

Source: World Tourism Organization (UNWTO) ©

Jordan
International Tourist Arrivals at Frontiers (by nationality)

	1995	2000	2003	2004	2005*	Market share (%) 2000	Market share (%) 2005*	Growth rate (%) 04/03	Growth rate (%) 05*/04	Average per year (%) 2000-2005*
Total	**1,074,527**	**1,580,430**	**2,353,087**	**2,852,803**	**2,986,589**	**100**	**100**	**21.2**	**4.7**	**13.6**
From Middle East	*566,561*	*730,365*	*1,464,910*	*1,780,755*	*1,828,735*	*46.2*	*61.2*	*21.6*	*2.7*	*20.1*
Syrian Arab Republic	..	161,215	653,433	792,410	695,364	10.2	23.3	21.3	-12.2	34.0
Saudi Arabia	452,860	129,807	305,587	347,498	388,311	8.2	13.0	13.7	11.7	24.5
Iraq	..	272,880	190,208	35,993	324,869	17.3	10.9	-81.1	802.6	3.5
Egypt	..	34,773	140,883	167,536	147,810	2.2	4.9	18.9	-11.8	33.6
Kuwait	46,279	11,545	34,078	283,767	71,566	0.7	2.4	732.7	-74.8	44.0
Lebanon	..	19,031	41,472	43,467	60,560	1.2	2.0	4.8	39.3	26.1
Palestine	..	15,920	23,887	29,867	47,540	1.0	1.6	25.0	59.2	24.5
Bahrain	40,163	7,270	32,252	33,785	38,708	0.5	1.3	4.8	14.6	39.7
Yemen	..	24,529	14,553	14,132	14,165	1.6	0.5	-2.9	0.2	-10.4
Libyan Arab Jamahiriya	..	27,278	10,000	11,948	11,649	1.7	0.4	19.5	-2.5	-15.6
Untd Arab Emirates	11,267	6,507	7,930	9,135	10,852	0.4	0.4	15.2	18.8	10.8
Qatar	6,610	3,833	4,204	4,729	8,979	0.2	0.3	12.5	89.9	18.6
Oman	9,382	4,759	6,401	6,448	8,362	0.3	0.3	0.7	29.7	11.9
Other Middle East	..	11,018	22	40	..	0.7		81.8		
From other regions	*507,966*	*504,690*	*467,857*	*585,849*	*641,193*	*31.9*	*21.5*	*25.2*	*9.4*	*4.9*
Israel	100,079	99,737	105,807	121,506	124,540	6.3	4.2	14.8	2.5	4.5
United States	83,853	72,100	52,046	76,055	92,245	4.6	3.1	46.1	21.3	5.1
Turkey	..	9,352	80,802	80,392	74,340	0.6	2.5	-0.5	-7.5	51.4
United Kingdom	44,959	32,677	25,292	38,369	40,276	2.1	1.3	51.7	5.0	4.3
Germany	44,804	34,522	14,675	19,839	21,179	2.2	0.7	35.2	6.8	-9.3
Spain	13,995	17,214	5,912	10,940	20,465	1.1	0.7	85.0	87.1	3.5
France	30,075	35,075	12,984	16,359	20,458	2.2	0.7	26.0	25.1	-10.2
India	..	12,351	12,141	17,801	19,605	0.8	0.7	46.6	10.1	9.7
Indonesia	14,044	7,813	11,980	14,554	18,083	0.5	0.6	21.5	24.2	18.3
Italy	29,274	37,734	7,268	11,605	13,933	2.4	0.5	59.7	20.1	-18.1
Canada	11,816	10,114	9,049	12,513	13,234	0.6	0.4	38.3	5.8	5.5
Russian Federation	21,213	4,367	6,925	9,624	12,858	0.3	0.4	39.0	33.6	24.1
Philippines	..	2,040	6,213	6,652	9,683	0.1	0.3	7.1	45.6	36.5
Sri Lanka	..	2,459	8,179	8,431	9,505	0.2	0.3	3.1	12.7	31.1
Australia	10,455	10,170	5,849	9,841	9,476	0.6	0.3	68.3	-3.7	-1.4
Pakistan	..	2,582	3,666	7,069	8,935	0.2	0.3	92.8	26.4	28.2
Sudan	..	5,525	6,008	6,753	8,908	0.3	0.3	12.4	31.9	10.0
Netherlands	15,441	12,128	5,808	6,505	7,573	0.8	0.3	12.0	16.4	-9.0
Japan	6,669	7,445	5,287	6,296	6,677	0.5	0.2	19.1	6.1	-2.2
Korea, Republic of	..	2,410	5,377	6,786	6,173	0.2	0.2	26.2	-9.0	20.7
Sweden	5,985	4,651	4,490	4,720	5,198	0.3	0.2	5.1	10.1	2.2
China	..	2,454	3,828	5,419	5,106	0.2	0.2	41.6	-5.8	15.8
Algeria	..	2,345	2,581	2,388	4,859	0.1	0.2	-7.5	103.5	15.7
Morocco	..	1,471	2,243	2,555	4,618	0.1	0.2	13.9	80.7	25.7
South Africa	2,300	2,091	1,796	3,744	3,993	0.1	0.1	108.5	6.7	13.8
Other interregional	73,004	73,863	61,651	79,133	79,273	4.7	2.7	28.4	0.2	1.4
Nationals residing abroad	*..*	*340,293*	*412,963*	*479,683*	*511,915*	*21.5*	*17.1*	*16.2*	*6.7*	*8.5*
Other World/Not specified	*..*	*5,082*	*7,357*	*6,516*	*4,746*	*0.3*	*0.2*	*-11.4*	*-27.2*	*-1.4*

Source: World Tourism Organization (UNWTO) ©   (Data as collected by UNWTO for TMT 2006 Edition)

World Tourism Organization ©

III.1.5   Kuwait   Middle East

Profile

Kuwait

Middle East

Capital	Kuwait
Year of entry in UNWTO	2003
Area (100 km²)	178
Population (2005, million)	2.3
Gross Domestic Product (GDP) (2005, US$ million)	74,598
GDP per capita (2005, US$)	26,020

GDP growth (real, %)
'-> 2004: 6.2;   2005: 8.5;   2006*: 6.2;   2007*: 4.7

	2003	2004	2005*	2004/2003	2005*/2004
International Arrivals					
Visitors (1000)	2,602	3,056	..	17.4	
Tourists (overnight visitors) (1000)	94	91	..	-3.2	
- per 100 of inhabitants	4	4	..		
Tourism accommodation					
Number of rooms	3,980	4,281	4,267	7.6	-0.3
Nights spent in hotels and similar establishments (1000)					
by non-residents (inbound tourism)	315	281	..	-10.8	
Outbound Tourism					
Trips abroad (1000)	1,774	1,928	..	8.7	
- per 100 of inhabitants	81	85	..		
Receipts and Expenditure for International Tourism					
International Tourism Receipts (US$ million)	117	176	164	50.2	-6.8
- per Tourist Arrival (US$)	1,249	1,939	..	55.2	
- per Visitor Arrival (US$)	45	58	..	27.9	
- per capita (US$)	54	78	70		
International Fare Receipts (US$ million)	211	234	243	10.9	3.8
International Tourism Expenditure (US$ million)	3,349	3,702	4,277	10.5	15.5
- per trip (US$)	1,888	1,920	..	1.7	
- per capita (US$)	1,534	1,640	1,831		
International Fare Expenditure (US$ million)	403	448	466	11.2	4.0
Δ International Tourism Balance (US$ million)	-3,231	-3,526	-4,113		
Δ International Fare Balance (US$ million)	-192	-214	-223		

Source: World Tourism Organization (UNWTO)   (Data as collected by UNWTO for TMT 2006 Edition)
See annex for methodological notes and reference of external sources used.

International Tourism by Origin

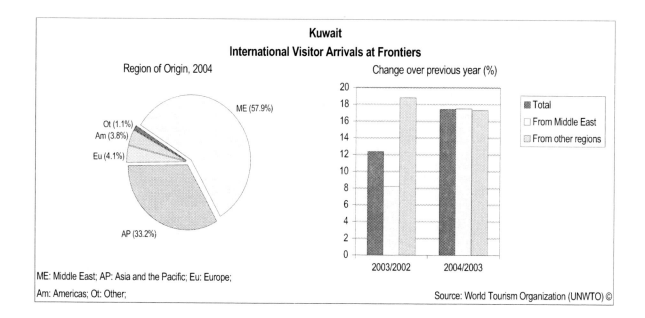

Kuwait
International Visitor Arrivals at Frontiers

Region of Origin, 2004

ME: Middle East; AP: Asia and the Pacific; Eu: Europe;
Am: Americas; Ot: Other;

Source: World Tourism Organization (UNWTO) ©

Kuwait
International Visitor Arrivals at Frontiers (by nationality)

	1995	2000	2002	2003	2004	Market share (%)		Growth rate (%)		Average per year (%)
						2000	2004	03/02	04/03	2000-2004
Total	1,443,069	1,944,233	2,315,568	2,602,300	3,056,093	100	100	12.4	17.4	12.0
From Middle East	879,387	1,191,168	1,391,296	1,505,733	1,769,220	61.3	57.9	8.2	17.5	10.4
Saudi Arabia	432,432	641,691	725,025	777,831	896,102	33.0	29.3	7.3	15.2	8.7
Egypt	194,206	219,553	256,867	289,401	327,460	11.3	10.7	12.7	13.2	10.5
Syrian Arab Republic	120,543	143,020	176,375	185,946	234,726	7.4	7.7	5.4	26.2	13.2
Bahrain	36,336	50,024	74,979	77,512	84,934	2.6	2.8	3.4	9.6	14.1
Lebanon	44,652	48,642	61,687	63,735	74,629	2.5	2.4	3.3	17.1	11.3
Jordan	20,120	36,221	37,706	42,140	50,938	1.9	1.7	11.8	20.9	8.9
Iraq	3,398	4,602	4,690	15,793	36,539	0.2	1.2	236.7	131.4	67.9
Qatar	8,580	15,727	19,564	18,385	23,065	0.8	0.8	-6.0	25.5	10.0
Untd Arab Emirates	7,081	15,122	13,588	13,173	16,783	0.8	0.5	-3.1	27.4	2.6
Oman	6,264	8,269	11,554	11,880	12,424	0.4	0.4	2.8	4.6	10.7
Palestine	4,540	5,479	5,473	5,489	5,935	0.3	0.2	0.3	8.1	2.0
Yemen	1,047	2,532	3,407	4,200	5,374	0.1	0.2	23.3	28.0	20.7
Libyan Arab Jamahiriya	188	286	381	248	311	0.0	0.0	-34.9	25.4	2.1
From other regions	554,420	741,324	921,322	1,094,329	1,283,649	38.1	42.0	18.8	17.3	14.7
India	153,202	225,642	314,054	363,724	413,109	11.6	13.5	15.8	13.6	16.3
Pakistan	62,393	74,429	84,224	111,055	123,128	3.8	4.0	31.9	10.9	13.4
Iran	76,588	100,328	99,066	100,474	121,642	5.2	4.0	1.4	21.1	4.9
Bangladesh	54,137	54,466	75,423	90,327	111,060	2.8	3.6	19.8	23.0	19.5
United States	18,566	27,588	35,219	85,988	92,761	1.4	3.0	144.2	7.9	35.4
Philippines	34,521	43,310	56,335	60,264	73,656	2.2	2.4	7.0	22.2	14.2
Sri Lanka	67,364	54,804	62,586	63,269	62,676	2.8	2.1	1.1	-0.9	3.4
United Kingdom	22,110	29,859	33,202	39,663	50,648	1.5	1.7	19.5	27.7	14.1
Indonesia	1,098	30,928	35,990	39,969	43,647	1.6	1.4	11.1	9.2	9.0
Canada	4,350	9,601	12,718	14,551	19,399	0.5	0.6	14.4	33.3	19.2
Nepal	..	3,313	4,183	9,990	16,639	0.2	0.5	138.8	66.6	49.7
Turkey	3,911	3,021	4,301	6,602	10,413	0.2	0.3	53.5	57.7	36.3
Germany	4,045	5,811	6,403	6,208	9,157	0.3	0.3	-3.0	47.5	12.0
France	3,391	5,950	6,375	6,369	9,058	0.3	0.3	-0.1	42.2	11.1
Morocco	4,306	5,975	10,348	8,867	8,873	0.3	0.3	-14.3	0.1	10.4
Japan	..	3,895	4,432	3,982	8,826	0.2	0.3	-10.2	121.6	22.7
Australia	2,940	3,841	4,286	5,767	8,049	0.2	0.3	34.6	39.6	20.3
Afghanistan	4,213	5,016	8,492	6,776	7,334	0.3	0.2	-20.2	8.2	10.0
Korea, Republic of	1,438	2,966	3,256	3,560	6,569	0.2	0.2	9.3	84.5	22.0
China	2,642	3,435	3,879	2,819	6,558	0.2	0.2	-27.3	132.6	17.5
Bulgaria	1,343	1,476	2,506	3,474	6,016	0.1	0.2	38.6	73.2	42.1
Italy	2,662	3,290	3,641	3,734	5,374	0.2	0.2	2.6	43.9	13.1
Sudan	746	1,508	2,323	3,235	4,759	0.1	0.2	39.3	47.1	33.3
Netherlands	1,209	1,757	2,557	2,999	4,469	0.1	0.1	17.3	49.0	26.3
Thailand	3,660	3,591	5,958	4,648	4,274	0.2	0.1	-22.0	-8.0	4.4
Other interregional	23,585	35,524	39,565	46,015	55,555	1.8	1.8	16.3	20.7	11.8
Other World/Not specified	9,262	11,741	2,950	2,238	3,224	0.6	0.1	-24.1	44.1	-27.6

Source: World Tourism Organization (UNWTO) ©   (Data as collected by UNWTO for TMT 2006 Edition)

III.1.6   Lebanon   Middle East

Promotional: www.destinationlebanon.com
Institutional/corporate: www.destinationlebanon.com

Profile

Lebanon

Capital	Beirut
Year of entry in UNWTO	1975
Area (100 km²)	104
Population (2005, million)	3.8
Gross Domestic Product (GDP) (2005, US$ million)	22,053
GDP per capita (2005, US$)	6,034
GDP growth (real, %)	

Middle East

'-> 2004: 6.0;   2005: 1.0;   2006*: -3.2;   2007*: 5.0

	2003	2004	2005*	2004/2003	2005*/2004
International Arrivals					
Tourists (overnight visitors) (1000)	1,016	1,278	1,140	25.9	-10.9
- per 100 of inhabitants	27	34	30		
Tourism accommodation					
Number of rooms	16,202	16,171	16,735	-0.2	3.5
Nights spent in hotels and similar establishments (1000)					
by non-residents (inbound tourism)	1,180	1,484	1,133	25.8	-23.7
Receipts and Expenditure for International Tourism					
International Tourism Receipts (US$ million)	6,374	5,411	5,432	-15.1	0.4
- per Tourist Arrival (US$)	6,275	4,232	4,767	-32.6	12.6
- per capita (US$)	1,710	1,433	1,420		
International Fare Receipts (US$ million)	408	520	437	27.5	-16.0
International Tourism Expenditure (US$ million)	2,943	3,170	2,878	7.7	-9.2
- per capita (US$)	789	839	752		
International Fare Expenditure (US$ million)	376	549	657	46.0	19.7
Δ International Tourism Balance (US$ million)	3,431	2,241	2,554		
Δ International Fare Balance (US$ million)	32	-29	-220		

Source: World Tourism Organization (UNWTO)   (Data as collected by UNWTO for TMT 2006 Edition)
See annex for methodological notes and reference of external sources used.

World Tourism Organization ©

International Tourism by Origin

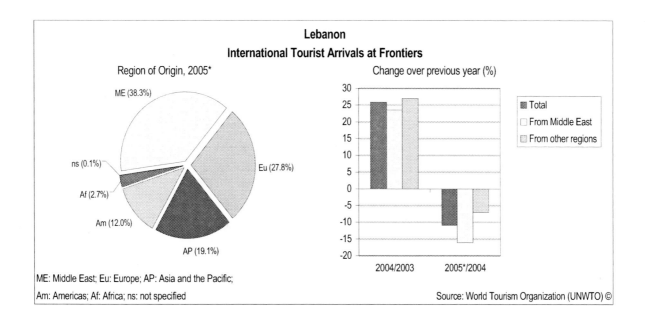

Lebanon
International Tourist Arrivals at Frontiers

Region of Origin, 2005*

ME (38.3%)
ns (0.1%)
Af (2.7%)
Am (12.0%)
AP (19.1%)
Eu (27.8%)

Change over previous year (%)

- Total
- From Middle East
- From other regions

ME: Middle East; Eu: Europe; AP: Asia and the Pacific;
Am: Americas; Af: Africa; ns: not specified

Source: World Tourism Organization (UNWTO) ©

Lebanon

International Tourist Arrivals at Frontiers (by nationality)

	1995	2000	2003	2004	2005*	Market share (%) 2000	2005*	Growth rate (%) 04/03	05*/04	Average per year (%) 2000-2005*
Total	**449,809**	**741,648**	**1,015,793**	**1,278,469**	**1,139,524**	**100**	**100**	**25.9**	**-10.9**	**9.0**
From Middle East	*145,666*	*288,083*	*421,148*	*520,230*	*436,549*	*38.8*	*38.3*	*23.5*	*-16.1*	*8.7*
Jordan	50,274	69,625	87,798	92,840	135,227	9.4	11.9	5.7	45.7	14.2
Saudi Arabia	34,711	98,343	162,230	200,899	124,687	13.3	10.9	23.8	-37.9	4.9
Kuwait	20,931	47,630	55,959	79,830	64,193	6.4	5.6	42.7	-19.6	6.2
Egypt	20,656	35,691	39,022	46,056	34,271	4.8	3.0	18.0	-25.6	-0.8
Iraq	2,924	6,183	7,863	17,159	20,677	0.8	1.8	118.2	20.5	27.3
Bahrain	3,683	8,024	25,002	27,184	17,624	1.1	1.5	8.7	-35.2	17.0
Untd Arab Emirates	4,296	9,742	20,261	26,837	17,044	1.3	1.5	32.5	-36.5	11.8
Qatar	2,256	4,802	10,728	14,819	12,064	0.6	1.1	38.1	-18.6	20.2
Oman	958	2,205	4,424	5,392	3,742	0.3	0.3	21.9	-30.6	11.2
Libyan Arab Jamahiriya	1,325	3,028	3,451	4,297	3,519	0.4	0.3	24.5	-18.1	3.1
Yemen	1,725	2,808	4,410	4,917	3,500	0.4	0.3	11.5	-28.8	4.5
Other Middle East	1,927	2	..	..	1	0.0	0.0			-12.9
From other regions	*265,556*	*450,056*	*594,385*	*755,012*	*701,666*	*60.7*	*61.6*	*27.0*	*-7.1*	*9.3*
Iran	6,536	23,180	70,400	89,770	92,863	3.1	8.1	27.5	3.4	32.0
France	42,739	64,766	76,409	94,347	80,480	8.7	7.1	23.5	-14.7	4.4
United States	16,568	43,343	60,050	78,827	68,361	5.8	6.0	31.3	-13.3	9.5
Germany	18,969	35,396	37,942	48,370	51,948	4.8	4.6	27.5	7.4	8.0
Canada	19,830	30,209	43,136	52,425	48,453	4.1	4.3	21.5	-7.6	9.9
Australia	18,986	30,628	31,854	45,915	38,577	4.1	3.4	44.1	-16.0	4.7
United Kingdom	16,077	24,281	28,024	34,532	35,538	3.3	3.1	23.2	2.9	7.9
Philippines	4,360	8,948	18,069	25,296	30,655	1.2	2.7	40.0	21.2	27.9
Sri Lanka	8,561	16,497	17,124	22,089	20,436	2.2	1.8	29.0	-7.5	4.4
Sweden	6,817	10,412	14,732	20,218	18,314	1.4	1.6	37.2	-9.4	12.0
Italy	12,038	14,706	13,119	15,567	14,104	2.0	1.2	18.7	-9.4	-0.8
Denmark	3,696	6,861	10,479	13,487	13,367	0.9	1.2	28.7	-0.9	14.3
India	3,887	7,224	9,603	11,240	11,111	1.0	1.0	17.0	-1.1	9.0
Russian Federation	9,178	5,044	7,881	8,994	9,157	0.7	0.8	14.1	1.8	12.7
Cyprus	2,616	4,396	8,032	12,347	8,955	0.6	0.8	53.7	-27.5	15.3
Turkey	5,382	4,638	6,799	9,629	8,618	0.6	0.8	41.6	-10.5	13.2
Netherlands	4,325	7,215	6,839	9,071	8,567	1.0	0.8	32.6	-5.6	3.5
Spain	2,740	5,126	5,646	7,868	8,442	0.7	0.7	39.4	7.3	10.5
Belgium	4,272	7,466	7,136	9,048	8,342	1.0	0.7	26.8	-7.8	2.2
Switzerland	4,335	7,095	6,957	9,931	8,239	1.0	0.7	42.7	-17.0	3.0
Brazil	6,022	5,901	6,200	8,031	7,432	0.8	0.7	29.5	-7.5	4.7
Greece	3,720	4,372	5,628	7,397	6,424	0.6	0.6	31.4	-13.2	8.0
Ukraine	1,266	3,647	5,262	6,140	6,048	0.5	0.5	16.7	-1.5	10.6
Japan	1,827	6,839	3,046	4,753	5,475	0.9	0.5	56.0	15.2	-4.4
Indonesia	1,120	3,334	6,466	8,263	5,401	0.4	0.5	27.8	-34.6	10.1
Other interregional	39,689	68,532	87,552	101,457	86,359	9.2	7.6	15.9	-14.9	4.7
Other World/Not specified	*38,587*	*3,509*	*260*	*3,227*	*1,309*	*0.5*	*0.1*	*1141.2*	*-59.4*	*-17.9*

Source: World Tourism Organization (UNWTO) ©   (Data as collected by UNWTO for TMT 2006 Edition)

World Tourism Organization ©

III.1.7   Libyan Arab Jamahiriya   Middle East

Profile

Libyan Arab Jamahiriya

Middle East

Capital	Tripoli
Year of entry in UNWTO	1977
Area (1000 km²)	1,760
Population (2005, million)	5.8
Gross Domestic Product (GDP) (2005, US$ million)	38,738
GDP per capita (2005, US$)	6,696
GDP growth (real, %)	
'-> 2004: 4.6; 2005: 3.5; 2006*: 5.0; 2007*: 4.6	

	2003	2004	2005*	2004/2003	2005*/2004
International Arrivals					
Visitors (1000)	958	999	..	4.3	
Tourists (overnight visitors) (1000)	142	149	..	4.9	
- per 100 of inhabitants	3	3	..		
Same-day visitors (1000)	816	850	..	4.2	
Tourism accommodation					
Number of rooms	12,405	12,704	..	2.4	
Nights spent in collective establishments (1000)					
by residents (domestic tourism)	968	964	..	-0.4	
Nights spent in hotels and similar establishments (1000)					
by non-residents (inbound tourism)	477	502	..	5.2	
Receipts and Expenditure for International Tourism					
International Tourism Receipts (US$ million)	205	218	250	6.3	14.7
- per Tourist Arrival (US$)	1,444	1,463	..	1.3	
- per Visitor Arrival (US$)	214	218	..	2.0	
- per capita (US$)	37	39	43		
International Fare Receipts (US$ million)	38	43	51	13.2	18.6
International Tourism Expenditure (US$ million)	557	603	680	8.3	12.8
- per capita (US$)	101	107	118		
International Fare Expenditure (US$ million)	132	186	240	40.9	29.0
Δ International Tourism Balance (US$ million)	-352	-385	-430		
Δ International Fare Balance (US$ million)	-94	-143	-189		

Source: World Tourism Organization (UNWTO)   (Data as collected by UNWTO for TMT 2006 Edition)

See annex for methodological notes and reference of external sources used.

International Tourism by Origin

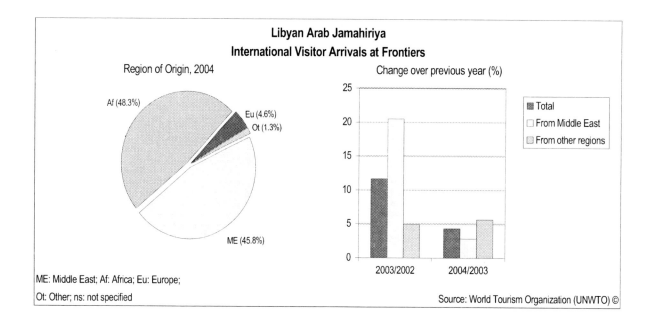

Libyan Arab Jamahiriya
International Visitor Arrivals at Frontiers

Region of Origin, 2004

Af (48.3%)
Eu (4.6%)
Ot (1.3%)
ME (45.8%)

Change over previous year (%)

■ Total
□ From Middle East
▒ From other regions

ME: Middle East; Af: Africa; Eu: Europe;
Ot: Other; ns: not specified

Source: World Tourism Organization (UNWTO) ©

Libyan Arab Jamahiriya
International Visitor Arrivals at Frontiers (by nationality)

	1995	2000	2002	2003	2004	Market share (%)		Growth rate (%)		Average per year (%)
						2000	2004	03/02	04/03	2000-2004
Total	**1,831,884**	**962,559**	**857,952**	**957,896**	**999,343**	**100**	**100**	**11.6**	**4.3**	**0.9**
From Middle East	*810,000*	*391,747*	*369,774*	*445,561*	*458,124*	*40.7*	*45.8*	*20.5*	*2.8*	*4.0*
All Middle East	810,000	..	..	..	..					
Egypt	..	372,914	354,189	429,220	441,230	38.7	44.2	21.2	2.8	4.3
Syrian Arab Republic	..	7,495	5,680	6,742	6,878	0.8	0.7	18.7	2.0	-2.1
Iraq	..	6,968	6,110	5,668	5,940	0.7	0.6	-7.2	4.8	-3.9
Jordan	..	2,380	2,021	2,141	2,267	0.2	0.2	5.9	5.9	-1.2
Palestine	..	865	771	778	801	0.1	0.1	0.9	3.0	-1.9
Lebanon	..	412	367	371	350	0.0	0.0	1.1	-5.7	-4.0
Yemen	..	250	223	225	236	0.0	0.0	0.9	4.9	-1.4
Saudi Arabia	..	250	223	225	198	0.0	0.0	0.9	-12.0	-5.7
Kuwait	..	93	83	84	89	0.0	0.0	1.2	6.0	-1.1
Untd Arab Emirates	..	67	60	60	77	0.0	0.0	0.0	28.3	3.5
Qatar	..	19	17	17	22	0.0	0.0	0.0	29.4	3.7
Bahrain	..	19	17	17	20	0.0	0.0	0.0	17.6	1.3
Oman	..	15	13	13	16	0.0	0.0	0.0	23.1	1.6
From other regions	*1,021,884*	*570,812*	*488,178*	*512,335*	*541,208*	*59.3*	*54.2*	*4.9*	*5.6*	*-1.3*
All North Africa	966,000	..	..	..	..					
Tunisia	..	400,843	329,145	346,331	366,871	41.6	36.7	5.2	5.9	-2.2
Algeria	..	85,181	70,416	71,657	73,459	8.8	7.4	1.8	2.5	-3.6
Morocco	..	23,088	19,076	19,120	20,803	2.4	2.1	0.2	8.8	-2.6
Sudan	..	20,536	16,302	16,897	17,335	2.1	1.7	3.6	2.6	-4.1
Italy	4,800	7,488	8,266	7,289	7,982	0.8	0.8	-11.8	9.5	1.6
France	2,079	5,271	4,022	6,514	6,951	0.5	0.7	62.0	6.7	7.2
Germany	3,070	6,739	3,442	6,190	6,759	0.7	0.7	79.8	9.2	0.1
United Kingdom	5,296	2,525	4,784	5,642	5,803	0.3	0.6	17.9	2.9	23.1
Malta	2,232	3,530	3,496	3,243	3,587	0.4	0.4	-7.2	10.6	0.4
Philippines	4,944	583	2,268	2,287	2,356	0.1	0.2	0.8	3.0	41.8
India	2,061	358	1,958	2,045	2,089	0.0	0.2	4.4	2.2	55.4
Canada	1,380	518	1,504	1,541	1,684	0.1	0.2	2.5	9.3	34.3
Austria	932	1,540	1,014	1,415	1,526	0.2	0.2	39.5	7.8	-0.2
Serbia & Montenegro	920	617	1,254	1,453	1,478	0.1	0.1	15.9	1.7	24.4
Spain	444	1,512	638	1,389	1,452	0.2	0.1	117.7	4.5	-1.0
Korea, Republic of	3,520	393	1,174	1,255	1,307	0.0	0.1	6.9	4.1	35.0
Mauritania	..	1,841	1,028	1,159	1,179	0.2	0.1	12.7	1.7	-10.5
Turkey	7,633	516	1,206	1,021	1,142	0.1	0.1	-15.3	11.9	22.0
Thailand	337	27	972	1,012	1,042	0.0	0.1	4.1	3.0	149.2
Bulgaria	2,244	193	932	894	910	0.0	0.1	-4.1	1.8	47.4
China	827	141	552	644	853	0.0	0.1	16.7	32.5	56.8
Ireland	258	102	644	743	792	0.0	0.1	15.4	6.6	66.9
Ukraine	232	89	560	715	785	0.0	0.1	27.7	9.8	72.3
Poland	1,541	296	726	701	776	0.0	0.1	-3.4	10.7	27.2
Other interregional	11,134	6,885	12,799	11,178	12,287	0.7	1.2	-12.7	9.9	15.6
Other World/Not specified	*..*	*..*	*..*	*..*	*11*		*0.0*			

Source: World Tourism Organization (UNWTO) ©   (Data as collected by UNWTO for TMT 2006 Edition)

III.1.8   Oman   Middle East

Research and data: www.oman.org/tourism.htm ; www.omanchamber.com ;
www.moneoman.gov.om

Profile

Oman

Capital	Muscat
Year of entry in UNWTO	2004
Area (1000 km²)	310
Population (2005, million)	3.0
Gross Domestic Product (GDP) (2005, US$ million)	30,734
GDP per capita (2005, US$)	12,664

Middle East

GDP growth (real, %)
'-> 2004: 5.6;   2005: 6.7;   2006*: 7.1;   2007*: 5.7

	2003	2004	2005*	2004/2003	2005*/2004
International Arrivals					
Visitors (1000)	1,210	1,407	..	16.3	
Tourists (overnight visitors) (1000)	1,039	1,195	..	15.0	
- per 100 of inhabitants	37	41	..		
Same-day visitors (1000)	171	212	..	24.0	
Tourism accommodation					
Number of rooms	6,462	6,980	7,247	8.0	3.8
Nights spent in hotels and similar establishments (1000)	1,078	1,321	1,748	22.5	32.3
by non-residents (inbound tourism)	777	995	1,394	28.1	40.1
by residents (domestic tourism)	301	326	354	8.3	8.6
Receipts and Expenditure for International Tourism					
International Tourism Receipts (US$ million)	385	414	481	7.4	16.4
- per Tourist Arrival (US$)	370	346	..	-6.6	
- per Visitor Arrival (US$)	318	294	..	-7.6	
- per capita (US$)	137	142	160		
International Fare Receipts (US$ million)	161	190	198	18.0	4.2
International Tourism Expenditure (US$ million)	577	616	645	6.8	4.6
- per capita (US$)	206	212	215		
International Fare Expenditure (US$ million)	174	180	195	3.4	8.3
Δ International Tourism Balance (US$ million)	-192	-203	-164		

Source: World Tourism Organization (UNWTO)   (Data as collected by UNWTO for TMT 2006 Edition)
See annex for methodological notes and reference of external sources used.

International Tourism by Origin

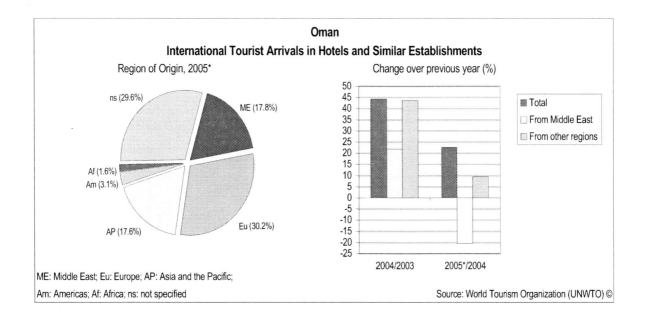

Oman
International Tourist Arrivals in Hotels and Similar Establishments

Region of Origin, 2005*

ns (29.6%)
ME (17.8%)
Af (1.6%)
Am (3.1%)
AP (17.6%)
Eu (30.2%)

Change over previous year (%)

Total
From Middle East
From other regions

2004/2003   2005*/2004

ME: Middle East; Eu: Europe; AP: Asia and the Pacific;
Am: Americas; Af: Africa; ns: not specified

Source: World Tourism Organization (UNWTO) ©

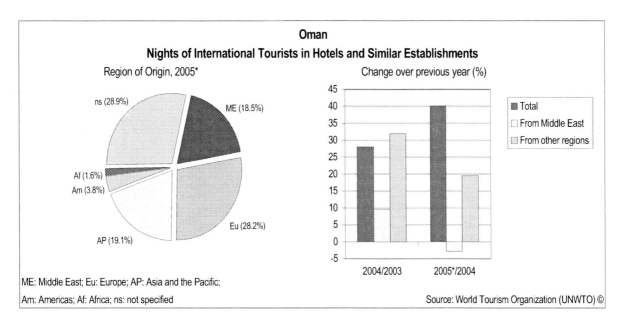

Oman
Nights of International Tourists in Hotels and Similar Establishments

Region of Origin, 2005*

ns (28.9%)
ME (18.5%)
Af (1.6%)
Am (3.8%)
AP (19.1%)
Eu (28.2%)

Change over previous year (%)

Total
From Middle East
From other regions

2004/2003   2005*/2004

ME: Middle East; Eu: Europe; AP: Asia and the Pacific;
Am: Americas; Af: Africa; ns: not specified

Source: World Tourism Organization (UNWTO) ©

Oman

International Tourist Arrivals in Hotels and Similar Establishments (by nationality)

	1995	2000	2003	2004	2005*	Market share (%) 2000	2005*	Growth rate (%) 04/03	05*/04	Average per year (%) 2000-2005*
Total	**279,000**	**571,110**	**629,525**	**908,466**	**1,114,498**	**100**	**100**	**44.3**	**22.7**	**14.3**
From Middle East	*40,000*	*127,676*	*204,586*	*249,285*	*198,577*	*22.4*	*17.8*	*21.8*	*-20.3*	*9.2*
Untd Arab Emirates	..	55,984	87,407	103,317	75,292	9.8	6.8	18.2	-27.1	6.1
All Middle East	40,000	..	..	..	..					
Bahrain	..	15,827	29,881	26,536	31,539	2.8	2.8	-11.2	18.9	14.8
Saudi Arabia	..	17,260	22,163	31,066	25,233	3.0	2.3	40.2	-18.8	7.9
Egypt	..	9,207	16,886	20,276	15,922	1.6	1.4	20.1	-21.5	11.6
Jordan	..	3,954	9,167	11,953	10,572	0.7	0.9	30.4	-11.6	21.7
Kuwait	..	10,196	11,218	15,564	10,226	1.8	0.9	38.7	-34.3	0.1
Qatar	..	5,774	8,697	12,998	9,186	1.0	0.8	49.5	-29.3	9.7
Lebanon	..	3,602	5,437	9,481	7,435	0.6	0.7	74.4	-21.6	15.6
Syrian Arab Republic	..	2,115	5,206	7,081	4,759	0.4	0.4	36.0	-32.8	17.6
Libyan Arab Jamahiriya	..	42	..	..	..	0.0				
Other Middle East	..	3,715	8,524	11,013	8,413	0.7	0.8	29.2	-23.6	17.8
From other regions	*177,000*	*443,434*	*372,243*	*534,683*	*585,615*	*77.6*	*52.5*	*43.6*	*9.5*	*5.7*
United Kingdom	..	66,555	60,532	92,887	118,411	11.7	10.6	53.5	27.5	12.2
India	..	52,313	83,065	106,456	104,778	9.2	9.4	28.2	-1.6	14.9
All Europe	99,000	..	..	..	..					
Germany	..	58,357	31,133	78,129	92,481	10.2	8.3	151.0	18.4	9.6
All Asia	45,000	..	..	..	..					
Switzerland	..	18,810	9,735	17,203	23,463	3.3	2.1	76.7	36.4	4.5
United States	..	26,789	24,620	26,910	22,708	4.7	2.0	9.3	-15.6	-3.3
France	..	16,718	14,803	23,495	21,289	2.9	1.9	58.7	-9.4	5.0
All Americas	18,000	..	..	..	..					
Pakistan	..	9,065	12,017	16,506	17,125	1.6	1.5	37.4	3.8	13.6
Sweden	..	2,850	2,061	3,554	15,741	0.5	1.4	72.4	342.9	40.7
All Africa	15,000	..	..	..	..					
Austria	..	5,201	3,139	7,850	11,309	0.9	1.0	150.1	44.1	16.8
Italy	..	7,663	8,901	10,218	10,413	1.3	0.9	14.8	1.9	6.3
Australia	..	4,742	6,379	7,177	9,069	0.8	0.8	12.5	26.4	13.8
Netherlands	..	11,746	9,052	11,408	8,605	2.1	0.8	26.0	-24.6	-6.0
Japan	..	8,803	6,572	7,279	7,350	1.5	0.7	10.8	1.0	-3.5
Canada	..	6,759	5,246	8,931	7,009	1.2	0.6	70.2	-21.5	0.7
China	..	1,456	4,351	3,667	6,317	0.3	0.6	-15.7	72.3	34.1
Philippines	..	12,704	5,609	5,986	4,991	2.2	0.4	6.7	-16.6	-17.0
Tanzania	..	6,368	6,202	7,828	4,520	1.1	0.4	26.2	-42.3	-6.6
Morocco	..	613	1,892	6,836	4,465	0.1	0.4	261.3	-34.7	48.8
Denmark	..	1,910	1,766	3,045	3,258	0.3	0.3	72.4	7.0	11.3
Sri Lanka	..	2,756	4,032	3,969	3,098	0.5	0.3	-1.6	-21.9	2.4
Belgium	..	..	..	..	2,643		0.2			
Other interregional	..	121,256	71,136	85,349	86,572	21.2	7.8	20.0	1.4	-6.5
Other World/Not specified	*62,000*	*..*	*52,696*	*124,498*	*330,306*		*29.6*	*136.3*	*165.3*	

Source: World Tourism Organization (UNWTO) ©   (Data as collected by UNWTO for TMT 2006 Edition)

World Tourism Organization ©

Oman

Nights of International Tourists in Hotels and Similar Establishments (by nationality)

	1995	2000	2003	2004	2005*	Market share (%) 2000	Market share (%) 2005*	Growth rate (%) 04/03	Growth rate (%) 05*/04	Average per year (%) 2000-2005*
Total	..	..	**777,154**	**995,032**	**1,393,919**		**100**	**28.0**	**40.1**	
From Middle East	..	..	*242,074*	*265,499*	*258,004*		*18.5*	*9.7*	*-2.8*	
Untd Arab Emirates	..	..	88,217	98,616	84,173		6.0	11.8	-14.6	
Bahrain	..	..	31,121	30,935	39,677		2.8	-0.6	28.3	
Saudi Arabia	..	..	26,262	28,708	32,638		2.3	9.3	13.7	
Egypt	..	..	24,135	28,471	25,522		1.8	18.0	-10.4	
Jordan	..	..	14,350	15,890	16,564		1.2	10.7	4.2	
Kuwait	..	..	14,054	15,083	14,963		1.1	7.3	-0.8	
Lebanon	..	..	11,206	13,319	13,000		0.9	18.9	-2.4	
Qatar	..	..	9,562	11,876	12,433		0.9	24.2	4.7	
Syrian Arab Republic	..	..	9,107	10,286	8,832		0.6	12.9	-14.1	
Other Middle East	..	..	14,060	12,315	10,202		0.7	-12.4	-17.2	
From other regions	..	..	*464,486*	*613,114*	*733,296*		*52.6*	*32.0*	*19.6*	
India	..	..	113,993	133,101	141,401		10.1	16.8	6.2	
United Kingdom	..	..	68,244	96,579	132,787		9.5	41.5	37.5	
Germany	..	..	32,626	72,567	105,849		7.6	122.4	45.9	
United States	..	..	32,925	31,212	35,112		2.5	-5.2	12.5	
Switzerland	..	..	7,648	16,588	27,043		1.9	116.9	63.0	
France	..	..	14,741	23,566	24,545		1.8	59.9	4.2	
Pakistan	..	..	15,082	18,732	21,398		1.5	24.2	14.2	
Sweden	..	..	2,279	4,115	16,856		1.2	80.6	309.6	
Australia	..	..	9,822	14,352	15,209		1.1	46.1	6.0	
Netherlands	..	..	10,881	13,962	12,970		0.9	28.3	-7.1	
Italy	..	..	16,530	12,240	12,840		0.9	-26.0	4.9	
Austria	..	..	2,920	7,587	11,884		0.9	159.8	56.6	
Japan	..	..	8,835	10,996	11,540		0.8	24.5	4.9	
Canada	..	..	7,560	12,600	11,271		0.8	66.7	-10.5	
Philippines	..	..	8,330	8,556	9,502		0.7	2.7	11.1	
China	..	..	6,856	5,649	9,018		0.6	-17.6	59.6	
Russian Federation	..	..	..	..	4,834		0.3			
Tanzania	..	..	6,803	8,285	4,624		0.3	21.8	-44.2	
Sri Lanka	..	..	4,725	4,199	4,449		0.3	-11.1	6.0	
Denmark	..	..	2,101	5,721	4,003		0.3	172.3	-30.0	
Sudan	..	..	3,399	4,566	3,874		0.3	34.3	-15.2	
South Africa	..	..	4,433	5,280	3,821		0.3	19.1	-27.6	
Iran	..	..	4,360	4,285	3,359		0.2	-1.7	-21.6	
Belgium	..	..	..	..	3,343		0.2			
Morocco	..	..	2,984	6,546	3,212		0.2	119.4	-50.9	
Other interregional	..	..	76,409	91,830	98,552		7.1	20.2	7.3	
Other World/Not specified	..	..	*70,594*	*116,419*	*402,619*		*28.9*	*64.9*	*245.8*	

Source: World Tourism Organization (UNWTO) ©   (Data as collected by UNWTO for TMT 2006 Edition)

III.1.9 Palestine — Middle East

Profile

Palestine

Middle East

Year of entry in UNWTO			1999
Area (10 km²)			38
Population (2005, million)			1.4

	2003	2004	2005*	2004/2003	2005*/2004
International Arrivals					
Visitors (1000)	46	..	..		
Tourists (overnight visitors) (1000)	37	56	88	51.4	57.1
- per 100 of inhabitants	3	4	6		
Tourism accommodation					
Number of rooms	3,050	3,554	3,691	16.5	3.9
Nights spent in collective establishments (1000)					
by non-residents (inbound tourism)	239	..	..		
Nights spent in hotels and similar establishments (1000)	199	268	350	34.7	30.6
by non-residents (inbound tourism)	113	164	251	45.1	53.0
by residents (domestic tourism)	86	104	99	20.9	-4.8
Receipts and Expenditure for International Tourism					
International Tourism Receipts (US$ million)	107	56	..	-47.7	
- per Tourist Arrival (US$)	2,892	1,000	..	-65.4	
- per Visitor Arrival (US$)	2,308	..	..		
- per capita (US$)	84	42	..		
International Tourism Expenditure (US$ million)	317	286	..	-9.8	
- per capita (US$)	249	216	..		
Δ International Tourism Balance (US$ million)	-210	-230	..		

Source: World Tourism Organization (UNWTO)   (Data as collected by UNWTO for TMT 2006 Edition)

See annex for methodological notes and reference of external sources used.

International Tourism by Origin

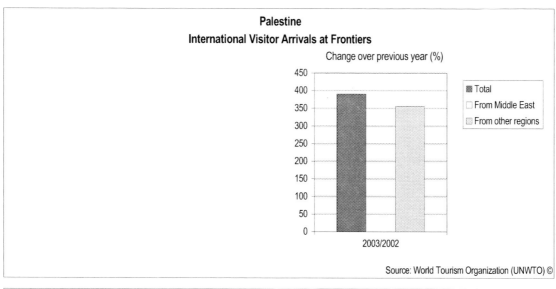

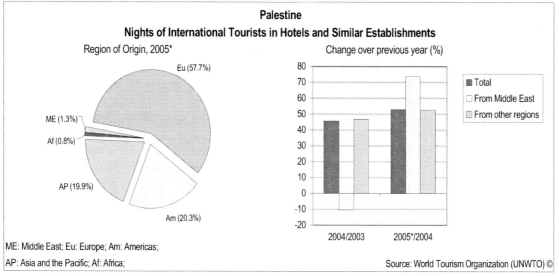

ME: Middle East; Eu: Europe; Am: Americas;
AP: Asia and the Pacific; Af: Africa;

Source: World Tourism Organization (UNWTO) ©

Palestine

Nights of International Tourists in Hotels and Similar Establishments (by nationality)

	1995	2000	2003	2004	2005*	Market share (%) 2000	Market share (%) 2005*	Growth rate (%) 04/03	Growth rate (%) 05*/04	Average per year (%) 2000-2005*
Total	..	**964,052**	**112,807**	**164,375**	**251,357**	**100**	**100**	**45.7**	**52.9**	**-23.6**
From Middle East	..	*21,602*	*2,076*	*1,860*	*3,230*	*2.2*	*1.3*	*-10.4*	*73.7*	*-31.6*
All Middle East	..	21,602	2,076	1,860	3,230	2.2	1.3	-10.4	73.7	-31.6
From other regions	..	*942,450*	*110,731*	*162,515*	*248,127*	*97.8*	*98.7*	*46.8*	*52.7*	*-23.4*
All Asia	..	44,031	13,458	26,241	49,179	4.6	19.6	95.0	87.4	2.2
Canada, USA	..	105,911	24,645	33,603	48,943	11.0	19.5	36.3	45.7	-14.3
Israel	..	44,797	16,754	23,319	30,400	4.6	12.1	39.2	30.4	-7.5
All Africa	..	6,817	1,560	1,374	2,077	0.7	0.8	-11.9	51.2	-21.2
Australia, New Zealand	..	8,589	845	665	948	0.9	0.4	-21.3	42.6	-35.6
Other Americas	..	23,774	807	1,578	2,038	2.5	0.8	95.5	29.2	-38.8
Other Europe	..	708,531	52,662	75,735	114,542	73.5	45.6	43.8	51.2	-30.5

Source: World Tourism Organization (UNWTO) ©   (Data as collected by UNWTO for TMT 2006 Edition)

Palestine

International Visitor Arrivals at Frontiers (by residence)

	1995	2000	2002	2003	2004	Market share (%) 2000	2004	Growth rate (%) 03/02	04/03	Average per year (%) 2000-2004
Total	..	**1,055,000**	**9,453**	**46,356**	..	**100**		**390.4**		
From Middle East	..	*42,000*	..	..	..	*4.0*				
All Middle East	..	42,000	..	..	..	4.0				
From other regions	..	*1,013,000*	*7,332*	*33,414*	..	*96.0*		*355.7*		
Italy	..	132,002	664	5,081	..	12.5		665.2		
Philippines	..	..	61	4,128	..			6667.2		
United States	..	122,961	1,144	3,910	..	11.7		241.8		
France	..	40,315	599	2,481	..	3.8		314.2		
Indonesia	..	..	417	2,090	..			401.2		
Spain	..	38,193	354	2,066	..	3.6		483.6		
Romania	..	..	716	1,567	..			118.9		
Germany	..	81,301	404	1,246	..	7.7		208.4		
United Kingdom	..	69,221	344	1,065	..	6.6		209.6		
Russian Federation	..	57,554	335	1,056	..	5.5		215.2		
Japan	..	10,280	131	1,014	..	1.0		674.0		
Greece	..	36,905	419	725	..	3.5		73.0		
Poland	..	28,424	209	709	..	2.7		239.2		
India	..	4,401	113	561	..	0.4		396.5		
Mexico	..	..	18	528	..			2833.3		
Korea, Republic of	..	..	265	420	..			58.5		
Canada	..	4,561	100	353	..	0.4		253.0		
Israel	..	4,933	..	330	..	0.5				
Sweden	..	..	73	314	..			330.1		
Czech Rep	..	..	36	269	..			647.2		
Netherlands	..	..	42	246	..			485.7		
Brazil	..	8,216	..	187	..	0.8				
Austria	..	2,119	68	185	..	0.2		172.1		
Cyprus	..	2,711	17	168	..	0.3		888.2		
Australia	..	..	25	154	..			516.0		
Other interregional	..	368,903	778	2,561	..	35.0		229.2		
Other World/Not specified	..	..	*2,121*	*12,942*	..			*510.2*		

Source: World Tourism Organization (UNWTO) ©　　　　　　　　　　　(Data as collected by UNWTO for TMT 2006 Edition)

Note: 2001-2003: Arrivals to the west bank only, excluding jerusalem and the gaza strip due to the lack of control on the borders of these regions.

World Tourism Organization ©

III.1.10   Qatar   Middle East

Profile

Qatar

Capital	Doha
Year of entry in UNWTO	2002
Area (100 km²)	110
Population (2005, 1000)	863
Gross Domestic Product (GDP) (2005, US$ million)	34,341
GDP per capita (2005, US$)	43,110
GDP growth (real, %)	

Middle East
-> 2004: 11.2;   2005: 6.5;   2006*: 6.7;   2007*: 4.7

	2003	2004	2005*	2004/2003	2005*/2004
International Arrivals					
Tourists (overnight visitors) (1000)	557	732	913	31.5	24.6
- per 100 of inhabitants	68	87	106		
Tourism accommodation					
Number of rooms	3,858	3,792	4,180	-1.7	10.2
Nights spent in hotels and similar establishments (1000)					
by non-residents (inbound tourism)	848	983	1,024	15.9	4.2
Receipts and Expenditure for International Tourism					
International Tourism Receipts (US$ million)	369	498	760	35.0	52.8
- per Tourist Arrival (US$)	662	680	833	2.7	22.6
- per capita (US$)	451	592	881		
International Tourism Expenditure (US$ million)	471	691	1,759	46.8	154.6
- per capita (US$)	576	822	2,038		
Δ International Tourism Balance (US$ million)	-102	-193	-999		

Source: World Tourism Organization (UNWTO)   (Data as collected by UNWTO for TMT 2006 Edition)
See annex for methodological notes and reference of external sources used.

International Tourism by Origin

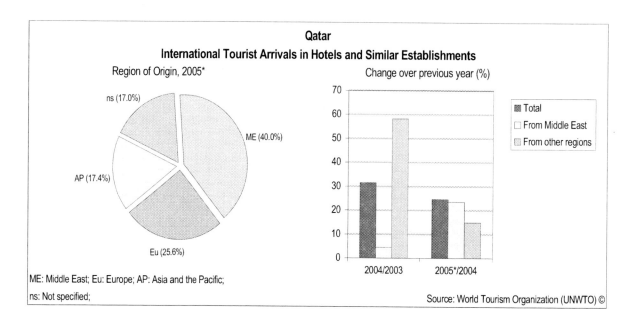

Qatar
International Tourist Arrivals in Hotels and Similar Establishments

Region of Origin, 2005*

ns (17.0%)
ME (40.0%)
AP (17.4%)
Eu (25.6%)

Change over previous year (%)

Total
From Middle East
From other regions

2004/2003   2005*/2004

ME: Middle East; Eu: Europe; AP: Asia and the Pacific;
ns: Not specified;

Source: World Tourism Organization (UNWTO) ©

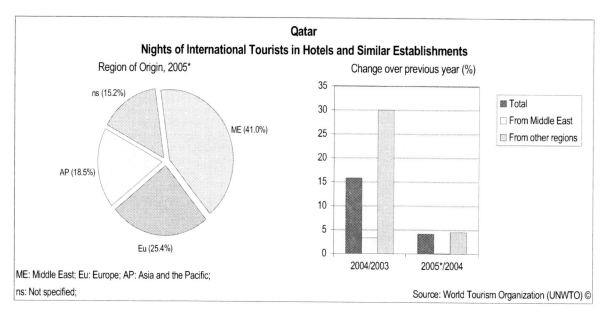

Qatar
Nights of International Tourists in Hotels and Similar Establishments

Region of Origin, 2005*

ns (15.2%)
ME (41.0%)
AP (18.5%)
Eu (25.4%)

Change over previous year (%)

Total
From Middle East
From other regions

2004/2003   2005*/2004

ME: Middle East; Eu: Europe; AP: Asia and the Pacific;
ns: Not specified;

Source: World Tourism Organization (UNWTO) ©

Qatar

International Tourist Arrivals in Hotels and Similar Establishments (by residence)

	1995	2000	2003	2004	2005*	Market share (%) 2000	Market share (%) 2005*	Growth rate (%) 04/03	Growth rate (%) 05*/04	Average per year (%) 2000-2005*
Total	..	**377,979**	**556,965**	**732,454**	**912,997**	**100**	**100**	**31.5**	**24.6**	**19.3**
From Middle East	..	*166,375*	*282,538*	*295,335*	*364,977*	*44.0*	*40.0*	*4.5*	*23.6*	*17.0*
All Middle East	..	166,375	282,538	295,335	364,977	44.0	40.0	4.5	23.6	17.0
From other regions	..	*167,789*	*215,968*	*341,706*	*392,594*	*44.4*	*43.0*	*58.2*	*14.9*	*18.5*
All Europe	..	105,758	88,620	195,732	233,315	28.0	25.6	120.9	19.2	17.1
All Asia	..	62,031	127,348	145,974	159,279	16.4	17.4	14.6	9.1	20.8
Other World/Not specified	..	*43,815*	*58,459*	*95,413*	*155,426*	*11.6*	*17.0*	*63.2*	*62.9*	*28.8*

Source: World Tourism Organization (UNWTO) ©   (Data as collected by UNWTO for TMT 2006 Edition)

Qatar

Nights of International Tourists in Hotels and Similar Establishments (by residence)

	1995	2000	2003	2004	2005*	Market share (%) 2000	Market share (%) 2005*	Growth rate (%) 04/03	Growth rate (%) 05*/04	Average per year (%) 2000-2005*
Total	..	**434,901**	**848,395**	**982,619**	**1,023,698**	**100**	**100**	**15.8**	**4.2**	**18.7**
From Middle East	..	*179,989*	*405,781*	*419,185*	*419,532*	*41.4*	*41.0*	*3.3*	*0.1*	*18.4*
All Middle East	..	179,989	405,781	419,185	419,532	41.4	41.0	3.3	0.1	18.4
From other regions	..	*196,025*	*330,395*	*429,600*	*449,065*	*45.1*	*43.9*	*30.0*	*4.5*	*18.0*
All Europe	..	110,671	165,335	243,446	260,095	25.4	25.4	47.2	6.8	18.6
All Asia	..	85,354	165,060	186,154	188,970	19.6	18.5	12.8	1.5	17.2
Other World/Not specified	..	*58,887*	*112,219*	*133,834*	*155,101*	*13.5*	*15.2*	*19.3*	*15.9*	*21.4*

Source: World Tourism Organization (UNWTO) ©   (Data as collected by UNWTO for TMT 2006 Edition)

III.1.11 Saudi Arabia — Middle East

Promotional: www.sauditourism.gov.sa
Institutional/corporate: www.sct.gov.sa
Research and data: www.mas.gov.sa

Profile

Saudi Arabia

Capital	Riyadh
Year of entry in UNWTO	2002
Area (1000 km²)	2,150
Population (2005, million)	26.4
Gross Domestic Product (GDP) (2005, US$ million)	309,945
GDP per capita (2005, US$)	13,410
GDP growth (real, %)	

Middle East   '-> 2004: 5.3;   2005: 6.6;   2006*: 5.8;   2007*: 6.5

	2003	2004	2005*	2004/2003	2005*/2004
International Arrivals					
Visitors (1000)	..	11,083	10,417		-6.0
Tourists (overnight visitors) (1000)	7,332	8,599	8,037	17.3	-6.5
- per 100 of inhabitants	29	33	30		
Same-day visitors (1000)	..	2,484	2,380		-4.2
Tourism accommodation					
Number of rooms	81,197	96,144	104,093	18.4	8.3
Nights spent in collective establishments (1000)		327,776	288,096		-12.1
by non-residents (inbound tourism)	..	112,556	91,359		-18.8
by residents (domestic tourism)	284,900	215,220	196,737	-24.5	-8.6
Nights spent in hotels and similar establishments (1000)		174,997	165,358		-5.5
by non-residents (inbound tourism)	..	63,341	62,120		-1.9
by residents (domestic tourism)	..	111,656	103,238		-7.5
Outbound Tourism					
Trips abroad (1000)	4,104	4,235	5,009	3.2	18.3
- per 100 of inhabitants	16	16	19		
Receipts and Expenditure for International Tourism					
International Tourism Receipts (US$ million)	3,413	6,486	5,177	90.0	-20.2
- per Tourist Arrival (US$)	466	754	644	62.0	-14.6
- per Visitor Arrival (US$)	..	585	497		-15.1
- per capita (US$)	136	251	196		
International Fare Receipts (US$ million)	..	852	1,280		50.2
International Tourism Expenditure (US$ million)	4,160	4,256	3,775	2.3	-11.3
- per trip (US$)	1,014	1,005	754	-0.9	-25.0
- per capita (US$)	165	165	143		
International Fare Expenditure (US$ million)	..	172	203		18.0
Δ International Tourism Balance (US$ million)	-747	2,230	1,402		
Δ International Fare Balance (US$ million)	..	680	1,077		

Source: World Tourism Organization (UNWTO)   (Data as collected by UNWTO for TMT 2006 Edition)
See annex for methodological notes and reference of external sources used.

World Tourism Organization ©

International Tourism by Origin

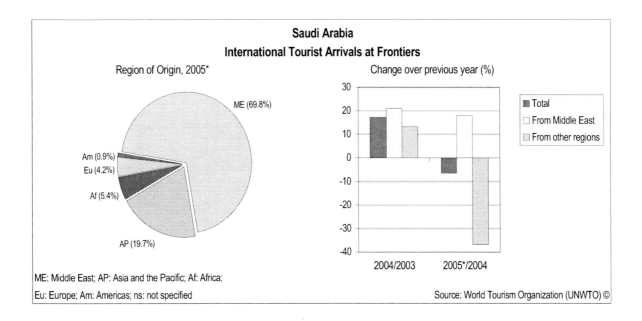

Saudi Arabia
International Tourist Arrivals at Frontiers

Region of Origin, 2005*

ME (69.8%)
Am (0.9%)
Eu (4.2%)
Af (5.4%)
AP (19.7%)

Change over previous year (%)

Total
From Middle East
From other regions

2004/2003   2005*/2004

ME: Middle East; AP: Asia and the Pacific; Af: Africa;
Eu: Europe; Am: Americas; ns: not specified

Source: World Tourism Organization (UNWTO) ©

Saudi Arabia
International Tourist Arrivals at Frontiers (by nationality)

	1995	2000	2003	2004	2005*	Market share (%) 2000	Market share (%) 2005*	Growth rate (%) 04/03	Growth rate (%) 05*/04	Average per year (%) 2000-2005*
Total	..	6,585,326	7,332,233	8,599,430	8,036,613	100	100	17.3	-6.5	4.1
From Middle East	..	*3,598,746*	*3,923,873*	*4,752,257*	*5,607,356*	*54.6*	*69.8*	*21.1*	*18.0*	*9.3*
Kuwait	..	907,521	971,341	1,238,382	1,462,879	13.8	18.2	27.5	18.1	10.0
Untd Arab Emirates	..	158,679	189,471	238,536	1,043,076	2.4	13.0	25.9	337.3	45.7
Egypt	..	888,585	787,277	976,931	799,665	13.5	10.0	24.1	-18.1	-2.1
Syrian Arab Republic	..	479,251	541,894	726,752	576,950	7.3	7.2	34.1	-20.6	3.8
Qatar	..	322,185	388,239	434,944	511,143	4.9	6.4	12.0	17.5	9.7
Bahrain	..	214,463	281,875	277,618	356,163	3.3	4.4	-1.5	28.3	10.7
Jordan	..	250,495	240,356	306,495	279,288	3.8	3.5	27.5	-8.9	2.2
Yemen	..	125,048	212,292	220,759	261,520	1.9	3.3	4.0	18.5	15.9
Oman	..	94,247	136,389	118,695	137,562	1.4	1.7	-13.0	15.9	7.9
Lebanon	..	51,646	63,793	74,591	68,703	0.8	0.9	16.9	-7.9	5.9
Iraq	..	22,027	25,099	43,063	52,477	0.3	0.7	71.6	21.9	19.0
Libyan Arab Jamahiriya	..	44,229	39,546	48,149	49,108	0.7	0.6	21.8	2.0	2.1
Palestine	..	40,370	46,301	47,342	8,822	0.6	0.1	2.2	-81.4	-26.2
From other regions	..	*2,968,705*	*3,386,937*	*3,838,823*	*2,428,021*	*45.1*	*30.2*	*13.3*	*-36.8*	*-3.9*
Iran	..	321,370	618,897	386,507	519,865	4.9	6.5	-37.5	34.5	10.1
Pakistan	..	462,064	539,471	654,059	351,672	7.0	4.4	21.2	-46.2	-5.3
Indonesia	..	390,953	396,709	486,869	226,037	5.9	2.8	22.7	-53.6	-10.4
Sudan	..	121,779	108,742	157,548	130,098	1.8	1.6	44.9	-17.4	1.3
India	..	293,944	362,609	474,467	117,101	4.5	1.5	30.8	-75.3	-16.8
Malaysia	..	108,768	84,473	98,608	101,206	1.7	1.3	16.7	2.6	-1.4
Turkey	..	174,909	177,467	236,267	100,167	2.7	1.2	33.1	-57.6	-10.5
Nigeria	..	102,263	99,028	119,553	96,671	1.6	1.2	20.7	-19.1	-1.1
United Kingdom	..	77,672	69,552	82,602	62,023	1.2	0.8	18.8	-24.9	-4.4
Bangladesh	..	199,270	209,560	255,402	52,633	3.0	0.7	21.9	-79.4	-23.4
Morocco	..	78,971	70,238	80,322	52,123	1.2	0.6	14.4	-35.1	-8.0
Germany	..	11,574	12,007	18,406	51,682	0.2	0.6	53.3	180.8	34.9
United States	..	41,461	35,405	39,096	48,498	0.6	0.6	10.4	24.0	3.2
Sri Lanka	..	67,231	81,695	98,403	42,445	1.0	0.5	20.5	-56.9	-8.8
Philippines	..	71,016	79,490	98,707	35,253	1.1	0.4	24.2	-64.3	-13.1
Nepal	..	21,215	23,843	29,662	31,305	0.3	0.4	24.4	5.5	8.1
France	..	15,028	15,237	17,539	30,946	0.2	0.4	15.1	76.4	15.5
Tunisia	..	40,906	32,573	35,717	30,194	0.6	0.4	9.7	-15.5	-5.9
Afghanistan	..	13,140	31,481	33,313	25,918	0.2	0.3	5.8	-22.2	14.6
Algeria	..	90,632	85,352	112,924	23,465	1.4	0.3	32.3	-79.2	-23.7
China	..	9,842	15,136	21,398	22,837	0.1	0.3	41.4	6.7	18.3
Ethiopia	..	18,496	26,332	43,212	19,914	0.3	0.2	64.1	-53.9	1.5
Singapore	..	17,387	7,149	6,969	15,390	0.3	0.2	-2.5	120.8	-2.4
Italy	..	5,985	5,615	5,446	13,500	0.1	0.2	-3.0	147.9	17.7
Canada	..	10,067	9,081	12,591	13,405	0.2	0.2	38.7	6.5	5.9
Other interregional	..	202,762	189,795	233,236	213,673	3.1	2.7	22.9	-8.4	1.1
Other World/Not specified	..	*17,875*	*21,423*	*8,350*	*1,236*	*0.3*	*0.0*	*-61.0*	*-85.2*	*-41.4*

Source: World Tourism Organization (UNWTO) ©   (Data as collected by UNWTO for TMT 2006 Edition)

III.1.12 Syrian Arab Republic   Middle East

Promotional: www.syriatourism.org
Institutional/corporate: www.syriatourism.org
Research and data: www.syriatourism.org

Profile

Syrian Arab Republic

Capital	Damascus
Year of entry in UNWTO	1975
Area (1000 km²)	185
Population (2005, million)	18.4
Gross Domestic Product (GDP) (2005, US$ million)	27,297
GDP per capita (2005, US$)	1,464

GDP growth (real, %)

Middle East   '-> 2004: 3.1;   2005: 2.9;   2006*: 3.2;   2007*: 3.7

	2003	2004	2005*	2004/2003	2005*/2004
International Arrivals					
Visitors (1000)	4,388	6,154	5,838	40.2	-5.1
Tourists (overnight visitors) (1000)	2,085|	3,033	3,368		11.0
- per 100 of inhabitants	12	17	18		
Same-day visitors (1000)	2,303	3,121	2,470	35.5	-20.9
Tourism accommodation					
Number of rooms	16,966	17,267	18,798	1.8	8.9
Nights spent in collective establishments (1000)					
by non-residents (inbound tourism)	20,700	27,930	30,948	34.9	10.8
Nights spent in hotels and similar establishments (1000)	6,827	8,976	9,767	31.5	8.8
by non-residents (inbound tourism)	5,775	7,995	8,803	38.4	10.1
by residents (domestic tourism)	1,052	981	964	-6.7	-1.7
Outbound Tourism					
Trips abroad (1000)	3,997	4,309	4,564	7.8	5.9
- per 100 of inhabitants	23	24	25		
Receipts and Expenditure for International Tourism					
International Tourism Receipts (US$ million)	773	1,800	2,175	132.9	20.8
- per Tourist Arrival (US$)	371	593	646	60.1	8.8
- per Visitor Arrival (US$)	176	292	373	66.0	27.4
- per capita (US$)	44	100	118		
International Fare Receipts (US$ million)	104	88	108	-15.4	22.7
International Tourism Expenditure (US$ million)	741	804	550	8.5	-31.6
- per trip (US$)	185	187	121	0.6	-35.4
- per capita (US$)	42	45	30		
International Fare Expenditure (US$ million)	34	48	43	41.2	-10.4
Δ International Tourism Balance (US$ million)	32	996	1,625		
Δ International Fare Balance (US$ million)	70	40	65		

Source: World Tourism Organization (UNWTO)   (Data as collected by UNWTO for TMT 2006 Edition)

See annex for methodological notes and reference of external sources used.

| : change of series.

International Tourism by Origin

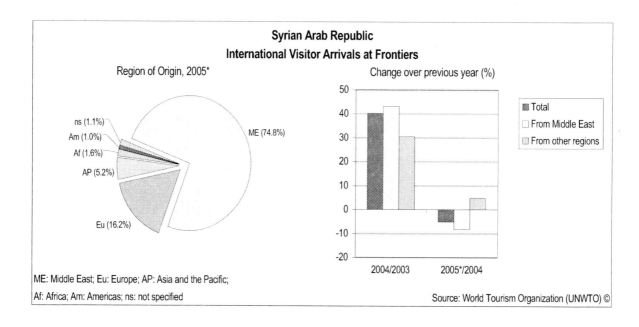

Syrian Arab Republic
International Visitor Arrivals at Frontiers

Region of Origin, 2005*

Change over previous year (%)

ME: Middle East; Eu: Europe; AP: Asia and the Pacific;
Af: Africa; Am: Americas; ns: not specified

Source: World Tourism Organization (UNWTO) ©

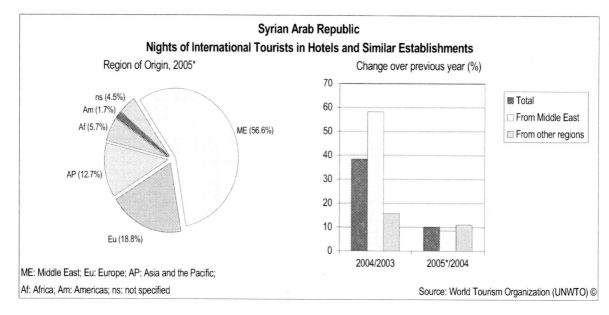

Syrian Arab Republic
Nights of International Tourists in Hotels and Similar Establishments

Region of Origin, 2005*

Change over previous year (%)

ME: Middle East; Eu: Europe; AP: Asia and the Pacific;
Af: Africa; Am: Americas; ns: not specified

Source: World Tourism Organization (UNWTO) ©

Syrian Arab Republic
International Visitor Arrivals at Frontiers (by nationality)

	1995	2000	2003	2004	2005*	Market share (%) 2000	Market share (%) 2005*	Growth rate (%) 04/03	Growth rate (%) 05*/04	Average per year (%) 2000-2005*
Total	**2,252,787**	**3,014,758**	**4,388,119**	**6,153,653**	**5,837,980**	**100**	**100**	**40.2**	**-5.1**	**14.1**
From Middle East	*1,581,703*	*2,196,287*	*3,325,490*	*4,760,773*	*4,369,669*	*72.9*	*74.8*	*43.2*	*-8.2*	*14.7*
Lebanon	839,308	995,235	1,654,001	2,262,733	1,681,158	33.0	28.8	36.8	-25.7	11.1
Jordan	421,072	538,493	752,935	851,095	940,413	17.9	16.1	13.0	10.5	11.8
Iraq	4,171	85,439	253,120	804,131	913,266	2.8	15.6	217.7	13.6	60.6
Saudi Arabia	143,502	283,653	361,758	461,035	469,118	9.4	8.0	27.4	1.8	10.6
Kuwait	38,300	69,075	72,693	105,715	103,474	2.3	1.8	45.4	-2.1	8.4
Palestine	17,643	37,082	52,087	56,884	65,839	1.2	1.1	9.2	15.7	12.2
Bahrain	25,156	32,263	60,648	67,163	55,854	1.1	1.0	10.7	-16.8	11.6
Egypt	50,075	32,320	31,423	44,533	36,398	1.1	0.6	41.7	-18.3	2.4
Untd Arab Emirates	9,438	14,698	24,274	30,538	28,188	0.5	0.5	25.8	-7.7	13.9
Libyan Arab Jamahiriya	3,556	24,358	18,230	20,102	22,957	0.8	0.4	10.3	14.2	-1.2
Yemen	17,858	19,656	22,046	28,760	19,123	0.7	0.3	30.5	-33.5	-0.5
Qatar	5,490	5,160	9,883	14,411	17,126	0.2	0.3	45.8	18.8	27.1
Other Middle East	6,134	58,855	12,392	13,673	16,755	2.0	0.3	10.3	22.5	-22.2
From other regions	*636,068*	*768,828*	*1,023,442*	*1,335,734*	*1,401,273*	*25.5*	*24.0*	*30.5*	*4.9*	*12.8*
Turkey	162,091	182,801	470,900	689,581	688,978	6.1	11.8	46.4	-0.1	30.4
Iran	203,406	221,380	213,931	196,699	247,662	7.3	4.2	-8.1	25.9	2.3
Former U.S.S.R.	58,995	18,871	28,696	35,188	42,000	0.6	0.7	22.6	19.4	17.4
Germany	24,308	38,297	25,036	34,878	38,408	1.3	0.7	39.3	10.1	0.1
United States	10,881	25,094	29,023	38,939	38,343	0.8	0.7	34.2	-1.5	8.8
Algeria	20,001	18,340	25,382	33,073	32,983	0.6	0.6	30.3	-0.3	12.5
France	22,476	36,059	26,910	33,599	31,191	1.2	0.5	24.9	-7.2	-2.9
Tunisia	12,139	18,139	21,048	28,021	30,500	0.6	0.5	33.1	8.8	11.0
United Kingdom	9,938	20,101	16,908	19,902	20,508	0.7	0.4	17.7	3.0	0.4
Sudan	15,895	21,778	17,303	17,859	17,885	0.7	0.3	3.2	0.1	-3.9
Indonesia	2,909	6,949	13,513	18,559	17,119	0.2	0.3	37.3	-7.8	19.8
Sweden	4,204	11,141	12,950	19,069	16,548	0.4	0.3	47.3	-13.2	8.2
Spain	4,494	9,168	6,890	11,329	15,744	0.3	0.3	64.4	39.0	11.4
Italy	11,293	20,441	8,859	11,729	13,898	0.7	0.2	32.4	18.5	-7.4
Canada	4,074	8,123	9,864	13,571	13,474	0.3	0.2	37.6	-0.7	10.7
Cyprus	1,672	6,130	6,627	11,163	11,990	0.2	0.2	68.4	7.4	14.4
India	3,665	10,685	9,560	11,936	11,875	0.4	0.2	24.9	-0.5	2.1
Netherlands	6,596	10,015	7,862	12,880	11,790	0.3	0.2	63.8	-8.5	3.3
Australia	4,481	8,973	7,597	12,542	11,254	0.3	0.2	65.1	-10.3	4.6
Morocco	4,466	7,874	9,754	10,711	11,217	0.3	0.2	9.8	4.7	7.3
Pakistan	5,383	9,921	4,217	8,634	8,789	0.3	0.2	104.7	1.8	-2.4
Denmark	1,748	4,402	5,616	9,188	8,770	0.1	0.2	63.6	-4.5	14.8
Japan	4,476	8,166	4,787	5,751	6,715	0.3	0.1	20.1	16.8	-3.8
Austria	4,394	5,166	3,730	4,631	5,231	0.2	0.1	24.2	13.0	0.3
Belgium	3,253	5,930	3,376	4,709	5,074	0.2	0.1	39.5	7.8	-3.1
Other interregional	28,830	34,884	33,103	41,593	43,327	1.2	0.7	25.6	4.2	4.4
Other World/Not specified	*35,016*	*49,643*	*39,187*	*57,146*	*67,038*	*1.6*	*1.1*	*45.8*	*17.3*	*6.2*

Source: World Tourism Organization (UNWTO) ©   (Data as collected by UNWTO for TMT 2006 Edition)
Note: Excluding nationals residing abroad

Syrian Arab Republic
Nights of International Tourists in Hotels and Similar Establishments (by nationality)

	1995	2000	2003	2004	2005*	Market share (%) 2000	2005*	Growth rate (%) 04/03	05*/04	Average per year (%) 2000-2005*
Total	1,822,650	1,836,879	5,774,524	7,995,088	8,803,464	100	100	38.5	10.1	36.8
From Middle East	*591,993*	*624,740*	*2,903,850*	*4,594,297*	*4,985,408*	*34.0*	*56.6*	*58.2*	*8.5*	*51.5*
Iraq	8,434	36,904	373,922	1,626,703	2,013,112	2.0	22.9	335.0	23.8	122.5
Jordan	128,857	145,448	744,395	810,698	1,039,870	7.9	11.8	8.9	28.3	48.2
Saudi Arabia	86,701	90,599	377,159	627,080	710,273	4.9	8.1	66.3	13.3	51.0
Lebanon	182,924	193,784	745,768	763,089	568,376	10.5	6.5	2.3	-25.5	24.0
Kuwait	21,883	16,761	78,880	126,827	146,971	0.9	1.7	60.8	15.9	54.4
Bahrain	4,723	6,168	154,254	156,210	144,901	0.3	1.6	1.3	-7.2	88.0
Egypt	80,704	44,367	44,443	144,476	81,343	2.4	0.9	225.1	-43.7	12.9
Libyan Arab Jamahiriya	7,829	30,107	84,356	79,339	68,044	1.6	0.8	-5.9	-14.2	17.7
Yemen	41,341	27,549	159,262	122,857	65,667	1.5	0.7	-22.9	-46.6	19.0
Palestine	15,339	15,185	86,906	60,088	57,410	0.8	0.7	-30.9	-4.5	30.5
Untd Arab Emirates	..	8,294	27,195	45,772	48,339	0.5	0.5	68.3	5.6	42.3
Qatar	2,732	4,541	4,072	8,313	11,082	0.2	0.1	104.2	33.3	19.5
Other Middle East	10,526	5,033	23,238	22,845	30,020	0.3	0.3	-1.7	31.4	42.9
From other regions	*1,165,757*	*1,148,377*	*2,661,439*	*3,080,951*	*3,423,078*	*62.5*	*38.9*	*15.8*	*11.1*	*24.4*
Iran	196,152	199,592	1,042,389	711,977	904,069	10.9	10.3	-31.7	27.0	35.3
Turkey	19,253	17,945	32,496	129,935	327,255	1.0	3.7	299.8	151.9	78.7
Germany	89,009	115,935	128,557	209,965	213,725	6.3	2.4	63.3	1.8	13.0
Algeria	83,892	41,997	115,503	204,431	207,861	2.3	2.4	77.0	1.7	37.7
Former U.S.S.R.	242,267	100,112	153,223	170,220	191,125	5.5	2.2	11.1	12.3	13.8
Tunisia	43,625	48,693	96,846	154,137	166,507	2.7	1.9	59.2	8.0	27.9
France	108,345	140,348	142,297	177,445	159,319	7.6	1.8	24.7	-10.2	2.6
United Kingdom	32,712	36,830	139,689	135,886	121,573	2.0	1.4	-2.7	-10.5	27.0
Spain	17,449	31,118	49,797	87,566	120,820	1.7	1.4	75.8	38.0	31.2
Italy	58,345	91,730	62,169	84,808	100,381	5.0	1.1	36.4	18.4	1.8
Sudan	55,980	40,476	105,705	96,099	99,462	2.2	1.1	-9.1	3.5	19.7
Indonesia	81	..	72,153	103,233	92,350		1.0	43.1	-10.5	
United States	24,582	30,231	14,590	83,945	82,719	1.6	0.9	475.4	-1.5	22.3
Netherlands	34,119	28,996	41,979	82,612	75,348	1.6	0.9	96.8	-8.8	21.0
India	7,277	7,033	41,427	57,696	57,875	0.4	0.7	39.3	0.3	52.4
Austria	18,385	16,304	52,841	35,246	41,032	0.9	0.5	-33.3	16.4	20.3
Denmark	4,222	7,159	31,339	40,710	40,831	0.4	0.5	29.9	0.3	41.7
Canada	7,856	10,416	21,736	48,100	36,561	0.6	0.4	121.3	-24.0	28.5
Cyprus	3,227	23,547	17,249	34,043	34,637	1.3	0.4	97.4	1.7	8.0
Switzerland	10,341	19,683	22,579	34,593	34,363	1.1	0.4	53.2	-0.7	11.8
Sweden	5,544	6,975	33,928	42,063	32,526	0.4	0.4	24.0	-22.7	36.1
Belgium	15,243	20,341	14,564	26,185	32,214	1.1	0.4	79.8	23.0	9.6
Greece	5,092	8,194	13,630	27,235	27,752	0.4	0.3	99.8	1.9	27.6
Yugoslav SFR	1,247	1,373	28,534	25,593	27,178	0.1	0.3	-10.3	6.2	81.7
Morocco	6,670	25,377	9,277	32,288	26,392	1.4	0.3	248.0	-18.3	0.8
Other interregional	74,842	77,972	176,942	244,940	169,203	4.2	1.9	38.4	-30.9	16.8
Other World/Not specified	*64,900*	*63,762*	*209,235*	*319,840*	*394,978*	*3.5*	*4.5*	*52.9*	*23.5*	*44.0*

Source: World Tourism Organization (UNWTO) ©   (Data as collected by UNWTO for TMT 2006 Edition)

III.1.13 United Arab Emirates   Middle East

Promotional: www.dubaitourism.ae

Profile

United Arab Emirates

Capital	Abu Dhabi
Area (1000 km²)	84
Population (2005, million)	2.6
Gross Domestic Product (GDP) (2005, US$ million)	129,642
GDP per capita (2005, US$)	27,700
GDP growth (real, %)	

Middle East

-> 2004: 9.7;   2005: 8.5;   2006*: 11.5;   2007*: 5.8

	2003	2004	2005*	2004/2003	2005*/2004
International Arrivals					
Tourists (overnight visitors) (1000)	5,871	..	..		
- per 100 of inhabitants	236	..	..		
Tourism accommodation					
Number of rooms	38,402	..	..		
Nights spent in hotels and similar establishments (1000)					
by non-residents (inbound tourism)	14,192	..	..		
Receipts and Expenditure for International Tourism					
International Tourism Receipts (US$ million)	1,439	1,594	2,200	10.8	38.0
- per Tourist Arrival (US$)	245	..	..		
- per capita (US$)	579	632	858		
International Tourism Expenditure (US$ million)	3,956	4,472	5,255	13.0	17.5
- per capita (US$)	1,592	1,772	2,050		
Δ International Tourism Balance (US$ million)	-2,517	-2,878	-3,055		

Source: World Tourism Organization (UNWTO)   (Data as collected by UNWTO for TMT 2006 Edition)
See annex for methodological notes and reference of external sources used.

International Tourism by Origin

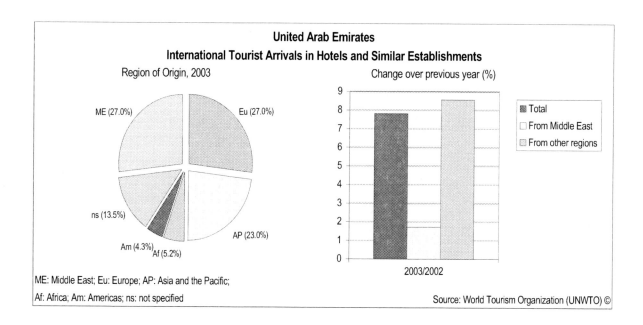

United Arab Emirates
International Tourist Arrivals in Hotels and Similar Establishments

Region of Origin, 2003

ME (27.0%)
Eu (27.0%)
ns (13.5%)
AP (23.0%)
Am (4.3%)
Af (5.2%)

Change over previous year (%)

Total
From Middle East
From other regions

2003/2002

ME: Middle East; Eu: Europe; AP: Asia and the Pacific;
Af: Africa; Am: Americas; ns: not specified

Source: World Tourism Organization (UNWTO) ©

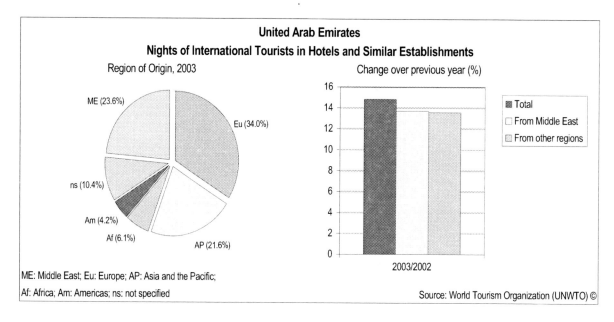

United Arab Emirates
Nights of International Tourists in Hotels and Similar Establishments

Region of Origin, 2003

ME (23.6%)
Eu (34.0%)
ns (10.4%)
Am (4.2%)
Af (6.1%)
AP (21.6%)

Change over previous year (%)

Total
From Middle East
From other regions

2003/2002

ME: Middle East; Eu: Europe; AP: Asia and the Pacific;
Af: Africa; Am: Americas; ns: not specified

Source: World Tourism Organization (UNWTO) ©

United Arab Emirates
International Tourist Arrivals in Hotels and Similar Establishments (by nationality)

	1995	2000	2002	2003	2004	Market share (%) 2000	2004	Growth rate (%) 03/02	04/03	Average per year (%) 2000-2004
Total	**2,314,659**	**3,906,545**	**5,445,367**	**5,871,023**	..	**100**		**7.8**		
From Middle East	*591,177*	*1,088,753*	*1,556,533*	*1,583,258*	..	*27.9*		*1.7*		
Egypt	44,958	94,058	111,822	121,221	..	2.4		8.4		
Lebanon	29,240	55,790	74,225	83,137	..	1.4		12.0		
Jordan	18,147	55,344	73,140	76,553	..	1.4		4.7		
Syrian Arab Republic	22,748	43,341	53,836	60,104	..	1.1		11.6		
Yemen	9,928	33,557	47,383	36,912	..	0.9		-22.1		
Iraq	1,570	13,137	18,521	18,401	..	0.3		-0.6		
Palestine	5,483	11,004	15,042	13,946	..	0.3		-7.3		
Other Middle East	459,103	782,522	1,162,564	1,172,984	..	20.0		0.9		
From other regions	*1,515,171*	*2,221,950*	*3,219,641*	*3,495,230*	..	*56.9*		*8.6*		
United Kingdom	164,312	337,865	491,604	496,147	..	8.6		0.9		
India	127,361	235,493	336,046	357,941	..	6.0		6.5		
Iran	41,402	154,861	270,350	334,453	..	4.0		23.7		
Russian Federation	25,062	228,785	267,655	324,484	..	5.9		21.2		
Germany	88,802	171,519	236,660	235,147	..	4.4		-0.6		
Pakistan	83,438	136,061	154,711	183,724	..	3.5		18.8		
United States	72,464	100,547	123,112	175,116	..	2.6		42.2		
France	37,379	60,955	90,735	98,624	..	1.6		8.7		
All Oceania	12,451	36,001	68,434	84,407	..	0.9		23.3		
Canada	11,761	27,859	95,878	55,297	..	0.7		-42.3		
Bangladesh	23,667	42,038	45,987	45,580	..	1.1		-0.9		
Netherlands	13,284	26,017	37,179	37,563	..	0.7		1.0		
Japan	19,159	28,079	32,876	37,549	..	0.7		14.2		
Sudan	8,489	18,841	31,211	35,347	..	0.5		13.3		
Somalia	7,630	9,443	..	..	..	0.2				
Other Africa	53,818	145,317	279,511	271,525	..	3.7		-2.9		
Other Americas	8,319	11,068	19,759	23,949	..	0.3		21.2		
Other Asia	226,106	199,529	293,751	305,550	..	5.1		4.0		
Other Europe	490,267	251,672	344,182	392,827	..	6.4		14.1		
Nationals residing abroad	*208,311*	*595,842*	*669,193*	*792,535*	..	*15.3*		*18.4*		

Source: World Tourism Organization (UNWTO) ©   (Data as collected by UNWTO for TMT 2006 Edition)

United Arab Emirates

Nights of International Tourists in Hotels and Similar Establishments (by nationality)

	1995	2000	2002	2003	2004	Market share (%) 2000	Market share (%) 2004	Growth rate (%) 03/02	Growth rate (%) 04/03	Average per year (%) 2000-2004
Total	**6.363.775**	**10.313.499**	**12.359.593**	**14.191.984**	..	100		**14,8**		
From Middle East	*1.336.139*	*2.453.001*	*2.941.737*	*3.345.105*	..	*23,8*		*13,7*		
Egypt	127.548	251.983	254.026	296.319	..	2,4		16,6		
Lebanon	82.084	155.527	165.598	195.412	..	1,5		18,0		
Jordan	47.141	140.433	158.968	175.979	..	1,4		10,7		
Syrian Arab Republic	62.861	108.880	121.456	136.658	..	1,1		12,5		
Yemen	24.099	77.109	99.859	79.599	..	0,7		-20,3		
Iraq	4.717	41.155	48.319	50.513	..	0,4		4,5		
Palestine	14.912	25.352	29.928	29.346	..	0,2		-1,9		
Other Middle East	972.777	1.652.562	2.063.583	2.381.279	..	16,0		15,4		
From other regions	*4.675.781*	*6.826.493*	*8.245.537*	*9.364.628*	..	*66,2*		*13,6*		
United Kingdom	479.770	1.065.594	1.451.979	1.574.331	..	10,3		8,4		
Russian Federation	87.425	1.001.440	910.063	1.054.744	..	9,7		15,9		
India	337.531	543.871	717.049	819.990	..	5,3		14,4		
Iran	130.297	403.941	580.214	816.580	..	3,9		40,7		
Germany	348.496	699.553	673.823	699.367	..	6,8		3,8		
United States	182.216	264.909	291.783	401.518	..	2,6		37,6		
Pakistan	181.390	285.879	301.002	380.683	..	2,8		26,5		
France	107.324	188.120	236.050	249.386	..	1,8		5,6		
All Oceania	55.177	83.633	130.007	167.597	..	0,8		28,9		
Canada	30.566	74.991	180.558	134.588	..	0,7		-25,5		
Netherlands	38.588	81.733	108.668	116.845	..	0,8		7,5		
Japan	60.385	80.844	82.536	102.956	..	0,8		24,7		
Bangladesh	61.685	75.713	92.326	89.090	..	0,7		-3,5		
Sudan	22.232	60.120	73.597	84.742	..	0,6		15,1		
Somalia	26.520	26.669	..	..	..	0,3				
Other Africa	175.894	492.565	732.768	788.003	..	4,8		7,5		
Other Americas	21.318	32.369	51.679	65.997	..	0,3		27,7		
Other Asia	508.591	467.520	612.347	685.930	..	4,5		12,0		
Other Europe	1.820.376	897.029	1.019.088	1.132.281	..	8,7		11,1		
Nationals residing abroad	*351.855*	*1.034.005*	*1.172.319*	*1.482.251*	..	*10,0*		*26,4*		

Source: World Tourism Organization (UNWTO) ©   (Data as collected by UNWTO for TMT 2006 Edition)

III.1.14 Yemen   Middle East

Promotional: www.yementourism.com

Profile

Yemen

Capital	Sanaa
Year of entry in UNWTO	1977
Area (1000 km²)	528
Population (2005, million)	20.7
Gross Domestic Product (GDP) (2005, US$ million)	15,193
GDP per capita (2005, US$)	586
GDP growth (real, %)	

Middle East   '-> 2004: 2.6;   2005: 3.8;   2006*: 3.9;   2007*: 2.5

	2003	2004	2005*	2004/2003	2005*/2004
International Arrivals					
Tourists (overnight visitors) (1000)	155	274	336	77.0	22.8
- per 100 of inhabitants	1	1	2		
Tourism accommodation					
Number of rooms	13,280	12,890	15,265	-2.9	18.4
Nights spent in hotels and similar establishments (1000)	4,287		6,189		
by non-residents (inbound tourism)	928	1,642	2,017	76.9	22.8
by residents (domestic tourism)	3,359	..	4,172		
Receipts and Expenditure for International Tourism					
International Tourism Receipts (US$ million)	139	139	181		30.2
- per Tourist Arrival (US$)	899	508	539	-43.5	6.1
- per capita (US$)	7	7	9		
International Tourism Expenditure (US$ million)	77	126	167	63.6	32.5
- per capita (US$)	4	6	8		
International Fare Expenditure (US$ million)	57	57	57		
Δ International Tourism Balance (US$ million)	62	13	14		

Source: World Tourism Organization (UNWTO)   (Data as collected by UNWTO for TMT 2006 Edition)
See annex for methodological notes and reference of external sources used.

International Tourism by Origin

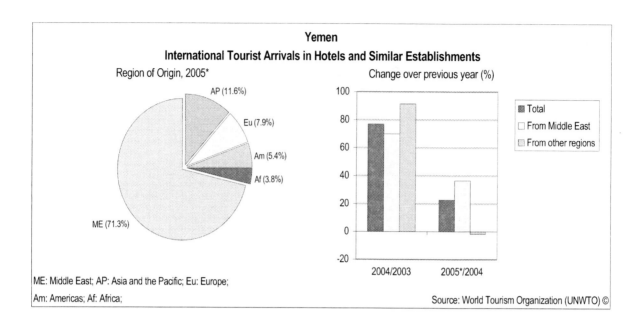

Yemen
International Tourist Arrivals in Hotels and Similar Establishments

Region of Origin, 2005*

AP (11.6%)
Eu (7.9%)
Am (5.4%)
Af (3.8%)
ME (71.3%)

Change over previous year (%)

Total
From Middle East
From other regions

2004/2003   2005*/2004

ME: Middle East; AP: Asia and the Pacific; Eu: Europe;
Am: Americas; Af: Africa;

Source: World Tourism Organization (UNWTO) ©

Yemen

International Tourist Arrivals in Hotels and Similar Establishments (by nationality)

	1995	2000	2003	2004	2005*	Market share (%) 2000	Market share (%) 2005*	Growth rate (%) 04/03	Growth rate (%) 05*/04	Average per year (%) 2000-2005*
Total	**61,346**	**72,836**	**154,667**	**273,732**	**336,070**	**100**	**100**	**77.0**	**22.8**	**35.8**
From Middle East	*9,719*	*25,404*	*103,409*	*175,679*	*239,701*	*34.9*	*71.3*	*69.9*	*36.4*	*56.7*
Saudi Arabia	2,415	9,842	59,669	123,799	162,160	13.5	48.3	107.5	31.0	75.1
Syrian Arab Republic	726	2,278	6,780	7,307	7,622	3.1	2.3	7.8	4.3	27.3
Egypt	1,455	3,355	3,677	8,464	6,947	4.6	2.1	130.2	-17.9	15.7
Jordan	1,475	2,352	2,689	5,129	3,483	3.2	1.0	90.7	-32.1	8.2
Iraq	1,045	2,543	2,846	3,945	1,687	3.5	0.5	38.6	-57.2	-7.9
Other Middle East	2,603	5,034	27,748	27,035	57,802	6.9	17.2	-2.6	113.8	62.9
From other regions	*51,627*	*47,432*	*51,258*	*98,053*	*96,369*	*65.1*	*28.7*	*91.3*	*-1.7*	*15.2*
United States	2,806	5,702	3,860	12,172	9,627	7.8	2.9	215.3	-20.9	11.0
United Kingdom	4,965	4,342	4,640	7,061	4,348	6.0	1.3	52.2	-38.4	0.0
France	8,297	4,535	1,882	3,101	3,078	6.2	0.9	64.8	-0.7	-7.5
Italy	7,610	4,748	1,731	2,332	3,054	6.5	0.9	34.7	31.0	-8.4
Germany	10,028	4,194	1,894	2,757	2,975	5.8	0.9	45.6	7.9	-6.6
Sudan	504	2,288	1,875	3,055	2,179	3.1	0.6	62.9	-28.7	-1.0
Japan	1,555	1,240	628	1,531	1,245	1.7	0.4	143.8	-18.7	0.1
Australia	750	446	377	733	1,177	0.6	0.4	94.4	60.6	21.4
Netherlands	1,413	1,014	801	1,117	932	1.4	0.3	39.5	-16.6	-1.7
Switzerland	1,105	502	229	337	345	0.7	0.1	47.2	2.4	-7.2
Other Africa	1,107	3,370	6,752	7,798	10,449	4.6	3.1	15.5	34.0	25.4
Other Americas	401	2,459	9,072	5,816	8,626	3.4	2.6	-35.9	48.3	28.5
Other Asia	3,030	7,102	15,661	38,340	36,610	9.8	10.9	144.8	-4.5	38.8
Other Europe	8,056	5,490	1,856	11,903	11,724	7.5	3.5	541.3	-1.5	16.4

Source: World Tourism Organization (UNWTO) ©   (Data as collected by UNWTO for TMT 2006 Edition)

World Tourism Organization ©

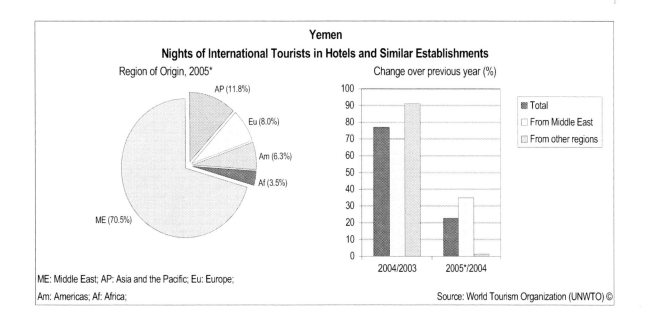

Yemen
Nights of International Tourists in Hotels and Similar Establishments

Region of Origin, 2005*

AP (11.8%)
Eu (8.0%)
Am (6.3%)
Af (3.5%)
ME (70.5%)

Change over previous year (%)

■ Total
□ From Middle East
▨ From other regions

ME: Middle East; AP: Asia and the Pacific; Eu: Europe;
Am: Americas; Af: Africa;

Source: World Tourism Organization (UNWTO) ©

Yemen
Nights of International Tourists in Hotels and Similar Establishments (by nationality)

	1995	2000	2003	2004	2005*	Market share (%) 2000	Market share (%) 2005*	Growth rate (%) 04/03	Growth rate (%) 05*/04	Average per year (%) 2000-2005*
Total	..	**473,434**	**928,002**	**1,642,392**	**2,017,497**	**100**	**100**	**77.0**	**22.8**	**33.6**
From Middle East	..	*156,715*	*620,454*	*1,054,074*	*1,421,374*	*33.1*	*70.5*	*69.9*	*34.8*	*55.4*
Saudi Arabia	..	55,718	358,014	742,794	973,860	11.8	48.3	107.5	31.1	77.2
Egypt	..	21,352	22,062	50,784	55,782	4.5	2.8	130.2	9.8	21.2
Syrian Arab Republic	..	8,974	40,680	43,842	45,730	1.9	2.3	7.8	4.3	38.5
Jordan	..	16,127	16,134	30,774	20,898	3.4	1.0	90.7	-32.1	5.3
Iraq	..	17,610	17,076	23,670	10,122	3.7	0.5	38.6	-57.2	-10.5
Other Middle East	..	36,934	166,488	162,210	314,982	7.8	15.6	-2.6	94.2	53.5
From other regions	..	*316,719*	*307,548*	*588,318*	*596,123*	*66.9*	*29.5*	*91.3*	*1.3*	*13.5*
United States	..	40,038	23,160	73,032	75,358	8.5	3.7	215.3	3.2	13.5
United Kingdom	..	30,587	27,840	42,366	33,559	6.5	1.7	52.2	-20.8	1.9
Italy	..	38,140	10,386	13,992	17,668	8.1	0.9	34.7	26.3	-14.3
France	..	36,923	11,292	18,606	17,264	7.8	0.9	64.8	-7.2	-14.1
Germany	..	36,529	11,364	16,542	17,094	7.7	0.8	45.6	3.3	-14.1
Sudan	..	10,657	11,250	18,330	13,074	2.3	0.6	62.9	-28.7	4.2
Japan	..	7,303	3,768	9,186	8,039	1.5	0.4	143.8	-12.5	1.9
Australia	..	2,382	2,262	4,398	6,636	0.5	0.3	94.4	50.9	22.7
Netherlands	..	8,920	4,806	6,702	6,580	1.9	0.3	39.5	-1.8	-5.9
Switzerland	..	3,598	1,374	2,022	2,000	0.8	0.1	47.2	-1.1	-11.1
Other Africa	..	11,158	40,512	46,788	56,703	2.4	2.8	15.5	21.2	38.4
Other Americas	..	10,215	54,432	29,562	50,821	2.2	2.5	-45.7	71.9	37.8
Other Asia	..	43,739	89,766	235,374	224,296	9.2	11.1	162.2	-4.7	38.7
Other Europe	..	36,530	15,336	71,418	67,031	7.7	3.3	365.7	-6.1	12.9

Source: World Tourism Organization (UNWTO) ©   (Data as collected by UNWTO for TMT 2006 Edition)

World Tourism Organization ©

III.2   North Africa

III.2.1   Algeria   North Africa

Promotional: www.algérie-tourisme.dz
Institutional/corporate: www.tourisme.dz

Profile

Algeria

Africa
North Africa

Capital	Algiers
Year of entry in UNWTO	1976
Area (1000 km²)	2,382
Population (2005, million)	32.5
Gross Domestic Product (GDP) (2005, US$ million)	102,026
GDP per capita (2005, US$)	3,086
GDP growth (real, %)	

'-> 2004: 5.2;   2005: 5.3;   2006*: 4.9;   2007*: 5.0

	2003	2004	2005*	2004/2003	2005*/2004
International Arrivals					
Visitors (1000)	1,166	1,234	1,443	5.8	17.0
- per 100 of inhabitants	4	4	4		
Tourism accommodation					
Number of bed-places	77,473	82,034	83,895	5.9	2.3
Nights spent in hotels and similar establishments (1000)	4,319	4,543	4,705	5.2	3.6
by non-residents (inbound tourism)	371	394	483	6.2	22.6
by residents (domestic tourism)	3,948	4,149	4,222	5.1	1.8
Outbound Tourism					
Trips abroad (1000)	1,254	1,417	1,513	13.0	6.8
- per 100 of inhabitants	4	4	5		
Receipts and Expenditure for International Tourism					
International Tourism Receipts (US$ million)	112	179	184	59.4	3.1
- per Visitor Arrival (US$)	96	145	128	50.7	-11.9
- per capita (US$)	4	6	6		
International Tourism Expenditure (US$ million)	255	341	370	33.7	8.5
- per trip (US$)	203	241	245	18.3	1.6
- per capita (US$)	8	11	11		
Δ International Tourism Balance (US$ million)	-143	-162	-186		

Source: World Tourism Organization (UNWTO)   (Data as collected by UNWTO for TMT 2006 Edition)
See annex for methodological notes and reference of external sources used.

International Tourism by Origin

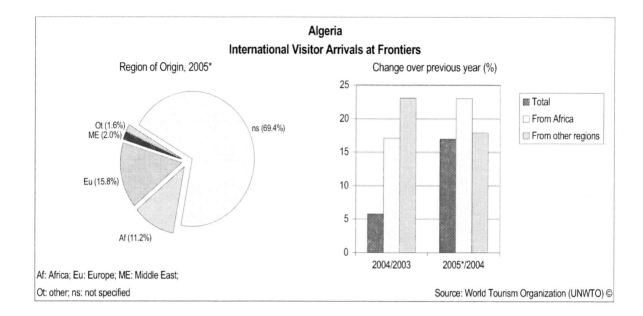

Algeria
International Visitor Arrivals at Frontiers (by nationality)

	1995	2000	2003	2004	2005*	Market share (%) 2000	Market share (%) 2005*	Growth rate (%) 04/03	Growth rate (%) 05*/04	Average per year (%) 2000-2005*
Total	**519,576**	**865,984**	**1,166,287**	**1,233,719**	**1,443,090**	**100**	**100**	**5.8**	**17.0**	**10.8**
From Africa	*42,878*	*55,508*	*111,941*	*131,066*	*161,182*	*6.4*	*11.2*	*17.1*	*23.0*	*23.8*
Tunisia	24,207	32,481	86,025	103,593	128,765	3.8	8.9	20.4	24.3	31.7
Mali	5,874	8,857	14,453	11,520	12,817	1.0	0.9	-20.3	11.3	7.7
Morocco	4,797	3,805	4,186	5,424	9,984	0.4	0.7	29.6	84.1	21.3
Mauritania	1,967	1,489	1,596	1,914	3,028	0.2	0.2	19.9	58.2	15.3
Niger	1,507	1,751	1,343	2,025	1,262	0.2	0.1	50.8	-37.7	-6.3
Other Africa	4,526	7,125	4,338	6,590	5,326	0.8	0.4	51.9	-19.2	-5.7
From other regions	*54,772*	*120,030*	*192,973*	*237,496*	*280,024*	*13.9*	*19.4*	*23.1*	*17.9*	*18.5*
France	26,349	64,839	106,042	138,473	153,398	7.5	10.6	30.6	10.8	18.8
Spain	1,621	7,048	8,600	11,030	14,007	0.8	1.0	28.3	27.0	14.7
Italy	2,791	7,158	10,571	10,642	13,676	0.8	0.9	0.7	28.5	13.8
Libyan Arab Jamahiriya	7,698	4,851	9,391	10,007	11,803	0.6	0.8	6.6	17.9	19.5
Germany	1,398	4,784	7,049	7,306	9,392	0.6	0.7	3.6	28.6	14.4
United Kingdom	935	2,313	4,549	6,956	8,126	0.3	0.6	52.9	16.8	28.6
Turkey	663	2,081	3,741	6,013	7,548	0.2	0.5	60.7	25.5	29.4
Belgium	508	2,163	3,801	4,769	5,393	0.2	0.4	25.5	13.1	20.0
United States	1,286	1,312	2,098	3,321	3,549	0.2	0.2	58.3	6.9	22.0
Canada	416	1,435	2,255	2,655	3,305	0.2	0.2	17.7	24.5	18.2
Switzerland	353	1,753	2,558	2,345	2,905	0.2	0.2	-8.3	23.9	10.6
Japan	78	815	1,236	1,435	1,721	0.1	0.1	16.1	19.9	16.1
Portugal	122	427	1,049	920	1,571	0.0	0.1	-12.3	70.8	29.8
Netherlands	117	844	1,525	1,496	1,536	0.1	0.1	-1.9	2.7	12.7
Sweden	223	639	945	984	1,275	0.1	0.1	4.1	29.6	14.8
Austria	114	688	959	665	900	0.1	0.1	-30.7	35.3	5.5
Norway	35	176	291	464	776	0.0	0.1	59.5	67.2	34.5
Greece	237	279	395	384	518	0.0	0.0	-2.8	34.9	13.2
Denmark	93	250	458	592	513	0.0	0.0	29.3	-13.3	15.5
Australia	35	180	281	333	420	0.0	0.0	18.5	26.1	18.5
Finland	26	94	239	202	245	0.0	0.0	-15.5	21.3	21.1
Brazil	82	56	83	144	233	0.0	0.0	73.5	61.8	33.0
Mexico	22	74	85	150	227	0.0	0.0	76.5	51.3	25.1
Argentina	60	93	118	111	200	0.0	0.0	-5.9	80.2	16.5
Luxembourg	27	58	73	94	89	0.0	0.0	28.8	-5.3	8.9
Other interregional	9,483	15,620	24,581	26,005	36,698	1.8	2.5	5.8	41.1	18.6
Nationals residing abroad	*421,926*	*690,446*	*861,373*	*865,157*	*1,001,884*	*79.7*	*69.4*	*0.4*	*15.8*	*7.7*

Source: World Tourism Organization (UNWTO) ©   (Data as collected by UNWTO for TMT 2006 Edition)

III.2.2   Morocco   North Africa

Promotional: www.tourism-in-morocco.com ; www.tourisme-marocain.com
Institutional/corporate: www.tourisme.gov.ma (site in progress)
Research and data: www.tourisme.gov.ma (site in progress)

Profile

Morocco

Capital	Rabat
Year of entry in UNWTO	1975
Area (1000 km²)	447
Population (2005, million)	32.7
Gross Domestic Product (GDP) (2005, US$ million)	51,621
GDP per capita (2005, US$)	1,713

Africa
North Africa

GDP growth (real, %)
'-> 2004: 4.2;   2005: 1.7;   2006*: 7.3;   2007*: 3.3

	2003	2004	2005*	2004/2003	2005*/2004
International Arrivals					
Visitors (1000)	5,021	5,732	6,077	14.2	6.0
Tourists (overnight visitors) (1000)	4,761	5,477	5,843	15.0	6.7
- per 100 of inhabitants	15	17	18		
Cruise passengers (1000)	260	256	233	-1.5	-9.0
Tourism accommodation					
Number of rooms	52,918	57,431	59,864	8.5	4.2
Nights spent in hotels and similar establishments (1000)	11,173	13,165	15,215	17.8	15.6
by non-residents (inbound tourism)	8,515	10,307	12,259	21.0	18.9
by residents (domestic tourism)	2,658	2,858	2,956	7.5	3.4
Outbound Tourism					
Trips abroad (1000)	1,612	1,603	2,247	-0.6	40.2
- per 100 of inhabitants	5	5	7		
Receipts and Expenditure for International Tourism					
International Tourism Receipts (US$ million)	3,225	3,924	4,621	21.6	17.8
- per Tourist Arrival (US$)	677	716	791	5.8	10.4
- per Visitor Arrival (US$)	642	684	760	6.6	11.1
- per capita (US$)	102	122	141		
International Fare Receipts (US$ million)	581	618	816	6.4	32.0
International Tourism Expenditure (US$ million)	548	575	614	4.9	6.9
- per trip (US$)	340	359	273	5.5	-23.8
- per capita (US$)	17	18	19		
International Fare Expenditure (US$ million)	297	338	387	13.8	14.5
Δ International Tourism Balance (US$ million)	2,677	3,349	4,007		
Δ International Fare Balance (US$ million)	284	280	429		

Source: World Tourism Organization (UNWTO)   (Data as collected by UNWTO for TMT 2006 Edition)
See annex for methodological notes and reference of external sources used.

International Tourism by Origin

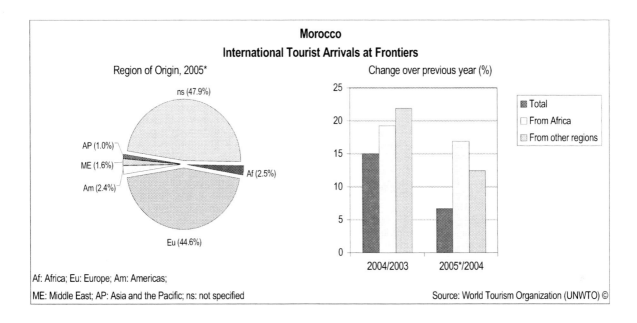

Morocco
International Tourist Arrivals at Frontiers

Region of Origin, 2005*

Change over previous year (%)

- Total
- From Africa
- From other regions

Af: Africa; Eu: Europe; Am: Americas;
ME: Middle East; AP: Asia and the Pacific; ns: not specified

Source: World Tourism Organization (UNWTO) ©

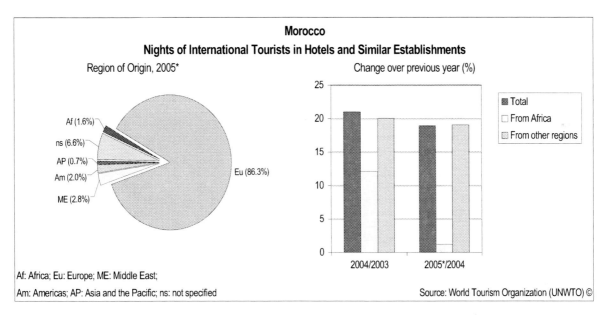

Morocco
Nights of International Tourists in Hotels and Similar Establishments

Region of Origin, 2005*

Change over previous year (%)

- Total
- From Africa
- From other regions

Af: Africa; Eu: Europe; ME: Middle East;
Am: Americas; AP: Asia and the Pacific; ns: not specified

Source: World Tourism Organization (UNWTO) ©

Morocco

International Tourist Arrivals at Frontiers (by nationality)

	1995	2000	2003	2004	2005*	Market share (%) 2000	Market share (%) 2005*	Growth rate (%) 04/03	Growth rate (%) 05*/04	Average per year (%) 2000-2005*
Total	**2,601,641**	**4,278,120**	**4,761,271**	**5,476,712**	**5,843,360**	**100**	**100**	**15.0**	**6.7**	**6.4**
From Africa	*66,258*	*88,689*	*103,194*	*123,070*	*143,855*	*2.1*	*2.5*	*19.3*	*16.9*	*10.2*
Algeria	13,178	20,251	23,095	29,744	37,298	0.5	0.6	28.8	25.4	13.0
Tunisia	27,689	26,495	24,645	23,904	25,709	0.6	0.4	-3.0	7.6	-0.6
Senegal ·	5,355	7,775	10,674	16,208	20,922	0.2	0.4	51.8	29.1	21.9
Mauritania	4,326	5,886	15,913	18,895	20,889	0.1	0.4	18.7	10.6	28.8
Guinea	2,755	5,926	8,907	11,218	10,175	0.1	0.2	25.9	-9.3	11.4
Côte d'Ivoire	1,568	1,969	3,314	4,121	5,982	0.0	0.1	24.4	45.2	24.9
Mali	3,893	6,145	4,507	4,679	5,603	0.1	0.1	3.8	19.7	-1.8
South Africa	1,586	3,072	1,950	2,233	3,093	0.1	0.1	14.5	38.5	0.1
Congo	107	1,350	1,346	1,747	2,288	0.0	0.0	29.8	31.0	11.1
Niger	799	1,887	1,366	1,496	2,161	0.0	0.0	9.5	44.5	2.7
Gabon	1,302	1,203	1,016	1,266	1,955	0.0	0.0	24.6	54.4	10.2
Other intraregional	3,700	6,730	6,461	7,559	7,780	0.2	0.1	17.0	2.9	2.9
From other regions	*1,455,696*	*2,230,277*	*2,113,727*	*2,577,109*	*2,897,930*	*52.1*	*49.6*	*21.9*	*12.4*	*5.4*
France	421,890	813,865	916,147	1,167,088	1,337,204	19.0	22.9	27.4	14.6	10.4
Spain	199,133	232,245	231,156	317,119	367,811	5.4	6.3	37.2	16.0	9.6
United Kingdom	128,913	137,247	134,059	150,398	193,565	3.2	3.3	12.2	28.7	7.1
Germany	161,748	211,039	129,391	141,210	144,200	4.9	2.5	9.1	2.1	-7.3
Belgium	44,102	79,918	80,062	105,821	125,890	1.9	2.2	32.2	19.0	9.5
Italy	101,212	142,426	100,001	112,807	120,955	3.3	2.1	12.8	7.2	-3.2
United States	80,168	121,068	64,445	76,889	82,980	2.8	1.4	19.3	7.9	-7.3
Netherlands	44,615	59,436	66,486	73,190	80,090	1.4	1.4	10.1	9.4	6.1
Switzerland	25,586	44,556	42,173	41,758	46,508	1.0	0.8	-1.0	11.4	0.9
Portugal	16,472	31,302	36,389	38,951	36,980	0.7	0.6	7.0	-5.1	3.4
Canada	24,725	34,320	27,606	31,321	36,825	0.8	0.6	13.5	17.6	1.4
Saudi Arabia	26,957	31,749	28,921	31,478	36,406	0.7	0.6	8.8	15.7	2.8
Sweden	12,000	29,725	24,094	26,723	26,638	0.7	0.5	10.9	-0.3	-2.2
Japan	17,206	23,643	13,982	15,723	17,044	0.6	0.3	12.5	8.4	-6.3
Austria	12,489	23,297	12,798	13,561	14,634	0.5	0.3	6.0	7.9	-8.9
Ireland	6,803	10,943	15,166	18,112	13,202	0.3	0.2	19.4	-27.1	3.8
Australia	4,505	11,636	10,047	12,544	12,327	0.3	0.2	24.9	-1.7	1.2
Turkey	3,031	4,616	8,012	7,900	12,161	0.1	0.2	-1.4	53.9	21.4
Denmark	7,669	14,619	15,593	15,143	12,115	0.3	0.2	-2.9	-20.0	-3.7
Egypt	4,290	9,427	9,648	9,890	11,553	0.2	0.2	2.5	16.8	4.2
Poland	5,535	8,628	5,457	8,913	10,632	0.2	0.2	63.3	19.3	4.3
Norway	6,258	21,826	17,651	13,988	10,585	0.5	0.2	-20.8	-24.3	-13.5
Libyan Arab Jamahiriya	11,369	11,357	9,572	9,426	9,653	0.3	0.2	-1.5	2.4	-3.2
Finland	19,084	11,765	9,661	10,012	9,290	0.3	0.2	3.6	-7.2	-4.6
Russian Federation	4,915	8,089	8,039	11,318	8,670	0.2	0.1	40.8	-23.4	1.4
Other interregional	65,021	101,535	97,171	115,826	120,012	2.4	2.1	19.2	3.6	3.4
Nationals residing abroad	*1,077,522*	*1,952,615*	*2,537,396*	*2,769,132*	*2,787,825*	*45.6*	*47.7*	*9.1*	*0.7*	*7.4*
Other World/Not specified	*2,165*	*6,539*	*6,954*	*7,401*	*13,750*	*0.2*	*0.2*	*6.4*	*85.8*	*16.0*

Source: World Tourism Organization (UNWTO) ©   (Data as collected by UNWTO for TMT 2006 Edition)

Morocco

Nights of International Tourists in Hotels and Similar Establishments (by nationality)

	1995	2000	2003	2004	2005*	Market share (%) 2000	Market share (%) 2005*	Growth rate (%) 04/03	Growth rate (%) 05*/04	Average per year (%) 2000-2005*
Total	**8,501,511**	**13,251,700**	**8,515,293**	**10,307,268**	**12,259,489**	**100**	**100**	**21.0**	**18.9**	**-1.5**
From Africa	*309,432*	*261,058*	*172,589*	*193,527*	*195,873*	*2.0*	*1.6*	*12.1*	*1.2*	*-5.6*
All Africa	309,432	..	..	..	..					
Algeria	..	37,243	33,478	54,997	59,556	0.3	0.5	64.3	8.3	9.8
Tunisia	..	50,623	38,882	38,582	42,085	0.4	0.3	-0.8	9.1	-3.6
Mauritania	..	88,713	21,929	17,159	9,327	0.7	0.1	-21.8	-45.6	-36.3
Other Africa	..	84,479	78,300	82,789	84,905	0.6	0.7	5.7	2.6	0.1
From other regions	*7,719,360*	*12,344,211*	*7,875,443*	*9,456,135*	*11,259,660*	*93.2*	*91.8*	*20.1*	*19.1*	*-1.8*
France	2,189,394	5,400,395	4,329,870	5,240,184	6,231,344	40.8	50.8	21.0	18.9	2.9
Germany	2,262,641	2,048,457	761,604	823,916	904,777	15.5	7.4	8.2	9.8	-15.1
United Kingdom	742,220	679,591	450,654	567,385	860,904	5.1	7.0	25.9	51.7	4.8
Spain	376,179	728,886	354,495	559,481	699,362	5.5	5.7	57.8	25.0	-0.8
Belgium	250,295	514,864	356,957	498,876	624,088	3.9	5.1	39.8	25.1	3.9
Italy	641,043	867,381	439,014	519,290	568,695	6.5	4.6	18.3	9.5	-8.1
Scandinavia	248,536	..	..	..	..					
All Middle East	240,145	..	..	..	..					
United States	260,216	390,824	133,333	153,725	184,634	2.9	1.5	15.3	20.1	-13.9
Netherlands	132,655	194,897	136,800	140,202	181,167	1.5	1.5	2.5	29.2	-1.5
Saudi Arabia	..	175,708	131,269	155,768	158,516	1.3	1.3	18.7	1.8	-2.0
Switzerland	162,631	213,793	129,539	131,133	145,623	1.6	1.2	1.2	11.0	-7.4
Sweden	..	240,368	112,706	125,153	117,957	1.8	1.0	11.0	-5.7	-13.3
Portugal	61,247	121,641	91,840	70,718	88,862	0.9	0.7	-23.0	25.7	-6.1
Japan	75,052	130,139	61,275	70,596	84,436	1.0	0.7	15.2	19.6	-8.3
Canada	77,106	101,731	43,293	46,609	57,927	0.8	0.5	7.7	24.3	-10.7
Finland	..	67,994	49,967	45,914	43,747	0.5	0.4	-8.1	-4.7	-8.4
Austria	..	72,425	40,432	48,790	41,161	0.5	0.3	20.7	-15.6	-10.7
Denmark	..	68,370	34,278	36,137	39,044	0.5	0.3	5.4	8.0	-10.6
Egypt	..	29,027	27,528	26,041	31,850	0.2	0.3	-5.4	22.3	1.9
Norway	..	120,124	38,340	27,961	21,080	0.9	0.2	-27.1	-24.6	-29.4
Untd Arab Emirates	..	10,609	15,945	16,213	16,761	0.1	0.1	1.7	3.4	9.6
Libyan Arab Jamahiriya	..	37,447	17,284	14,765	16,494	0.3	0.1	-14.6	11.7	-15.1
Commonwealth Indep. States	..	19,191	26,839	32,766	15,829	0.1	0.1	22.1	-51.7	-3.8
Syrian Arab Republic	..	9,323	8,556	10,446	13,012	0.1	0.1	22.1	24.6	6.9
Other interregional	..	101,026	83,625	94,066	112,390	0.8	0.9	12.5	19.5	2.2
Nationals residing abroad	*..*	*30,374*	*25,195*	*23,956*	*34,030*	*0.2*	*0.3*	*-4.9*	*42.1*	*2.3*
Other World/Not specified	*472,719*	*616,057*	*442,066*	*633,650*	*769,926*	*4.6*	*6.3*	*43.3*	*21.5*	*4.6*

Source: World Tourism Organization (UNWTO) ©   (Data as collected by UNWTO for TMT 2006 Edition)

III.2.3 Sudan   North Africa

Profile

Sudan

Capital	Khartoum
Year of entry in UNWTO	1975
Area (1000 km²)	2,506
Population (2005, million)	40.2
Gross Domestic Product (GDP) (2005, US$ million)	27,542
GDP per capita (2005, US$)	820

Africa
North Africa

GDP growth (real, %)
· 2004: 5.2;   2005: 7.9;   2006*: 12.1;   2007*: 11.3

	2003	2004	2005*	2004/2003	2005*/2004
International Arrivals					
Tourists (overnight visitors) (1000)	52	61	246	15.8	305.8
- per 100 of inhabitants	0	0	1		
Tourism accommodation					
Number of rooms	..	4,200	4,200		
Receipts and Expenditure for International Tourism					
International Tourism Receipts (US$ million)	18	21	89	16.7	324.4
- per Tourist Arrival (US$)	344	347	363	0.7	4.6
- per capita (US$)	0	1	2		
International Tourism Expenditure (US$ million)	119	176	667	47.9	279.2
- per capita (US$)	3	4	17		
Δ International Tourism Balance (US$ million)	-101	-155	-578		

Source: World Tourism Organization (UNWTO)   (Data as collected by UNWTO for TMT 2006 Edition)
See annex for methodological notes and reference of external sources used.

International Tourism by Origin

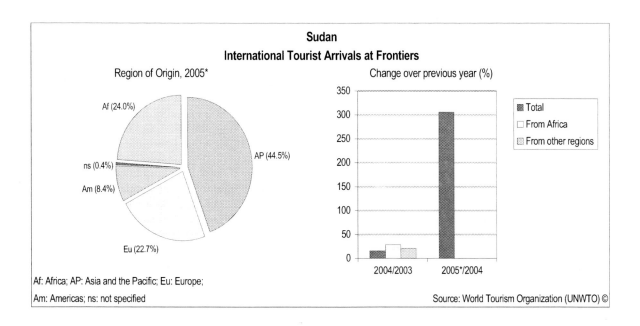

Sudan
International Tourist Arrivals at Frontiers

Region of Origin, 2005*

Af (24.0%)
ns (0.4%)
Am (8.4%)
Eu (22.7%)
AP (44.5%)

Change over previous year (%)

Total
From Africa
From other regions

2004/2003   2005*/2004

Af: Africa; AP: Asia and the Pacific; Eu: Europe;
Am: Americas; ns: not specified

Source: World Tourism Organization (UNWTO) ©

Sudan

International Tourist Arrivals at Frontiers (by nationality)

	1995	2000	2003	2004	2005*	Market share (%) 2000	Market share (%) 2005*	Growth rate (%) 04/03	Growth rate (%) 05*/04	Average per year (%) 2000-2005*
Total	**63,040**	**38,000**	**52,291**	**60,577**	**245,798**	**100**	**100**	**15.8**	**305.8**	**45.3**
From Africa	*5,715*	*5,000*	*7,000*	*9,000*	*58,991*	*13.2*	*24.0*	*28.6*	*555.5*	*63.8*
All Africa	..	5,000	7,000	9,000	58,991	13.2	24.0	28.6	555.5	63.8
Ethiopia	3,215	..	..	..	..					
Other Africa	2,500	..	..	..	..					
From other regions	*51,725*	*33,000*	*28,000*	*34,000*	*185,927*	*86.8*	*75.6*	*21.4*	*446.8*	*41.3*
All Asia	..	7,000	14,000	17,000	109,380	18.4	44.5	21.4	543.4	73.3
All Europe	..	9,000	14,000	17,000	55,796	23.7	22.7	21.4	228.2	44.0
All Americas	..	4,000	..	..	20,751	10.5	8.4			39.0
All Middle East	..	9,000	..	..	..	23.7				
All South Asia	..	4,000	..	..	..	10.5				
China	3,534	..	..	..	..					
Egypt	3,283	..	..	..	..					
Canada	3,237	..	..	..	..					
United States	3,125	..	..	..	..					
France	2,235	..	..	..	..					
Japan	2,158	..	..	..	..					
Greece	2,155	..	..	..	..					
All South America	2,110	..	..	..	..					
Yemen	1,795	..	..	..	..					
India	1,725	..	..	..	..					
Saudi Arabia	1,520	..	..	..	..					
Germany	1,322	..	..	..	..					
Pakistan	1,295	..	..	..	..					
Switzerland	1,235	..	..	..	..					
Lebanon	1,230	..	..	..	..					
Australia	1,225	..	..	..	..					
Netherlands	1,153	..	..	..	..					
Bulgaria	1,095	..	..	..	..					
Italy	1,092	..	..	..	..					
United Kingdom	1,022	..	..	..	..					
Other interregional	14,179	..	..	..	..					
Other World/Not specified	*5,600*	*..*	*17,291*	*17,577*	*880*		*0.4*	*1.7*	*-95.0*	

Source: World Tourism Organization (UNWTO) ©　　　　　　　　　　　(Data as collected by UNWTO for TMT 2006 Edition)

| III.2.4 | Tunisia | North Africa |

Promotional: www.tourismtunisia.com

Profile

Tunisia

Africa
North Africa

Capital	Tunis
Year of entry in UNWTO	1975
Area (1000 km²)	164
Population (2005, million)	10.1
Gross Domestic Product (GDP) (2005, US$ million)	28,674
GDP per capita (2005, US$)	2,829
GDP growth (real, %)	

'-> 2004: 6.0;   2005: 4.2;   2006*: 5.8;   2007*: 6.0

	2003	2004	2005*	2004/2003	2005*/2004
International Arrivals					
Visitors (1000)	5,492	6,419	6,975	16.9	8.7
Tourists (overnight visitors) (1000)	5,114	5,998	6,378	17.3	6.3
- per 100 of inhabitants	52	60	63		
Cruise passengers (1000)	378	421	597	11.4	41.8
Tourism accommodation					
Number of rooms	111,009	113,076	114,919	1.9	1.6
Nights spent in hotels and similar establishments (1000)	28,110	33,487	36,310	19.1	8.4
by non-residents (inbound tourism)	25,301	30,665	33,587	21.2	9.5
by residents (domestic tourism)	2,809	2,822	2,723	0.5	-3.5
Outbound Tourism					
Trips abroad (1000)	2,274	2,312	2,241	1.7	-3.1
- per 100 of inhabitants	23	23	22		
Receipts and Expenditure for International Tourism					
International Tourism Receipts (US$ million)	1,582	1,970	2,063	24.5	4.7
- per Tourist Arrival (US$)	309	329	323	6.2	-1.5
- per Visitor Arrival (US$)	288	307	296	6.5	-3.6
- per capita (US$)	160	198	205		
International Fare Receipts (US$ million)	352	462	658	31.3	42.4
International Tourism Expenditure (US$ million)	300	340	385	13.2	13.1
- per trip (US$)	132	147	172	11.4	16.7
- per capita (US$)	30	34	38		
International Fare Expenditure (US$ million)	56	87	78	55.9	-10.3
Δ International Tourism Balance (US$ million)	1,282	1,630	1,679		
Δ International Fare Balance (US$ million)	296	375	580		

Source: World Tourism Organization (UNWTO)   (Data as collected by UNWTO for TMT 2006 Edition)

See annex for methodological notes and reference of external sources used.

International Tourism by Origin

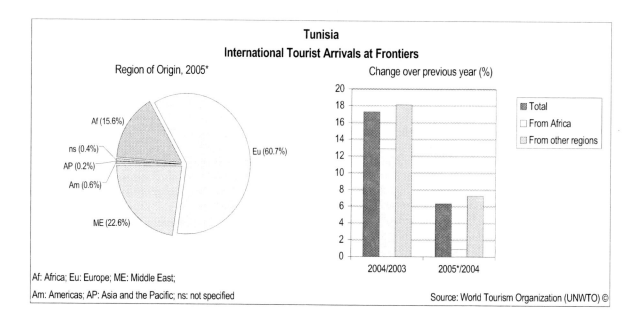

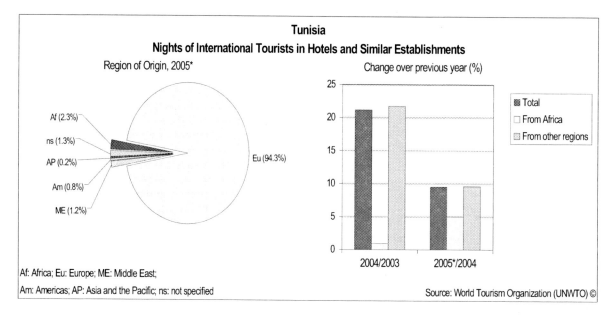

Tunisia
International Tourist Arrivals at Frontiers (by nationality)

	1995	2000	2003	2004	2005*	Market share (%) 2000	Market share (%) 2005*	Growth rate (%) 04/03	Growth rate (%) 05*/04	Average per year (%) 2000-2005*
Total	**4,119,847**	**5,057,513**	**5,114,304**	**5,997,929**	**6,378,435**	**100**	**100**	**17.3**	**6.3**	**4.8**
From Africa	*1,034,479*	*666,199*	*872,251*	*984,538*	*993,378*	*13.2*	*15.6*	*12.9*	*0.9*	*8.3*
Algeria	988,608	611,620	811,463	914,064	930,715	12.1	14.6	12.6	1.8	8.8
Morocco	26,689	37,689	35,003	35,897	29,912	0.7	0.5	2.6	-16.7	-4.5
Mauritania	6,367	5,558	6,962	8,111	7,871	0.1	0.1	16.5	-3.0	7.2
Sudan	..	387	691	774	1,038	0.0	0.0	12.0	34.1	21.8
Other Africa	12,815	10,945	18,132	25,692	23,842	0.2	0.4	41.7	-7.2	16.8
From other regions	*3,046,434*	*4,367,956*	*4,228,791*	*4,994,935*	*5,358,334*	*86.4*	*84.0*	*18.1*	*7.3*	*4.2*
Libyan Arab Jamahiriya	618,746	685,208	1,325,660	1,435,785	1,404,007	13.5	22.0	8.3	-2.2	15.4
France	465,103	997,882	833,989	1,020,810	1,170,100	19.7	18.3	22.4	14.6	3.2
Germany	837,116	1,011,298	488,481	569,475	571,934	20.0	9.0	16.6	0.4	-10.8
Italy	245,933	393,891	379,773	448,292	472,768	7.8	7.4	18.0	5.5	3.7
United Kingdom	239,567	299,376	223,189	300,784	327,542	5.9	5.1	34.8	8.9	1.8
Belgium	74,198	139,846	132,596	140,790	155,082	2.8	2.4	6.2	10.2	2.1
Spain	33,289	102,828	78,223	114,871	146,404	2.0	2.3	46.9	27.5	7.3
Czech Rep	32,749	54,762	90,038	128,404	145,881	1.1	2.3	42.6	13.6	21.6
Poland	19,772	49,837	54,443	75,133	122,627	1.0	1.9	38.0	63.2	19.7
Russian Federation	12,967	20,979	73,376	99,406	96,175	0.4	1.5	35.5	-3.3	35.6
Switzerland	74,539	118,449	85,765	99,117	92,766	2.3	1.5	15.6	-6.4	-4.8
Austria	65,036	110,160	70,065	84,383	86,412	2.2	1.4	20.4	2.4	-4.7
Netherlands	70,507	67,587	44,490	53,683	66,096	1.3	1.0	20.7	23.1	-0.4
Scandinavia	59,663	..	..	..	..					
Hungary	19,687	33,445	55,532	52,895	58,546	0.7	0.9	-4.7	10.7	11.8
Slovakia	6,970	18,412	21,898	34,733	39,966	0.4	0.6	58.6	15.1	16.8
Portugal	13,601	17,668	28,197	35,795	38,901	0.3	0.6	26.9	8.7	17.1
Denmark	..	19,574	10,487	17,266	36,982	0.4	0.6	64.6	114.2	13.6
Sweden	..	24,651	23,286	34,328	36,428	0.5	0.6	47.4	6.1	8.1
Ireland	13,275	32,945	22,713	20,736	21,163	0.7	0.3	-8.7	2.1	-8.5
Finland	..	18,257	11,009	13,942	19,902	0.4	0.3	26.6	42.7	1.7
Yugoslav SFR	4,676	6,986	14,419	15,325	19,795	0.1	0.3	6.3	29.2	23.2
Norway	..	13,312	25,599	15,273	18,711	0.3	0.3	-40.3	22.5	7.0
Canada	13,318	14,902	11,913	15,803	17,039	0.3	0.3	32.7	7.8	2.7
United States	11,499	16,373	10,279	13,205	15,737	0.3	0.2	28.5	19.2	-0.8
Other interregional	114,223	99,328	113,371	154,701	177,370	2.0	2.8	36.5	14.7	12.3
Other World/Not specified	*38,934*	*23,358*	*13,262*	*18,456*	*26,723*	*0.5*	*0.4*	*39.2*	*44.8*	*2.7*

Source: World Tourism Organization (UNWTO) ©   (Data as collected by UNWTO for TMT 2006 Edition)

Tunisia

Nights of International Tourists in Hotels and Similar Establishments (by nationality)

	1995	2000	2003	2004	2005*	Market share (%) 2000	Market share (%) 2005*	Growth rate (%) 04/03	Growth rate (%) 05*/04	Average per year (%) 2000-2005*
Total	23,514,405	33,168,301	25,301,322	30,664,500	33,587,183	100	100	21.2	9.5	0.3
From Africa	*682,609*	*563,431*	*726,309*	*732,914*	*769,590*	*1.7*	*2.3*	*0.9*	*5.0*	*6.4*
Algeria	592,398	437,757	581,137	564,544	630,719	1.3	1.9	-2.9	11.7	7.6
Morocco	50,952	59,135	52,119	54,045	44,500	0.2	0.1	3.7	-17.7	-5.5
Other Africa	39,259	66,539	93,053	114,325	94,371	0.2	0.3	22.9	-17.5	7.2
From other regions	*22,656,274*	*32,288,498*	*24,265,994*	*29,545,312*	*32,378,575*	*97.3*	*96.4*	*21.8*	*9.6*	*0.1*
France	3,546,073	7,205,700	5,671,187	6,835,348	7,798,901	21.7	23.2	20.5	14.1	1.6
Germany	10,282,862	11,284,300	5,498,718	6,535,380	6,641,427	34.0	19.8	18.9	1.6	-10.1
Italy	1,860,574	2,922,107	2,711,719	3,251,102	3,393,580	8.8	10.1	19.9	4.4	3.0
United Kingdom	2,303,954	3,036,300	2,289,934	2,963,841	3,234,237	9.2	9.6	29.4	9.1	1.3
Belgium	654,794	1,306,600	1,267,594	1,395,542	1,492,812	3.9	4.4	10.1	7.0	2.7
Czech Rep	322,677	503,709	984,417	1,288,584	1,432,338	1.5	4.3	30.9	11.2	23.2
Russian Federation	88,409	190,827	859,273	1,181,314	1,210,330	0.6	3.6	37.5	2.5	44.7
Spain	232,448	753,359	626,072	863,780	1,139,270	2.3	3.4	38.0	31.9	8.6
Poland	136,937	481,044	524,725	748,308	1,135,783	1.5	3.4	42.6	51.8	18.7
Switzerland	700,424	1,062,200	649,799	739,582	605,240	3.2	1.8	13.8	-18.2	-10.6
Scandinavia	478,839	617,800	..	..	..	1.9				
Austria	480,437	819,600	465,220	544,331	515,557	2.5	1.5	17.0	-5.3	-8.9
Netherlands	640,413	540,700	329,628	364,455	443,862	1.6	1.3	10.6	21.8	-3.9
Hungary	110,641	194,788	357,055	388,071	375,856	0.6	1.1	8.7	-3.1	14.0
Sweden	..	..	193,718	258,070	301,314		0.9	33.2	16.8	
Slovakia	18,609	88,847	133,816	217,774	295,534	0.3	0.9	62.7	35.7	27.2
Denmark	..	..	78,565	123,591	284,395		0.8	57.3	130.1	
Libyan Arab Jamahiriya	179,511	234,700	256,658	247,209	242,810	0.7	0.7	-3.7	-1.8	0.7
Canada	88,961	157,126	132,463	195,352	200,195	0.5	0.6	47.5	2.5	5.0
Finland	..	..	114,222	142,074	184,770		0.6	24.4	30.1	
Luxembourg	64,696	103,785	113,472	155,952	179,088	0.3	0.5	37.4	14.8	11.5
Yugoslav SFR	18,048	47,199	92,011	129,266	151,120	0.1	0.4	40.5	16.9	26.2
Norway	..	..	237,582	122,271	133,971		0.4	-48.5	9.6	
Portugal	75,955	85,200	88,140	143,148	116,162	0.3	0.3	62.4	-18.9	6.4
Malta	10,094	24,838	51,515	61,872	95,060	0.1	0.3	20.1	53.6	30.8
Other interregional	360,918	627,769	538,491	649,095	774,963	1.9	2.3	20.5	19.4	4.3
Nationals residing abroad	*..*	*..*	*7,036*	*12,328*	*17,239*		*0.1*	*75.2*	*39.8*	
Other World/Not specified	*175,522*	*316,372*	*301,983*	*373,946*	*421,779*	*1.0*	*1.3*	*23.8*	*12.8*	*5.9*

Source: World Tourism Organization (UNWTO) ©　　　　　　　　　　　　　(Data as collected by UNWTO for TMT 2006 Edition)

World Tourism Organization ©

Annex

Table of contents

1. International Tourist Arrivals

International Tourist Arrivals, 1950-2005*

	World	Africa	Americas	Asia and the Pacific	Europe	Middle East	World	Africa	Americas	Asia and the Pacific	Europe	Middle East
	International Tourist Arrivals (million)						Change over previous year (%)[1]					
1950	25.3	0.5	7.5	0.2	16.8	0.2						
1960	69.3	0.8	16.7	0.9	50.4	0.6						
1965	112.9	1.4	23.2	2.1	83.7	2.4						
1970	165.8	2.4	42.3	6.2	113.0	1.9						
1975	222.3	4.7	50.0	10.2	153.9	3.5						
1980	277.6	7.2	62.3	23.0	178.0	7.1						
1981	278.2	8.1	62.5	24.9	175.1	7.6	0.2	13.3	0.3	8.0	-1.6	7.3
1982	276.4	7.6	59.7	26.0	174.9	8.3	-0.6	-6.6	-4.5	4.5	-0.1	8.8
1983	281.2	8.2	59.9	26.6	179.0	7.5	1.7	8.4	0.4	2.3	2.4	-9.5
1984	306.2	8.8	67.4	29.5	192.8	7.7	8.9	7.5	12.5	10.8	7.7	2.3
1985	319.5	9.6	65.1	32.9	203.8	8.1	4.3	9.3	-3.4	11.6	5.7	5.6
1986	329.5	9.3	70.9	36.8	205.5	6.9	3.1	-3.1	8.9	12.1	0.9	-14.9
1987	359.0	9.8	76.6	42.1	223.3	7.2	8.9	5.1	8.0	14.3	8.6	4.0
1988	384.1	12.6	83.0	48.7	230.7	9.1	7.0	27.8	8.4	15.8	3.3	26.2
1989	409.0	13.8	86.9	49.4	249.6	9.2	6.5	10.3	4.7	1.4	8.2	1.9
1990	438.4	15.2	92.8	56.2	264.7	9.6	7.2	9.7	6.8	13.7	6.0	4.3
1991	441.3	16.3	95.3	58.0	262.8	8.9	0.6	7.1	2.7	3.3	-0.7	-7.1
1992	478.4	18.2	102.2	65.8	280.9	11.3	8.4	12.0	7.3	13.4	6.9	25.9
1993	494.2	18.8	102.2	72.3	289.5	11.4	3.3	3.2	0.0	10.0	3.0	1.4
1994	518.0	19.1	105.1	80.1	301.5	12.1	4.8	1.8	2.9	10.7	4.2	6.3
1995	538.5	20.1	109.0	82.5	313.2	13.7	3.9	4.9	3.7	3.0	3.9	12.9
1996	572.4	21.8	114.5	90.4	329.9	15.8	6.3	8.7	5.0	9.7	5.3	15.0
1997	596.0	22.8	116.2	89.7	350.6	16.7	4.1	4.5	1.5	-0.8	6.3	5.8
1998	614.3	25.2	119.2	89.4	362.5	18.0	3.1	10.6	2.5	-0.3	3.4	7.9
1999	637.4	26.7	122.0	98.8	368.4	21.5	3.8	6.0	2.4	10.5	1.6	19.5
2000	684.7	27.9	128.2	110.6	393.6	24.5	7.4	4.3	5.1	12.0	6.8	13.7
2001	684.4	28.8	122.2	115.8	393.1	24.5	0.0	3.2	-4.7	4.7	-0.1	0.3
2002	704.7	29.8	116.8	124.9	404.8	28.4	3.0	3.6	-4.4	7.8	3.0	16.0
2003	692.2	31.4	113.3	113.2	404.9	29.5	-1.8	5.3	-3.0	-9.4	0.0	3.7
2004	761.4	34.2	125.8	144.1	421.0	36.2	10.0	9.1	11.0	27.4	4.0	22.7
2005*	801.6	37.3	133.2	155.4	437.4	38.4	5.3	9.0	5.9	7.8	3.9	5.9

Average annual growth (%)						
1950-2000	6.8	8.3	5.8	13.1	6.5	10.1
1950-2005*	6.5	8.1	5.4	12.5	6.1	10.1
1950-1960	10.6	3.7	8.4	14.1	11.6	12.3
1960-1970	9.1	12.4	9.7	21.6	8.4	11.5
1970-1980	5.3	11.5	4.0	13.9	4.6	14.3
1980-1990	4.7	7.8	4.1	9.3	4.0	3.1
1980-1985	2.9	6.2	0.9	7.4	2.7	2.7
1985-1990	6.5	9.5	7.3	11.3	5.4	3.5
1990-2000	4.6	6.3	3.3	7.0	4.0	9.8
1990-1995	4.2	5.7	3.3	8.0	3.4	7.3
1995-2000	4.9	6.8	3.3	6.0	4.7	12.3
2000-2005*	3.2	6.0	0.8	7.0	2.1	9.4

Source: World Tourism Organization (UNWTO) © (Data as collected by UNWTO for TMT 2006 Edition)

[1] Before 1995, data are simple aggregates of country results and are not corrected for changes in series, so changes on previous year might not be in all cases correct.

International Tourist Arrivals by Country of Destination

	Series	International Tourist Arrivals (1000)						Market share in the region (%)			Change (%)		Average annual growth (%)	
		1990	1995	2000	2003	2004	2005*	1990	2000	2005*	04/03	05*/04	90-00	00-05*
Africa		*15,188*	*20,083*	*27,894*	*31,394*	*34,242*	*37,311*	*100*	*100*	*100*	*9.1*	*9.0*	*6.3*	*6.0*
North Africa		**8,398**	**7,271**	**10,240**	**11,094**	**12,769**	**13,911**	**55.3**	**36.7**	**37.3**	**15.1**	**8.9**	**2.0**	**6.3**
Algeria	VF	1,137	520	866	1,166	1,234	1,443	7.5	3.1	3.9	5.8	17.0	-2.7	10.8
Morocco	TF	4,024	2,602	4,278	4,761	5,477	5,843	26.5	15.3	15.7	15.0	6.7	0.6	6.4
Sudan	TF	33	29	38	52	61	246	0.2	0.1	0.7	15.8	305.8	1.4	45.3
Tunisia	TF	3,204	4,120	5,058	5,114	5,998	6,378	21.1	18.1	17.1	17.3	6.3	4.7	4.7
West Africa		**1,352**	**1,913**	**2,434**	**3,062**	**3,452**	**3,585**	**8.9**	**8.7**	**9.6**	**12.7**	**3.9**	**6.1**	**8.1**
Benin	TF	110	138	96	175	174	176	0.7	0.3	0.5	-0.9	1.4	-1.4	12.9
Burkina Faso	THS	74	124	126	163	222	245	0.5	0.5	0.7	36.2	10.1	5.5	14.2
Cape Verde	TF	24	28	115	150	157	198	0.2	0.4	0.5	4.7	26.0	17.0	11.5
Côte d'Ivoire	TF	196	188	..	180	..	..	1.3						
Gambia	TF	100	45	77	89	90	111	0.7	0.3	0.3	1.1	23.2	-2.5	7.5
Ghana	TF	146	286	399	531	584	429	1.0	1.4	1.1	10.0	-26.6	10.6	1.4
Guinea	TF	..	..	33	44	45	45		0.1	0.1	1.5	1.6		6.6
Mali	TF	44	42	86	110	113	143	0.3	0.3	0.4	2.1	26.8	7.0	10.6
Mauritania	TF	..	..	30	..	..	..		0.1					
Niger	TF	21	35	50	55	57	63	0.1	0.2	0.2	3.6	11.3	9.1	4.9
Nigeria	TF	190	656	813	924	962	1,010	1.3	2.9	2.7	4.1	5.0	15.6	4.4
Senegal	THS/TF	246	280	389	495	667	769	1.6	1.4	2.1	34.7	15.3	4.7	14.6
Sierra Leone	TF	98	38	16	38	44	40	0.6	0.1	0.1	14.3	-8.1	-16.6	20.1
Togo	THS	103	53	60	61	83	81	0.7	0.2	0.2	36.5	-2.3	-5.3	6.1
Central Africa		**365**	**357**	**666**	**636**	**728**	**792**	**2.4**	**2.4**	**2.1**	**14.4**	**8.9**	**6.2**	**3.5**
Angola	TF	67	9	51	107	194	210	0.4	0.2	0.6	82.3	8.0	-2.7	32.7
Cameroon	THS	89	100	277	..	190	176	0.6	1.0	0.5		-7.1	12.0	-8.6
Cent.Afr.Rep.	TF	..	26	11	6	8	12		0.0	0.0	43.4	47.1		1.4
Chad	THS	9	19	43	21	26	29	0.1	0.2	0.1	23.5	13.3	16.9	-7.3
Congo	THS	33	37	19	..	..	..	0.2	0.1				-5.4	
Dem.R.Congo	TF	55	35	103	35	30	61	0.4	0.4	0.2	-14.6	103.3	6.5	-9.9
Gabon	TF	109	125	155	222	..	..	0.7	0.6				3.6	
Sao Tome Prn	TF	3	6	7	14	11	11	0.0	0.0	0.0	-21.6	-1.9	9.0	8.1
East Africa		**2,842**	**4,752**	**6,338**	**7,206**	**7,614**	**8,059**	**18.7**	**22.7**	**21.6**	**5.7**	**5.8**	**8.4**	**4.9**
Burundi	TF	109	34	29	74	133	148	0.7	0.1	0.4	79.8	11.4	-12.4	38.6
Comoros	TF	8	23	24	14	18	20	0.1	0.1	0.1	23.7	11.1	11.6	-4.0
Djibouti	TF	33	21	20	23	26	30	0.2	0.1	0.1	13.4	14.8	-4.8	8.5
Eritrea	VF	..	315	70	80	87	83		0.3	0.2	9.1	-4.6		3.5
Ethiopia	TF	79	103	136	180	184	227	0.5	0.5	0.6	2.3	23.5	5.6	10.8
Kenya	TF	814	896	899	927	1,193	1,536	5.4	3.2	4.1	28.7	28.8	1.0	11.3
Madagascar	TF	53	75	160	139	229	277	0.3	0.6	0.7	64.6	21.3	11.7	11.6
Malawi	TF	130	192	228	424	427	438	0.9	0.8	1.2	0.8	2.4	5.8	13.9
Mauritius	TF	292	422	656	702	719	761	1.9	2.4	2.0	2.4	5.9	8.4	3.0
Mozambique	TF	..	..	..	441	470	578			1.5	6.6	23.0		
Reunion	TF	200	304	430	432	430	409	1.3	1.5	1.1	-0.5	-4.9	8.0	-1.0
Rwanda	TF	..	..	104	..	..	..		0.4					
Seychelles	TF	104	121	130	122	121	129	0.7	0.5	0.3	-1.0	6.5	2.3	-0.2
Tanzania	TF	..	285	459	552	566	590		1.6	1.6	2.5	4.2		5.1
Uganda	TF	69	160	193	305	512	468	0.5	0.7	1.3	68.2	-8.7	10.8	19.4
Zambia	TF	141	163	457	413	515	669	0.9	1.6	1.8	24.8	29.9	12.5	7.9
Zimbabwe	VF	636	1,416	1,967	2,256	1,854	1,559	4.2	7.1	4.2	-17.8	-15.9	12.0	-4.5
Southern Africa		**2,231**	**5,790**	**8,215**	**9,396**	**9,679**	**10,964**	**14.7**	**29.5**	**29.4**	**3.0**	**13.3**	**13.9**	**5.9**
Botswana	TF	543	521	1,104	1,406	1,523	1,675	3.6	4.0	4.5	8.3	10.0	7.4	8.7
Lesotho	VF	242	209	302	329	304	304	1.6	1.1	0.8	-7.8	0.0	2.2	0.1
Namibia	TF	..	272	656	695	..	778		2.4	2.1				3.5
South Africa	TF	..	4,488	5,872	6,505	6,678	7,369		21.1	19.7	2.7	10.3		4.6
Swaziland	THS	263	300	281	461	459	839	1.7	1.0	2.2	-0.4	82.8	0.7	24.5

Source: World Tourism Organization (UNWTO) ©

(Data as collected by UNWTO for TMT 2006 Edition)

World Tourism Organization ©

International Tourist Arrivals by Country of Destination

	Series	International Tourist Arrivals (1000)						Market share in the region (%)			Change (%)		Average annual growth (%)	
		1990	1995	2000	2003	2004	2005*	1990	2000	2005*	04/03	05*/04	90-00	00-05*
Americas		*92,804*	*109,028*	*128,193*	*113,293*	*125,792*	*133,198*	*100*	*100*	*100*	*11.0*	*5.9*	*3.3*	*0.8*
North America		**71,744**	**80,664**	**91,506**	**77,418**	**85,849**	**89,891**	**77.3**	**71.4**	**67.5**	**10.9**	**4.7**	**2.5**	**-0.4**
Canada	TF	15,209	16,932	19,627	17,534	19,145	18,771	16.4	15.3	14.1	9.2	-2.0	2.6	-0.9
Mexico	TF	17,172	20,241	20,641	18,665	20,618	21,915	18.5	16.1	16.5	10.5	6.3	1.9	1.2
United States	TF	39,363	43,491	51,238	41,218	46,086	49,206	42.4	40.0	36.9	11.8	6.8	2.7	-0.8
Caribbean		**11,392**	**14,023**	**17,086**	**17,080**	**18,095**	**18,802**	**12.3**	**13.3**	**14.1**	**5.9**	**3.9**	**4.1**	**1.9**
Anguilla	TF	31	39	44	47	54	62	0.0	0.0	0.0	15.1	15.0	3.6	7.1
Antigua,Barb	TF	206	220	207	224	245	245	0.2	0.2	0.2	9.6	0.0	0.0	3.5
Aruba	TF	433	619	721	642	728	733	0.5	0.6	0.5	13.4	0.6	5.2	0.3
Bahamas	TF	1,562	1,598	1,544	1,510	1,561	1,608	1.7	1.2	1.2	3.4	3.0	-0.1	0.8
Barbados	TF	432	442	545	531	552	548	0.5	0.4	0.4	3.8	-0.7	2.4	0.1
Bermuda	TF	435	387	332	257	272	270	0.5	0.3	0.2	5.9	-0.7	-2.7	-4.1
Bonaire	TF	37	59	51	62	63	63	0.0	0.0	0.0	1.6	-0.9	3.3	4.2
Br.Virgin Is	TF	160	219	272	318	307	337	0.2	0.2	0.3	-3.2	9.7	5.4	4.4
Cayman Islands	TF	253	361	354	294	260	168	0.3	0.3	0.1	-11.4	-35.4	3.4	-13.9
Cuba	TF	327	742	1,741	1,847	2,017	2,261	0.4	1.4	1.7	9.2	12.1	18.2	5.4
Curaçao	TF	219	224	191	221	223	222	0.2	0.1	0.2	0.9	-0.6	-1.4	3.1
Dominica	TF	45	60	70	73	80	79	0.0	0.1	0.1	9.4	-1.0	4.5	2.5
Dominican Rp	TF	1,305	1,776	2,978	3,282	3,450	3,691	1.4	2.3	2.8	5.1	7.0	8.6	4.4
Grenada	TF	76	108	129	142	134	98	0.1	0.1	0.1	-6.0	-26.6	5.4	-5.3
Guadeloupe	TCE	331	640	603	439	456	372	0.4	0.5	0.3	3.9	-18.4	6.2	-9.2
Haiti	TF	144	145	140	136	96	112	0.2	0.1	0.1	-29.1	16.4	-0.3	-4.3
Jamaica	TF	989	1,147	1,323	1,350	1,415	1,479	1.1	1.0	1.1	4.8	4.5	2.9	2.3
Martinique	TF	282	457	526	453	471	484	0.3	0.4	0.4	3.9	2.8	6.4	-1.6
Montserrat	TF	13	18	10	8	10	10	0.0	0.0	0.0	13.7	1.3	-2.3	-1.3
Puerto Rico	TF	2,560	3,131	3,341	3,238	3,541	3,686	2.8	2.6	2.8	9.3	4.1	2.7	2.0
Saba	TF	..	10	9	10	11	11		0.0	0.0	7.3	4.1		4.7
Saint Lucia	TF	141	231	270	277	298	318	0.2	0.2	0.2	7.8	6.5	6.7	3.3
St.Eustatius	TF	..	9	9	10	11	10		0.0	0.0	5.8	-6.3		2.6
St.Kitts-Nev	TF	73	79	73	91	118	127	0.1	0.1	0.1	29.7	8.0	0.0	11.7
St.Maarten	TF	545	449	432	428	475	468	0.6	0.3	0.4	11.1	-1.5	-2.3	1.6
St.Vincent,Grenadines	TF	54	60	73	79	87	96	0.1	0.1	0.1	10.4	10.1	3.1	5.5
Trinidad Tbg	TF	195	260	399	409	443	463	0.2	0.3	0.3	8.2	4.7	7.4	3.0
Turks,Caicos	TF	49	79	152	164	173	200	0.1	0.1	0.2	5.8	15.6	12.0	5.6
US.Virgin Is	TF	463	454	546	538	544	582	0.5	0.4	0.4	1.1	7.0	1.7	1.3
Central America		**1,945**	**2,611**	**4,346**	**4,900**	**5,554**	**6,288**	**2.1**	**3.4**	**4.7**	**13.4**	**13.2**	**8.4**	**7.7**
Belize	TF	197	131	196	221	231	237	0.2	0.2	0.2	4.7	2.5	-0.1	3.8
Costa Rica	TF	435	785	1,088	1,239	1,453	1,679	0.5	0.8	1.3	17.3	15.6	9.6	9.1
El Salvador	TF	194	235	795	857	812	969	0.2	0.6	0.7	-5.3	19.5	15.1	4.0
Guatemala	TF	509	563	826	880	1,182	1,316	0.5	0.6	1.0	34.2	11.4	5.0	9.8
Honduras	TF	290	271	471	611	641	673	0.3	0.4	0.5	5.0	5.0	5.0	7.4
Nicaragua	TF	106	281	486	526	615	712	0.1	0.4	0.5	16.9	15.9	16.4	8.0
Panama	TF	214	345	484	566	621	702	0.2	0.4	0.5	9.8	13.0	8.5	7.7
South America		**7,722**	**11,731**	**15,255**	**13,896**	**16,295**	**18,217**	**8.3**	**11.9**	**13.7**	**17.3**	**11.8**	**7.0**	**3.6**
Argentina	TF	1,930	2,289	2,909	2,995	3,457	3,823	2.1	2.3	2.9	15.4	10.6	4.2	5.6
Bolivia	TF	254	284	319	420	478	504	0.3	0.2	0.4	13.8	5.4	2.3	9.6
Brazil	TF	1,091	1,991	5,313	4,133	4,794	5,358	1.2	4.1	4.0	16.0	11.8	17.2	0.2
Chile	TF	943	1,540	1,742	1,614	1,785	2,027	1.0	1.4	1.5	10.6	13.6	6.3	3.1
Colombia	TF	813	1,399	557	625	791	933	0.9	0.4	0.7	26.6	18.0	-3.7	10.9
Ecuador	VF	362	440	627	761	819	860	0.4	0.5	0.6	7.6	5.0	5.6	6.5
French Guiana	TF	..	..	..	..	..	95			0.1				
Guyana	TF	64	106	105	101	122	117	0.1	0.1	0.1	20.9	-4.4	5.1	2.1
Paraguay	TF	280	438	289	268	309	341	0.3	0.2	0.3	15.3	10.2	0.3	3.4
Peru	TF	317	479	828	1,070	1,277	1,486	0.3	0.6	1.1	19.4	16.4	10.1	12.4
Suriname	TF	46	43	57	82	138	160	0.0	0.0	0.1	68.1	16.1	2.2	22.9
Uruguay	TF	..	2,022	1,968	1,420	1,756	1,808		1.5	1.4	23.7	2.9		-1.7
Venezuela	TF	525	700	469	337	486	706	0.6	0.4	0.5	44.3	45.2	-1.1	8.5

Source: World Tourism Organization (UNWTO) ©

(Data as collected by UNWTO for TMT 2006 Edition)

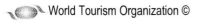 World Tourism Organization ©

International Tourist Arrivals by Country of Destination

	Series	International Tourist Arrivals (1000)						Market share in the region (%)			Change (%)		Average annual growth (%)	
		1990	1995	2000	2003	2004	2005*	1990	2000	2005*	04/03	05*/04	90-00	00-05*
Asia and the Pacific		*56,165*	*82,451*	*110,573*	*113,166*	*144,150*	*155,353*	*100*	*100*	*100*	*27.4*	*7.8*	*7.0*	*7.0*
North-East Asia		**26,394**	**41,313**	**58,349**	**61,732**	**79,412**	**87,576**	**47.0**	**52.8**	**56.4**	**28.6**	**10.3**	**8.3**	**8.5**
China	TF	10,484	20,034	31,229	32,970	41,761	46,809	18.7	28.2	30.1	26.7	12.1	11.5	8.4
Hong Kong (China)	TF	..	..	8,814	9,676	13,655	14,773		8.0	9.5	41.1	8.2		10.9
Japan	TF	3,236	3,345	4,757	5,212	6,138	6,728	5.8	4.3	4.3	17.8	9.6	3.9	7.2
Korea, D P Rp	*	115	..	..	..	..	..	0.2						
Korea, Republic of	VF	2,959	3,753	5,322	4,754	5,818	6,023	5.3	4.8	3.9	22.4	3.5	6.0	2.5
Macao (China)	TF	2,513	4,202	5,197	6,309	8,324	9,014	4.5	4.7	5.8	31.9	8.3	7.5	11.6
Mongolia	TF	147	108	137	201	301	338	0.3	0.1	0.2	49.4	12.4	-0.7	19.8
Taiwan (pr. of China)	VF	..	2,332	2,624	2,248	2,950	3,378		2.4	2.2	31.2	14.5		5.2
South-East Asia		**21,469**	**28,821**	**36,908**	**35,986**	**47,006**	**49,312**	**38.2**	**33.4**	**31.7**	**30.6**	**4.9**	**5.6**	**6.0**
Brunei Darussalam	VF	377	498	984	..	..	815	0.7	0.9	0.5			10.1	-3.7
Cambodia	TF	17	220	466	701	1,055	1,422	0.0	0.4	0.9	50.5	34.7	39.2	25.0
Indonesia	TF	2,178	4,324	5,064	4,467	5,321	5,002	3.9	4.6	3.2	19.1	-6.0	8.8	-0.2
Lao P.D.R.	TF	14	60	191	196	407	672	0.0	0.2	0.4	107.7	65.1	29.9	28.6
Malaysia	TF	7,446	7,469	10,222	10,577	15,703	16,431	13.3	9.2	10.6	48.5	4.6	3.2	10.0
Myanmar	TF	21	117	208	206	242	232	0.0	0.2	0.1	17.7	-4.0	25.8	2.2
Philippines	TF	1,025	1,760	1,992	1,907	2,291	2,623	1.8	1.8	1.7	20.1	14	6.9	5.7
Singapore	TF	4,842	6,070	6,062	4,703	6,553	7,080	8.6	5.5	4.6	39.3	8.0	2.3	3.2
Thailand	TF	5,299	6,952	9,579	10,082	11,737	11,567	9.4	8.7	7.4	16.4	-1.4	6.1	3.8
Vietnam	VF	250	1,351	2,140	2,429	2,928	3,468	0.4	1.9	2.2	20.6	18.4	24.0	10.1
Oceania		**5,152**	**8,084**	**9,230**	**9,023**	**10,118**	**10,488**	**9.2**	**8.3**	**6.8**	**12.1**	**3.7**	**6.0**	**2.6**
American Samoa	TF	26	34	44	..	..	25	0.0	0.0	0.0			5.4	-11.1
Australia	VF/TF	2,215	3,726	4,530	4,354	4,774	5,020	3.9	4.1	3.2	9.6	5.2	7.4	2.1
Cook Is	TF	34	48	73	78	83	88	0.1	0.1	0.1	6.4	6.1	7.9	3.9
Fiji	TF	279	318	294	431	504	550	0.5	0.3	0.4	17.0	9.1	0.5	13.3
French Polynesia	TF	132	172	252	213	212	208	0.2	0.2	0.1	-0.4	-1.8	6.7	-3.8
Guam	TF	780	1,362	1,287	910	1,160	1,228	1.4	1.2	0.8	27.5	5.8	5.1	-0.9
Kiribati	TF	3	4	5	5	4	3	0.0	0.0	0.0	-26.5	-22.4	4.8	-10.3
Marshall Is	TF	5	6	5	7	9	9	0.0	0.0	0.0	25.2	1.8	0.4	12.0
Micronesia (Fed.St.of)	TF	..	..	21	18	19	19		0.0	0.0	6.0	-1.6		-2.0
N.Mariana Is	TF	426	669	517	452	525	498	0.8	0.5	0.3	16.2	-5.1	2.0	-0.7
New Caledonia	TF	87	86	110	102	100	101	0.2	0.1	0.1	-2.4	1.1	2.4	-1.7
New Zealand	VF	976	1,409	1,787	2,104	2,334	2,366	1.7	1.6	1.5	10.9	1.3	6.2	5.8
Niue	TF	1	2	2	3	3	3	0.0	0.0	0.0	-5.8	9.5	6.6	8.0
Palau	TF	33	53	58	68	95	86	0.1	0.1	0.1	38.9	-9.2	5.8	8.2
Papua New Guinea	TF	41	42	58	56	59	69	0.1	0.1	0.0	4.9	17.3	3.5	3.6
Samoa	TF	48	68	88	92	98	102	0.1	0.1	0.1	6.1	3.7	6.2	3.0
Solomon Is	TF	9	11	5	7	..	9	0.0	0.0	0.0			-5.5	12.6
Tonga	TF	21	29	35	40	41	42	0.0	0.0	0.0	2.7	1.6	5.2	3.6
Tuvalu	TF	1	1	1	1	1	1	0.0	0.0	0.0	-6.3	-15.9	1.0	-0.3
Vanuatu	TF	35	44	58	50	61	62	0.1	0.1	0.0	21.9	1.0	5.2	1.4
South Asia		**3,150**	**4,233**	**6,086**	**6,426**	**7,613**	**7,977**	**5.6**	**5.5**	**5.1**	**18.5**	**4.8**	**6.8**	**5.6**
Bangladesh	TF	115	156	199	245	271	208	0.2	0.2	0.1	10.9	-23.4	5.6	0.9
Bhutan	TF	2	5	8	6	9	14	0.0	0.0	0.0	47.7	47.3	14.3	12.4
India	TF	1,707	2,124	2,649	2,726	3,457	3,919	3.0	2.4	2.5	26.8	13.3	4.5	8.1
Iran	TF	154	489	1,342	1,546	1,659	..	0.3	1.2		7.3		24.2	
Maldives	TF	195	315	467	564	617	395	0.3	0.4	0.3	9.4	-35.9	9.1	-3.3
Nepal	TF	255	363	464	338	385	375	0.5	0.4	0.2	13.9	-2.6	6.2	-4.1
Pakistan	TF	424	378	557	501	648	798	0.8	0.5	0.5	29.4	23.2	2.8	7.5
Sri Lanka	TF	298	403	400	501	566	549	0.5	0.4	0.4	13.1	-3.0	3.0	6.5

(Data as collected by UNWTO for TMT 2006 Edition)

World Tourism Organization ©

International Tourist Arrivals by Country of Destination

	Series	International Tourist Arrivals (1000)						Market share in the region (%)			Change (%)		Average annual growth (%)	
		1990	1995	2000	2003	2004	2005*	1990	2000	2005*	04/03	05*/04	90-00	00-05*
Europe		*264,657*	*313,198*	*393,615*	*404,862*	*421,044*	*437,360*	*100*	*100*	*100*	*4.0*	*3.9*	*4.0*	*2.1*
Northern Europe		**30,634**	**38,259**	**43,770**	**43,886**	**47,564**	**50,902**	**11.6**	**11.1**	**11.6**	**8.4**	**7.0**	**3.6**	**3.1**
Denmark	TCE	..	..	3,535	3,474	3,663	4,562		0.9	1.0	5.4	24.5		5.2
Finland	TF	..	1,779	2,714	2,756	2,840	3,140		0.7	0.7	3.0	10.6		3.0
Iceland	TCE	142	190	634	771	836	871	0.1	0.2	0.2	8.4	4.2	16.1	6.6
Ireland	TF	3,666	4,818	6,646	6,764	6,953	7,334	1.4	1.7	1.7	2.8	5.5	6.1	2.0
Norway	TF	1,955	2,880	3,104	3,269	3,628	3,824	0.7	0.8	0.9	11.0	5.4	4.7	4.3
Sweden	TCE	..	2,309	2,746	2,952	3,003	3,133		0.7	0.7	1.7	4.3		2.7
United Kingdom	TF	17,023	21,719	23,211	22,787	25,677	28,038	6.4	5.9	6.4	12.7	9.2	3.1	3.9
Western Europe		**108,626**	**112,184**	**139,658**	**136,076**	**139,043**	**142,598**	**41.0**	**35.5**	**32.6**	**2.2**	**2.6**	**2.5**	**0.4**
Austria	TCE	19,011	17,173	17,982	19,078	19,373	19,952	7.2	4.6	4.6	1.5	3.0	-0.6	2.1
Belgium	TCE	..	5,560	6,457	6,690	6,710	6,747		1.6	1.5	0.3	0.6		0.9
France	TF	52,497	60,033	77,190	75,048	75,121	75,910	19.8	19.6	17.4	0.1	1.1	3.9	-0.3
Germany	TCE	17,045	14,838	18,992	18,399	20,137	21,500	6.4	4.8	4.9	9.4	6.8	1.1	2.5
Liechtenstein	THS	78	59	62	49	49	50	0.0	0.0	0.0	-1.0	2.6	-2.3	-4.2
Luxembourg	TCE	820	768	852	867	878	913	0.3	0.2	0.2	1.2	4.0	0.4	1.4
Monaco	THS	245	233	300	235	250	286	0.1	0.1	0.1	6.6	14.2	2.0	-1.0
Netherlands	TCE	5,795	6,574	10,003	9,181	9,646	10,012	2.2	2.5	2.3	5.1	3.8	5.6	0.0
Switzerland	TH	7,963	6,946	7,821	6,530	..	7,229	3.0	2.0				-0.2	-1.6
Central/Eastern Europe		**31,490**	**60,035**	**69,431**	**78,134**	**85,927**	**87,050**	**11.9**	**17.6**	**19.9**	**10.0**	**1.3**	**8.2**	**4.6**
Armenia	TCE	..	12	45	206	263	319		0.0	0.1	27.6	21.1		47.9
Azerbaijan	TF	..	93	681	1,014	1,349	1,177		0.2	0.3	33.0	-12.7		11.6
Belarus	TF	..	161	60	64	67	91		0.0	0.0	4.8	34.9		8.6
Bulgaria	TF	..	3,466	2,785	4,048	4,630	4,837		0.7	1.1	14.4	4.5		11.7
Czech Rep	TCE	..	3,381	4,773	5,076	6,061	6,336		1.2	1.4	19.4	4.5		5.8
Estonia	TF	..	530	1,220	1,462	1,750	1,917		0.3	0.4	19.7	9.5		9.5
Former U.S.S.R.	TF	2,286	..	..	..	..	..	0.9						
Georgia	TF	..	85	387	313	368	560		0.1	0.1	17.5	52.1		7.7
Hungary	TF	..	..	..	..	12,212	10,048			2.3		-17.7		
Kazakhstan	TF	..	..	1,471	2,410	3,073	3,143		0.4	0.7	27.5	2.3		16.4
Kyrgyzstan	TF	..	36	59	342	398	315		0.0	0.1	16.4	-20.8		39.8
Latvia	TF	..	539	509	971	1,080	1,116		0.1	0.3	11.2	3.4		17.0
Lithuania	TF	..	650	1,083	1,491	1,800	2,000		0.3	0.5	20.7	11.1		13.1
Poland	TF	..	19,215	17,400	13,720	14,290	15,200		4.4	3.5	4.2	6.4		-2.7
Rep Moldova	TF	..	32	18	21	24	23		0.0	0.0	14.3	-4.2		5.0
Romania	TCE	1,432	766	867	1,105	1,359	1,430	0.5	0.2	0.3	23.0	5.2	-4.9	10.5
Russian Federation	TF	..	..	..	20,443	19,892	19,940			4.6	-2.7	0.2		
Slovakia	TCE	822	903	1,053	1,387	1,401	1,515	0.3	0.3	0.3	1.0	8.1	2.5	7.5
Tajikistan	TF	..	..	4	..	..	..		0.0					
Turkmenistan	TF	..	218	3	8	15	12		0.0	0.0	80.2	-21.5		27.8
Ukraine	TF	..	3,716	6,431	12,514	15,629	..		1.6		24.9			
Uzbekistan	TF	..	92	302	231	262	..		0.1		13.2			
Southern/Mediter. Eu.		**93,907**	**102,720**	**140,756**	**146,766**	**148,510**	**156,809**	**35.5**	**35.8**	**35.9**	**1.2**	**5.6**	**4.1**	**2.2**
Albania	THS	30	40	32	41	42	46	0.0	0.0	0.0	2.4	9.5	0.6	7.5
Andorra	TF	..	..	2,949	3,138	2,791	2,418				-11.0	-13.4		-3.9
Bosnia & Herzg	TCE	..	..	171	165	190	217		0.0	0.0	15.0	14.2		4.9
Croatia	TCE	..	1,485	5,831	7,409	7,912	8,467		1.5	1.9	6.8	7.0		7.7
Cyprus	TF	1,561	2,100	2,686	2,303	2,349	2,470	0.6	0.7	0.6	2.0	5.2	5.6	-1.7
F.Yug.Rp.Macedonia	TCE	..	147	224	158	165	197		0.1	0.0	4.8	19.3		-2.5
Greece	TF	8,873	10,130	13,096	13,969	13,313	14,276	3.4	3.3	3.3	-4.7	7.2	4.0	1.7
Israel	TF	1,063	2,215	2,417	1,063	1,506	1,903	0.4	0.6	0.4	41.6	26.4	8.6	-4.7
Italy	TF	26,679	31,052	41,181	39,604	37,071	36,513	10.1	10.5	8.3	-6.4	-1.5	4.4	-2.4
Malta	TF	872	1,116	1,216	1,118	1,156	1,171	0.3	0.3	0.3	3.4	1.3	3.4	-0.8
Portugal	TF	8,020	9,511	12,097	11,707	10,639	10,612	3.0	3.1	2.4	-9.1	-0.3	4.2	-2.6
San Marino	THS	45	28	43	41	42	50	0.0	0.0	0.0	2.4	19.0	-0.5	3.1
Serbia & Montenegro	TCE	..	228	239	481	580	725		0.1	0.2	20.5	25.0		24.8
Slovenia	TC	..	732	1,090	1,373	1,499	1,555		0.3	0.4	9.2	3.7		7.4
Spain	TF	34,085	34,920	47,898	50,854	52,430	55,916	12.9	12.2	12.8	3.1	6.6	3.5	3.1
Turkey	TF	4,799	7,083	9,586	13,341	16,826	20,273	1.8	2.4	4.6	26.1	20.5	7.2	16.2
Yugoslav SFR	TF	7,880	..	..	..	..	..	3.0						

Source: World Tourism Organization (UNWTO) ©

(Data as collected by UNWTO for TMT 2006 Edition)

International Tourist Arrivals by Country of Destination

	Series	International Tourist Arrivals (1000)						Market share in the region (%)			Change (%)		Average annual growth (%)	
		1990	1995	2000	2003	2004	2005*	1990	2000	2005*	04/03	05*/04	90-00	00-05*
Middle East		*9,630*	*13,704*	*24,451*	*29,509*	*36,220*	*38,358*	*100*	*100*	*100*	*22.7*	*5.9*	*9.8*	*9.4*
Bahrain	TF	1,376	1,396	2,420	2,955	3,514	3,914	14.3	9.9	10.2	18.9	11.4	5.8	10.1
Egypt	TF	2,411	2,871	5,116	5,746	7,795	8,244	25.0	20.9	21.5	35.7	5.8	7.8	10.0
Iraq	VF	748	61	78	..	..	..	7.8	0.3				-20.2	
Jordan	TF	572	1,075	1,580	2,353	2,853	2,987	5.9	6.5	7.8	21.2	4.7	10.7	13.6
Kuwait	THS	15	72	78	94	91	..	0.2	0.3		-3.2		17.9	
Lebanon	TF	..	450	742	1,016	1,278	1,140		3.0	3.0	25.9	-10.9		9.0
Libyan Arab Jamahiriya	TF	96	56	174	142	149	..	1.0	0.7		4.9		6.1	
Oman	THS/TF	149	279	571|	1,039	1,195	..	1.5	2.3		15.0		14.4	
Palestine	THS	..	..	310	37	56	88		1.3	0.2	51.4	57.1		-22.3
Qatar	TF	136	309	378	557	732	913	1.4	1.5	2.4	31.5	24.6	10.8	19.3
Saudi Arabia	TF	2,209	3,325|	6,585	7,332	8,599	8,037	22.9	26.9	21.0	17.3	-6.5	11.5	4.1
Syrian Arab Republic	TCE/TF	562	815	1,685	2,085	3,033	3,368	5.8	6.9	8.8	45.5	11.0	11.6	14.9
Untd Arab Emirates	THS	973	2,315	3,907	5,871	..	..	10.1	16.0				14.9	
Yemen	THS	52	61	73	155	274	336	0.5	0.3	0.9	77.0	22.8	3.5	35.7

Source: World Tourism Organization (UNWTO) ©

(Data as collected by UNWTO for TMT 2006 Edition)

| : change of series.

2. International Tourism Receipts

International Tourism Receipts, World

	International Tourism Receipts (billion)						Change current prices (%)				Change constant prices (%)			
	1990	1995	2000	2002	2003	2004	2005*	02/01	03/02	04/03	05*/04	02/01	03/02	04/03 05*/04
Local currencies								1.8	1.0	12.9	6.3	-0.5	-1.4	9.8 3.1
US$	263.9	404.7	474.1	480.1	527.2	629.0	675.7	3.9	9.8	19.3	7.4	2.2	7.3	16.2 3.9
Euro	207.2	309.4	513.3	507.7	466.0	505.7	543.1	-1.6	-8.2	8.5	7.4	-3.8	-10.1	6.3 5.1

Source: World Tourism Organization (UNWTO) ©   (Data as collected in UNWTO database November 2006)

International Tourism Receipts by (Sub)region

	Change Local currencies, constant prices (%)					US$ Receipts (billion)		Receipts per arrival	euro Receipts (billion)		Receipts per arrival	Market share (%)
	01/00	02/01	03/02	04/03	05*/04	2004	2005*	2005*	2004	2005*	2005*	2005*
World	-1.9	-0.5	-1.4	9.8	3.1	629.0	675.7	845	505.7	543.1	680	100
Africa	*17.1*	*5.3*	*23.9*	*5.9*	*10.4*	*18.9*	*21.6*	*580*	*15.2*	*17.4*	*465*	*3.2*
North Africa	21.3	-5.6	-2.3	13.4	15.0	6.1	7.0	505	4.9	5.6	405	1.0
West Africa	12.5	1.3	5.4	0.0	20.8	1.4	1.9	530	1.2	1.5	425	0.3
Central Africa	27.2	-2.2	14.1	-3.0	13.9	0.3	0.3	410	0.2	0.3	330	0.0
East Africa	14.5	0.7	8.0	18.2	2.2	3.8	4.1	505	3.1	3.3	405	0.6
Southern Africa	15.0	26.9	75.0	-4.0	8.8	7.3	8.3	760	5.9	6.7	610	1.2
Americas	*-10.3*	*-6.3*	*-2.1*	*11.6*	*3.8*	*132.0*	*144.5*	*1,085*	*106.1*	*116.2*	*870*	*21.4*
North America	-12.8	-6.7	-4.7	12.9	4.2	98.2	107.1	1,190	79.0	86.1	955	15.8
Caribbean	-3.7	-2.6	5.5	5.0	1.6	19.3	20.4	1,085	15.5	16.4	875	3.0
Central America	-7.4	3.4	13.2	12.1	10.9	4.0	4.6	740	3.2	3.7	595	0.7
South America	3.6	-12.0	5.2	12.9	1.7	10.6	12.4	680	8.5	10.0	545	1.8
Asia and the Pacific	*7.3*	*6.6*	*-8.7*	*25.1*	*4.0*	*123.9*	*134.5*	*865*	*99.6*	*108.1*	*695*	*19.9*
North-East Asia	8.7	12.3	-10.7	33.4	7.9	58.6	65.4	745	47.1	52.5	600	9.7
South-East Asia	8.4	-1.0	-16.8	26.1	-0.7	32.8	33.8	685	26.4	27.2	550	5.0
Oceania	3.1	3.7	2.9	7.6	0.9	23.8	25.6	2,445	19.1	20.6	1,965	3.8
South Asia	2.0	9.0	17.8	20.1	4.3	8.6	9.6	1,210	6.9	7.7	970	1.4
Europe	*-1.9*	*-0.9*	*-1.5*	*3.1*	*2.5*	*328.9*	*348.8*	*795*	*264.4*	*280.3*	*640*	*51.6*
Northern Europe	-3.5	2.3	-1.9	6.0	7.7	49.3	53.9	1,060	39.6	43.3	850	8.0
Western Europe	-1.0	-0.5	-3.3	2.0	1.7	117.9	122.5	860	94.8	98.4	690	18.1
Central/Eastern Europe	-4.5	-4.4	-2.6	5.3	0.9	28.9	32.4	375	23.3	26.1	300	4.8
Southern/Mediter. Eu.	-1.5	-1.6	0.6	2.7	1.5	132.8	140.0	895	106.8	112.5	715	20.7
Middle East	*4.8*	*6.0*	*27.5*	*25.3*	*-1.8*	*25.2*	*26.3*	*685*	*20.3*	*21.1*	*550*	*3.9*

Source: World Tourism Organization (UNWTO) ©   (Data as collected in UNWTO database November 2006)

International Tourism Receipts, 1950-2005*

	World	Africa	Americas	Asia and the Pacific	Europe	Middle East	World	Africa	Americas	Asia and the Pacific	Europe	Middle East
	International Tourism Receipts (US$, billion)						International Tourism Receipts (euro/ECU, billion)					
1950	2.1	0.1	1.1	0.04	0.9	0.03						
1960	6.9	0.2	2.5	0.2	3.9	0.1						
1965	11.6	0.3	3.4	0.5	7.2	0.3						
1970	17.9	0.5	4.8	1.2	11.0	0.4						
1975	40.7	1.3	10.2	2.5	25.9	0.9	32.8	1.0	8.2	2.0	20.8	0.7
1980	104.5	3.4	24.7	10.3	62.7	3.5	75.1	2.4	17.7	7.4	45.0	2.5
1981	106.0	3.7	27.8	12.1	58.1	4.4	95.0	3.3	24.9	10.8	52.1	3.9
1982	99.9	3.4	25.7	12.2	56.4	2.2	102.0	3.5	26.2	12.4	57.6	2.2
1983	103.0	3.5	26.3	12.8	56.0	4.4	115.7	3.9	29.6	14.3	62.9	5.0
1984	111.7	3.2	32.0	13.7	58.1	4.7	141.5	4.1	40.5	17.3	73.7	5.9
1985	118.5	3.1	33.3	14.5	63.4	4.2	155.3	4.0	43.7	19.0	83.1	5.5
1986	144.4	3.6	38.4	18.8	80.1	3.5	146.7	3.6	39.0	19.1	81.4	3.6
1987	178.1	4.6	43.1	24.8	101.1	4.5	154.3	4.0	37.3	21.5	87.6	3.9
1988	205.9	5.5	51.3	32.4	112.3	4.3	174.2	4.7	43.4	27.4	95.0	3.7
1989	262.9	5.7	60.2	36.1	155.8	5.2	238.6	5.2	54.7	32.7	141.4	4.7
1990	264.1	6.4	69.2	41.1	143.1	4.3	207.4	5.0	54.3	32.3	112.4	3.4
1991	277.7	6.0	76.3	42.9	148.1	4.5	224.1	4.8	61.5	34.7	119.5	3.6
1992	320.7	6.8	83.7	51.0	172.7	6.6	247.0	5.3	64.4	39.3	133.0	5.1
1993	327.3	6.9	89.1	57.0	167.3	6.9	279.5	5.9	76.1	48.7	142.9	5.9
1994	356.4	7.6	92.4	67.3	181.1	8.1	299.6	6.4	77.7	56.6	152.2	6.8
1995	405.0	8.5	98.4	75.9	212.3	9.8	309.6	6.5	75.3	58.0	162.3	7.5
1996	438.6	9.7	108.2	84.8	224.8	11.0	345.4	7.7	85.2	66.8	177.1	8.7
1997	442.0	9.5	114.4	82.2	223.7	12.1	389.7	8.4	100.9	72.5	197.3	10.7
1998	444.2	10.2	115.2	72.1	234.8	11.9	396.3	9.1	102.7	64.3	209.5	10.6
1999	457.4	10.8	119.9	79.0	233.9	13.9	429.2	10.2	112.5	74.1	219.4	13.1
2000	474.3	10.4	130.8	85.2	232.7	15.2	513.6	11.3	141.6	92.3	252.0	16.4
2001	462.5	11.5	119.8	88.0	227.7	15.6	516.4	12.8	133.7	98.3	254.3	17.4
2002	480.4	11.9	113.4	96.3	242.5	16.2	508.0	12.6	120.0	101.8	256.5	17.2
2003	527.5	16.0	114.1	93.5	284.1	19.7	466.3	14.2	100.9	82.7	251.1	17.5
2004	629.4	18.9	132.0	123.9	329.3	25.2	506.0	15.2	106.1	99.6	264.7	20.3
2005*	676.1	21.6	144.5	134.5	349.2	26.3	543.5	17.4	116.2	108.1	280.7	21.1

Source: World Tourism Organization (UNWTO) ©   (Data as collected by UNWTO for TMT 2006 Edition)

[1] Receipts data are in current US$ and euro (based on the average annual exchange rate for euro or ECU to US$) and can be strongly influenced by exchange rate fluctuations.

World Tourism Organization ©

See for tables in euro values pages Annex - 16 to Annex - 20

International Tourism Receipts by Country of Destination

	International Tourism Receipts (US$, million)						Market share in the region (%)			Change (%)		Receipts per arrival[1]	Receipts per capita[1]
	1990	1995	2000	2003	2004	2005*	1990	2000	2005*	04/03	05*/04		US$
Africa	*6,402*	*8,504*	*10,404*	*16,032*	*18,934*	*21,642*	*100*	*100*	*100*	*18.1*	*14.3*	*580*	*27*
North Africa	**2,333**	**2,867**	**3,822**	**4,938**	**6,093**	**7,018**	**36.4**	**36.7**	**32.4**	**23.4**	**15.2**	**505**	**61**
Algeria	105	33	96	112	179	184	1.6	0.9	0.9	59.4	3.1	130	6
Morocco	1,259	1,296	2,039	3,225	3,924	4,621	19.7	19.6	21.4	21.6	17.8	790	141
Sudan	21	8	5	18	21	89	0.3	0.0	0.4	16.7	324.4	365	2
Tunisia	948	1,530	1,682	1,582	1,970	2,124	14.8	16.2	9.8	24.5	7.8	335	211
West Africa	**605**	**541**	**944**	**1,329**	**1,442**	**1,891**	**9.5**	**9.1**	**8.7**	**8.5**	**31.1**	**530**	**7**
Benin	55	85	77	106	119	..	0.9	0.7		12.3		685	16
Burkina Faso	11	..	19	29	45	..	0.2	0.2		55.3		205	3
Cape Verde	6	10	41	87	99	127	0.1	0.4	0.6	13.9	28.5	645	305
Côte d'Ivoire	51	89	49	69	82	83	0.8	0.5	0.4	18.8	1.2	385	5
Gambia	26	28	48	51	58	62	0.4	0.5	0.3	12.5	8.2	560	39
Ghana	81	11	335	414	466	796	1.3	3.2	3.7	12.6	70.8	1,855	36
Guinea	30	1	12	31	30	..	0.5	0.1		-3.2		670	3
Guinea-Bissau	..	..	..	2	1	..				-50.0			1
Mali	47	25	40	128	140	148	0.7	0.4	0.7	9.4	5.7	1,035	13
Mauritania	9	11	..	..	..	..	0.1						
Niger	17	7	23	28	31	34	0.3	0.2	0.2	10.7	9.7	535	3
Nigeria	25	17	101	49	21	18	0.4	1.0	0.1	-57.6	-14.2	20	0
Senegal	167	168	144	209	212	..	2.6	1.4		1.4		320	19
Sierra Leone	19	57	11	60	58	64	0.3	0.1	0.3	-3.3	10.3	1,600	11
Togo	58	13	8	15	19	..	0.9	0.1		26.7		230	4
Central Africa	**98**	**133**	**143**	**261**	**274**	**323**	**1.5**	**1.4**	**1.5**	**5.0**	**18.0**	**410**	**3**
Angola	13	10	18	49	66	88	0.2	0.2	0.4	34.3	34.0	420	7
Cameroon	53	36	57	114	..	..	0.8	0.5					7
Cent.Afr.Rep.	3	4	5	4	4	..	0.0	0.0		0.0		490	1
Chad	8	43	14	..	..	..	0.1	0.1					
Congo	8	14	12	29	22	34	0.1	0.1	0.2	-24.1	54.5		9
Dem.R.Congo	7	..	..	1	1	..	0.1			2.3		30	0
Equatorial Guinea	1	1	5	..	..	..	0.0	0.0					
Gabon	3	18	20	15	10	..	0.0	0.2		-33.3		70	7
Sao Tome Prn	2	..	10	11	13	14	0.0	0.1	0.1	20.8	6.3	1,295	73
East Africa	**1,285**	**2,323**	**2,377**	**3,065**	**3,802**	**4,074**	**20.1**	**22.8**	**18.8**	**24.0**	**7.2**	**505**	**15**
Burundi	4	1	1	1	1	2	0.1	0.0	0.0	71.4	25.0	10	0
Comoros	2	22	15	11	13	14	0.0	0.1	0.1	16.8	12.8	720	21
Djibouti	..	4	..	7	7	7			0.0	-1.8	4.3	235	15
Eritrea	..	58	36	74	73	66		0.3	0.3	-1.4	-9.6	790	14
Ethiopia	25	16	57	114	174	168	0.4	0.5	0.8	52.6	-3.3	740	2
Kenya	443	486	283	347	486	579	6.9	2.7	2.7	39.8	19.2	375	17
Madagascar	40	58	121	44	56	62	0.6	1.2	0.3	27.3	10.7	225	3
Malawi	16	17	25	23	24	24	0.2	0.2	0.1	2.9	-0.1	55	2
Mauritius	244	430	542	696	853	871	3.8	5.2	4.0	22.5	2.2	1,145	708
Mozambique	..	..	74	98	95	130		0.7	0.6	-2.4	36.0	225	7
Reunion	..	283	296	413	448	442		2.8	2.0	8.5	-1.3	1,080	569
Rwanda	10	2	4	26	44	49	0.2	0.0	0.2	69.1	11.4		6
Seychelles	126	129	139	171	172	192	2.0	1.3	0.9	0.3	11.9	1,495	2,366
Tanzania	65	502	377	647	746	824	1.0	3.6	3.8	15.4	10.4	1,395	22
Uganda	10	78	165	184	256	381	0.2	1.6	1.8	39.1	48.8	815	14
Zambia	41	47	111	149	161	164	0.6	1.1	0.8	8.1	1.9	245	15
Zimbabwe	60	145	125	61	194	99	0.9	1.2	0.5	217.5	-48.9	65	8
Southern Africa	**2,081**	**2,640**	**3,118**	**6,439**	**7,323**	**8,336**	**32.5**	**30.0**	**38.5**	**13.7**	**13.8**	**760**	**163**
Botswana	117	162	222	457	549	562	1.8	2.1	2.6	20.2	2.3	335	343
Lesotho	17	27	24	28	34	30	0.3	0.2	0.1	21.4	-11.8	100	15
Namibia	85	278	160	330	403	348	1.3	1.5	1.6	22.1	-13.8	445	171
South Africa	1,832	2,125	2,675	5,523	6,282	7,327	28.6	25.7	33.9	13.7	16.6	995	165
Swaziland	30	48	37	101	54	69	0.5	0.4	0.3	-46.5	27.8	80	61

Source: World Tourism Organization (UNWTO) ©

(Data as collected by UNWTO for TMT 2006 Edition)

International Tourism Receipts by Country of Destination

	International Tourism Receipts (US$, million)						Market share in the region (%)			Change (%)		Receipts per arrival[1]	Receipts per capita[1]
	1990	1995	2000	2003	2004	2005*	1990	2000	2005*	04/03	05*/04	US$	US$
Americas	*69,191*	*98,438*	*130,800*	*114,116*	*132,023*	*144,523*	*100*	*100*	*100*	*15.7*	*9.5*	*1,085*	*164*
North America	**54,872**	**77,491**	**101,472**	**84,256**	**98,213**	**107,067**	**79.3**	**77.6**	**74.1**	**16.6**	**9.0**	**1,190**	**246**
Canada	6,339	7,917	10,778	10,546	12,871	13,584	9.2	8.2	9.4	22.0	5.5	725	414
Mexico	5,526	6,179	8,294	9,362	10,796	11,803	8.0	6.3	8.2	15.3	9.3	540	111
United States	43,007	63,395	82,400	64,348	74,547	81,680	62.2	63.0	56.5	15.8	9.6	1,660	276
Caribbean	**8,639**	**12,236**	**17,154**	**17,842**	**19,292**	**20,415**	**12.5**	**13.1**	**14.1**	**8.1**	**5.8**	**1,085**	**526**
Anguilla	35	50	56	60	69	86	0.1	0.0	0.1	15.3	24.7	1,390	6,512
Antigua,Barb	298	247	291	300	338	327	0.4	0.2	0.2	12.7	-3.3	1,330	4,758
Aruba	350	521	814	859	1,056	1,091	0.5	0.6	0.8	22.9	3.4	1,490	15,245
Bahamas	1,333	1,346	1,734	1,757	1,884	2,072	1.9	1.3	1.4	7.2	9.9	1,290	6,865
Barbados	494	622	723	758	776	776	0.7	0.6	0.5	2.3	0.1	1,420	2,784
Bermuda	490	488	431	348	426	430	0.7	0.3	0.3	22.4	0.9	1,595	6,578
Bonaire	18	37	59	84	84	85	0.0	0.0	0.1	-0.7	1.7	1,360	
Br.Virgin Is	132	211	345	342	393	437	0.2	0.3	0.3	14.9	11.2	1,295	19,302
Cayman Islands	236	394	559	518	519	353	0.3	0.4	0.2	0.2	-32.0	2,105	7,974
Cuba	243	963	1,737	1,846	1,915	1,920	0.4	1.3	1.3	3.7	0.3	850	169
Curaçao	120	175	189	223	222	239	0.2	0.1	0.2	-0.4	7.5	1,075	
Dominica	25	42	48	54	61	56	0.0	0.0	0.0	12.3	-7.2	710	815
Dominican Rp	818	1,571	2,860	3,128	3,152	3,518	1.2	2.2	2.4	0.8	11.6	955	389
Grenada	38	76	93	104	83	71	0.1	0.1	0.0	-19.5	-14.4	725	798
Guadeloupe	197	458	418	..	..	246	0.3	0.3	0.2			660	548
Haiti	46	90	128	93	87	110	0.1	0.1	0.1	-6.5	26.4	980	14
Jamaica	740	1,069	1,333	1,355	1,438	1,545	1.1	1.0	1.1	6.1	7.4	1,045	565
Martinique	240	384	302	247	291	280	0.3	0.2	0.2	17.8	-3.8	580	647
Montserrat	7	17	9	7	9	9	0.0	0.0	0.0	17.1	4.7	925	962
Puerto Rico	1,366	1,828	2,388	2,677	3,024	3,239	2.0	1.8	2.2	13.0	7.1	880	828
Saint Lucia	154	230	281	282	326	356	0.2	0.2	0.2	15.5	9.3	1,120	2,140
St.Kitts-Nev	58	63	58	75	103	107	0.1	0.0	0.1	37.3	4.1	845	2,753
St.Maarten	316	349	511	538	613	619	0.5	0.4	0.4	13.9	1.1	1,325	
St.Vincent,Grenadines	56	53	82	91	96	105	0.1	0.1	0.1	5.5	9.4	1,100	893
Trinidad Tbg	95	77	213	249	341	453	0.1	0.2	0.3	36.9	32.8	980	421
Turks,Caicos	37	53	285	..	..	..	0.1	0.2					
US.Virgin Is	697	822	1,206	1,257	1,356	1,491	1.0	0.9	1.0	7.9	10.0	2,560	13,715
Central America	**735**	**1,523**	**2,958**	**3,421**	**3,965**	**4,645**	**1.1**	**2.3**	**3.2**	**15.9**	**17.2**	**740**	**120**
Belize	44	78	111	117	133	214	0.1	0.1	0.1	13.5	60.7	905	760
Costa Rica	275	681	1,302	1,199	1,359	1,570	0.4	1.0	1.1	13.3	15.6	935	391
El Salvador	18	85	217	383	441	543	0.0	0.2	0.4	15.1	23.2	560	81
Guatemala	185	213	482	621	776	869	0.3	0.4	0.6	25.0	12.0	660	72
Honduras	29	107	260	356	414	464	0.0	0.2	0.3	16.3	12.1	690	65
Nicaragua	12	50	129	160	192	206	0.0	0.1	0.1	19.9	7.4	290	38
Panama	172	309	458	585	651	780	0.2	0.4	0.5	11.3	19.8	1,110	248
South America	**4,946**	**7,189**	**9,216**	**8,597**	**10,553**	**12,397**	**7.1**	**7.0**	**8.6**	**22.8**	**17.5**	**680**	**33**
Argentina	1,131	2,222	2,904	2,006	2,235	2,729	1.6	2.2	1.9	11.4	22.1	715	69
Bolivia	55	55	68	167	192	239	0.1	0.1	0.2	15.1	24.5	475	27
Brazil	1,492	972	1,810	2,479	3,222	3,861	2.2	1.4	2.7	30.0	19.8	720	21
Chile	540	911	819	883	1,095	1,109	0.8	0.6	0.8	24.0	1.3	545	69
Colombia	406	657	1,030	893	1,058	1,218	0.6	0.8	0.8	18.5	15.1	1,305	28
Ecuador	188	255	402	406	462	486	0.3	0.3	0.3	13.8	5.0	565	36
French Guiana	..	..	..	..	..	45			0.0			475	230
Guyana	27	33	75	26	27	35	0.0	0.1	0.0	3.8	29.6	300	46
Paraguay	128	137	73	64	70	78	0.2	0.1	0.1	9.5	11.5	230	12
Peru	217	428	837	963	1,142	1,308	0.3	0.6	0.9	18.6	14.6	880	47
Suriname	1	21	16	4	17	45	0.0	0.0	0.0	325.0	164.7	280	103
Uruguay	238	611	713	345	494	594	0.3	0.5	0.4	43.3	20.3	330	174
Venezuela	496	849	423	331	502	650	0.7	0.3	0.4	51.7	29.5	920	26

Source: World Tourism Organization (UNWTO) ©

(Data as collected by UNWTO for TMT 2006 Edition)

World Tourism Organization ©

International Tourism Receipts by Country of Destination

	International Tourism Receipts (US$, million)						Market share in the region (%)			Change (%)		Receipts per arrival[1]	Receipts per capita[1]
	1990	1995	2000	2003	2004	2005*	1990	2000	2005*	04/03	05*/04		US$
Asia and the Pacific	*41,138*	*75,928*	*85,224*	*93,536*	*123,900*	*134,475*	*100*	*100*	*100*	*32.5*	*8.5*	*865*	*37*
North-East Asia	**17,284**	**31,339**	**39,428**	**42,336**	**58,627**	**65,368**	**42.0**	**46.3**	**48.6**	**38.5**	**11.5**	**745**	**42**
China	2,218	8,730	16,231	17,406	25,739	29,296	5.4	19.0	21.8	47.9	13.8	625	22
Hong Kong (China)	4,682	7,760	5,907	7,137	8,999	10,292	11.4	6.9	7.7	26.1	14.4	695	1,492
Japan	3,578	3,224	3,373	8,817	11,269	6,630	8.7	4.0	4.9	27.8	-41.2	985	52
Korea, D P Rp	29	..	..	..	..	..	0.1						
Korea, Republic of	3,559	5,150	6,834	5,358	6,069	5,806	8.7	8.0	4.3	13.3	-4.3	965	119
Macao (China)	1,473	3,102	3,208	5,155	7,479	7,980	3.6	3.8	5.9	45.1	6.7	885	17,765
Mongolia	5	21	36	143	185	177	0.0	0.0	0.1	29.4	-4.4	525	63
Taiwan (pr. of China)	1,740	3,286	3,738	2,977	4,054	4,977	4.2	4.4	3.7	36.2	22.8	1,475	217
South-East Asia	**14,479**	**27,354**	**26,710**	**25,084**	**32,843**	**33,847**	**35.2**	**31.3**	**25.2**	**30.9**	**3.1**	**685**	**59**
Cambodia	..	53	304	389	604	840		0.4	0.6	55.1	39.2	590	62
Indonesia	2,105	5,229	4,975	4,037	4,798	4,521	5.1	5.8	3.4	18.8	-5.8	905	19
Lao P.D.R.	3	51	114	87	119	147	0.0	0.1	0.1	36.7	23.4	220	24
Malaysia	1,667	3,969	5,011	5,898	8,198	8,543	4.1	5.9	6.4	39.0	4.2	520	357
Myanmar	9	151	162	56	84	..	0.0	0.2		50.0		345	2
Philippines	1,306	1,136	2,156	1,544	2,017	2,265	3.2	2.5	1.7	30.6	12.3	865	26
Singapore	4,937	7,611	5,142	3,781	5,221	5,908	12.0	6.0	4.4	38.1	13.2	835	1,335
Thailand	4,326	8,039	7,468	7,828	10,034	9,591	10.5	8.8	7.1	28.2	-4.4	830	149
Vietnam	85	..	..	1,400	1,700	1,880	0.2			21.4	10.6	540	23
Oceania	**7,321**	**13,831**	**14,289**	**19,386**	**23,802**	**25,622**	**17.8**	**16.8**	**19.1**	**22.8**	**7.6**	**2,445**	**783**
American Samoa	10	..	..	..	..	..	0.0						
Australia	4,246	8,125	9,274	12,349	15,191	16,866	10.3	10.9	12.5	23.0	11.0	3,360	840
Cook Is	16	28	36	69	72	92	0.0	0.0	0.1	4.3	27.8	1,040	4,301
Fiji	202	291	182	340	420	434	0.5	0.2	0.3	23.3	3.3	790	485
French Polynesia	171	326	..	480	523	522	0.4		0.4	8.9	-0.3	2,505	1,928
Guam	936	..	..	..	..	..	2.3						
Kiribati	1	2	3	..	..	..	0.0	0.0					
Marshall Is	..	3	4	..	..	..		0.0					
Micronesia (Fed.St.of)	..	..	15	17	17	17		0.0	0.0	-1.2	3.6	900	158
N.Mariana Is	455	655	..	..	..	..	1.1						
New Caledonia	94	108	111	196	241	253	0.2	0.1	0.2	22.7	5.1	2,515	1,170
New Zealand	1,030	2,318	2,267	3,981	4,790	4,865	2.5	2.7	3.6	20.3	1.6	2,055	1,206
Niue	..	2	..	..	..	1			0.0			430	
Palau	..	..	53	76	97	97		0.1	0.1	28.2	0.3	1,130	4,789
Papua New Guinea	41	25	21	16	18	4	0.1	0.0	0.0	16.1	-80.3	50	1
Samoa	20	35	41	54	70	77	0.0	0.0	0.1	29.6	10.0	755	434
Solomon Is	7	16	4	2	4	2	0.0	0.0	0.0	127.4	-56.2	165	3
Tonga	9	10	7	14	15	11	0.0	0.0	0.0	7.1	-26.7	265	98
Vanuatu	39	45	56	52	64	74	0.1	0.1	0.1	23.1	15.6	1,190	360
South Asia	**2,055**	**3,404**	**4,797**	**6,729**	**8,628**	**9,638**	**5.0**	**5.6**	**7.2**	**28.2**	**11.7**	**1,210**	**6**
Bangladesh	11	25	50	57	67	70	0.0	0.1	0.1	17.2	4.8	335	0
Bhutan	2	5	10	8	12	19	0.0	0.0	0.0	50.0	48.6	1,360	8
India	1,539	2,581	3,460	4,463	6,170	7,524	3.7	4.1	5.6	38.2	21.9	1,920	7
Iran	61	67	467	1,033	1,044	992	0.1	0.5	0.7	1.1	-5.0	630	15
Maldives	89	211	321	402	408	287	0.2	0.4	0.2	1.6	-29.7	725	821
Nepal	64	177	158	200	230	132	0.2	0.2	0.1	15.0	-42.7	350	5
Pakistan	156	110	81	122	179	181	0.4	0.1	0.1	46.7	1.1	225	1
Sri Lanka	132	226	248	441	513	429	0.3	0.3	0.3	16.3	-16.4	780	21

Source: World Tourism Organization (UNWTO) ©   (Data as collected by UNWTO for TMT 2006 Edition)

International Tourism Receipts by Country of Destination

	International Tourism Receipts (US$, million)						Market share in the region (%)			Change (%)		Receipts per arrival[1]	Receipts per capita[1]
	1990	1995	2000	2003	2004	2005*	1990	2000	2005*	04/03	05*/04		US$
Europe	142,885	212,105	232,446	283,753	328,888	348,765	100	100	100	15.9	6.0	795	396
Northern Europe	26,267	33,916	35,938	41,399	49,275	53,891	18.4	15.5	15.5	19.0	9.4	1,060	605
Denmark	3,645	3,673	3,694	5,265	5,670	4,956	2.6	1.6	1.4	7.7	-12.6	1,085	912
Finland	1,167	1,641	1,411	1,873	2,076	2,186	0.8	0.6	0.6	10.8	5.3	695	419
Iceland	151	186	229	320	372	409	0.1	0.1	0.1	16.2	10.1	470	1,378
Ireland	1,453	2,208	2,633	3,856	4,398	4,744	1.0	1.1	1.4	14.1	7.9	645	1,181
Norway	1,570	2,238	2,050	2,659	3,136	3,495	1.1	0.9	1.0	18.0	11.5	915	761
Sweden	2,906	3,471	4,064	5,297	6,196	7,427	2.0	1.7	2.1	17.0	19.9	2,370	825
United Kingdom	15,375	20,500	21,857	22,656	28,221	30,675	10.8	9.4	8.8	24.6	8.7	1,095	508
Western Europe	63,114	80,776	82,774	103,183	117,870	122,459	44.2	35.6	35.1	14.2	3.9	860	658
Austria	13,417	12,927	9,931	13,954	15,582	16,012	9.4	4.3	4.6	11.7	2.8	800	1,956
Belgium	..	4,548	6,592	8,191	9,233	9,868		2.8	2.8	12.7	6.9	1,465	952
Belgium/Luxembourg	3,702	..	..	..	..	..							
France	20,184	27,541	30,757	36,593	40,841	42,276	14.1	13.2	12.1	11.6	3.5	555	697
Germany	14,245	18,001	18,693	23,106	27,668	29,173	10.0	8.0	8.4	19.7	5.4	1,355	354
Luxembourg	..	1,721	1,806	2,994	3,657	3,616		0.8	1.0	22.2	-1.1	3,960	7,716
Netherlands	4,155	6,578	7,217	9,159	10,333	10,475	2.9	3.1	3.0	12.8	1.4	1,045	638
Switzerland	7,411	9,459	7,777	9,186	10,556	11,040	5.2	3.3	3.2	14.9	4.6	1,525	1,474
Central/Eastern Europe	2,097	19,633	20,350	24,047	28,930	32,445	1.5	8.8	9.3	20.3	12.2	375	85
Armenia	..	1	38	73	85	141		0.0	0.0	16.4	65.9	445	47
Azerbaijan	228	70	63	58	65	77	0.2	0.0	0.0	12.1	18.5	65	10
Belarus	..	23	93	267	270	253		0.0	0.1	1.1	-6.3	2,785	25
Bulgaria	320	473	1,076	1,693	2,221	2,430	0.2	0.5	0.7	31.2	9.4	500	326
Czech Rep	419	2,880	2,973	3,556	4,172	4,668	0.3	1.3	14.4	17.3	11.9	735	456
Estonia	..	357	508	669	891	951		0.2	0.3	33.2	6.8	495	714
Georgia	..	..	97	147	177	241		0.0	0.1	20.1	36.7	430	52
Hungary	824	2,953	3,757	4,046	4,061	4,271	0.6	1.6	1.2	0.4	5.2	425	427
Kazakhstan	..	122	356	564	718	701		0.2	0.2	27.3	-2.4	225	46
Kyrgyzstan	..	5	15	48	76	73		0.0	0.0	58.3	-3.9	230	14
Latvia	..	20	131	222	267	341		0.1	0.1	20.1	27.8	305	149
Lithuania	..	77	391	638	776	921		0.2	0.3	21.7	18.7	460	256
Poland	358	6,614	5,677	4,069	5,833	6,274	0.3	2.4	1.8	43.4	7.6	415	163
Rep Moldova	..	57	39	58	96	107		0.0	0.0	65.5	11.1	4,635	24
Romania	106	590	359	448	505	1,060	0.1	0.2	0.3	12.7	109.9	740	47
Russian Federation	..	4,312	3,429	4,502	5,225	5,564		1.5	1.6	16.1	6.5	280	39
Slovakia	70	623	433	865	901	1,210	0.0	0.2	0.3	4.2	34.3	800	223
Tajikistan	..	..	..	2	1	2			0.0	-50.0	100.0		0
Ukraine	..	191	394	935	2,560	3,125		0.2	0.9		22.1	165	66
Uzbekistan	..	..	27	24	28	..		0.0		16.7		105	1
Southern/Mediter. Eu.	51,408	77,781	93,385	115,124	132,812	139,970	36.0	40.2	40.1	15.4	5.4	895	624
Albania	4	65	389	522	727	860	0.0	0.2	0.2	39.3	18.3	18,705	241
Bosnia & Herzg	..	..	233	376	483	514		0.1	0.1	28.5	6.5	2,365	116
Croatia	..	1,349	2,782	6,304	6,848	7,463		1.2	2.1	8.6	9.0	880	1,660
Cyprus	1,258	1,798	1,941	2,091	2,252	2,331	0.9	0.8	0.7	7.7	3.5	945	2,988
F.Yug.Rp.Macedonia	..	19	38	57	72	84		0.0	0.0	26.6	16.9	425	41
Greece	2,587	4,135	9,219	10,741	12,872	13,731	1.8	4.0	3.9	19.8	6.7	960	1,287
Israel	1,396	2,993	4,088	2,060	2,380	2,853	1.0	1.8	0.8	15.6	19.9	1,500	455
Italy	16,458	28,731	27,493	31,247	35,656	35,398	11.5	11.8	10.1	14.1	-0.7	970	609
Malta	496	654	590	721	773	759	0.3	0.3	0.2	7.2	-1.9	650	1,903
Portugal	3,555	4,831	5,243	6,616	7,707	7,712	2.5	2.3	2.2	16.5	0.1	725	730
Serbia & Montenegro	..	42	30	201	..	..		0.0				420	19
Slovenia	..	1,082	965	1,340	1,630	1,801		0.4	0.5	21.6	10.5	1,160	895
Spain	18,484	25,252	29,968	39,645	45,248	47,970	12.9	12.9	13.8	14.1	6.0	860	1,189
Turkey	3,225	4,957	7,636	13,203	15,888	18,152	2.3	3.3	5.2	20.3	14.2	895	261
Yugoslav SFR	2,774	..	..	..	..	..	1.9						

Source: World Tourism Organization (UNWTO) ©

(Data as collected by UNWTO for TMT 2006 Edition)

World Tourism Organization ©

International Tourism Receipts by Country of Destination

	International Tourism Receipts (US$, million)						Market share in the region (%)			Change (%)		Receipts per arrival[1]	Receipts per capita[1]
	1990	1995	2000	2003	2004	2005*	1990	2000	2005*	04/03	05*/04		US$
Middle East	*4,279*	*9,744*	*15,242*	*19,740*	*25,239*	*26,254*	*100*	*100*	*100*	*27.9*	*4.0*	*685*	*133*
Bahrain	135	247	573	720	864	920	3.2	3.8	3.5	20.0	6.5	235	1,337
Egypt	1,100	2,684	4,345	4,584	6,125	6,851	25.7	28.5	26.1	33.6	11.8	830	88
Iraq	173	18	2	..	..	..	4.1	0.0					
Jordan	512	660	723	1,062	1,330	1,441	12.0	4.7	5.5	25.2	8.3	480	250
Kuwait	132	121	98	117	176	164	3.1	0.6	0.6	50.2	-6.8	1,940	70
Lebanon	..	..	..	6,374	5,411	5,432			20.7	-15.1	0.4	4,765	1,420
Libyan Arab Jamahiriya	6	2	75	205	218	250	0.1	0.5	1.0	6.3	14.7	1,465	43
Oman	69	..	221	385	414	481	1.6	1.5	1.8	7.4	16.4	345	160
Palestine	..	255	283	107	56	..		1.9		-47.7		1,000	15
Qatar	..	..	128	369	498	760		0.8	2.9	35.0	52.8	835	881
Saudi Arabia	..	..	..	3,413	6,486	5,177			19.7	90.0	-20.2	645	196
Syrian Arab Republic	320	1,258	1,082	773	1,800	2,175	7.5	7.1	8.3	132.9	20.8	645	118
Untd Arab Emirates	315	632	1,063	1,439	1,594	2,200	7.4	7.0	8.4	10.8	38.0	245	858
Yemen	20	50	73	139	213	262	0.5	0.5	1.0	53.2	23.0	780	13

Source: World Tourism Organization (UNWTO) ©   (Data as collected by UNWTO for TMT 2006 Edition)

[1] Last year with data available

| : change of series.

See for tables in US$ values pages Annex - 11 to Annex – 15

International Tourism Receipts by Country of Destination

	International Tourism Receipts (euro, million)						Market share in the region (%)			Change (%)		Receipts per arrival¹	Receipts per capita¹
	1990	1995	2000	2003	2004	2005*	1990	2000	2005*	04/03	05*/04		euro
Africa	*5,027*	*6,502*	*11,264*	*14,173*	*15,221*	*17,396*	*100*	*100*	*100*	*7.4*	*14.3*	*465*	*22*
North Africa	**1,832**	**2,192**	**4,138**	**4,365**	**4,899**	**5,641**	**36.4**	**36.7**	**32.4**	**12.2**	**15.2**	**405**	**49**
Algeria	82	25	104	99	144	148	1.6	0.9	0.9	44.9	3.1	100	5
Morocco	989	991	2,208	2,851	3,154	3,714	19.7	19.6	21.4	10.6	17.8	635	114
Sudan	16	6	5	16	17	72	0.3	0.0	0.4	6.1	324.3	290	2
Tunisia	744	1,170	1,821	1,399	1,584	1,707	14.8	16.2	9.8	13.2	7.8	270	169
West Africa	**475**	**414**	**1,022**	**1,175**	**1,159**	**1,520**	**9.5**	**9.1**	**8.7**	**-1.3**	**31.1**	**425**	**6**
Benin	43	65	83	94	96	..	0.9	0.7		2.1		550	13
Burkina Faso	9	..	21	26	37	..	0.2	0.2		41.2		165	3
Cape Verde	5	8	44	77	80	102	0.1	0.4	0.6	3.6	28.5	520	245
Côte d'Ivoire	40	68	53	61	66	67	0.8	0.5	0.4	8.1	1.2	340	4
Gambia	20	21	52	45	46	50	0.4	0.5	0.3	2.3	8.2	450	31
Ghana	64	8	363	366	375	640	1.3	3.2	3.7	2.4	70.8	1,495	29
Guinea	24	1	13	27	24	..	0.5	0.1		-12.0		540	3
Guinea-Bissau	..	..	..	2	1	..				-54.5			1
Mali	37	19	43	113	113	119	0.7	0.4	0.7	-0.5	5.7	835	10
Mauritania	7	8	..	..	..	..	0.1						
Niger	13	5	25	25	25	27	0.3	0.2	0.2	0.7	9.7	430	2
Nigeria	20	13	109	44	17	14	0.4	1.0	0.1	-61.4	-14.2	15	0
Senegal	131	128	156	185	170	..	2.6	1.4		-7.8		255	15
Sierra Leone	15	44	12	53	47	51	0.3	0.1	0.3	-12.1	10.3	1,285	9
Togo	46	10	9	13	15	..	0.9	0.1		15.2		185	3
Central Africa	**77**	**102**	**155**	**230**	**220**	**260**	**1.5**	**1.4**	**1.5**	**-4.5**	**18.0**	**330**	**2**
Angola	10	8	19	43	53	71	0.2	0.2	0.4	22.1	34.0	340	6
Cameroon	42	28	62	101	..	..	0.8	0.5					6
Cent.Afr.Rep.	2	3	5	4	3	..	0.0	0.0		-9.1		395	1
Chad	6	33	15	..	..	..	0.1	0.1					
Congo	6	11	13	26	18	27	0.1	0.1	0.2	-31.0	54.5		8
Dem.R.Congo	5	..	..	1	1	..	0.1			-6.9		25	0
Equatorial Guinea	1	1	5	..	..	..	0.0	0.0					
Gabon	2	14	22	13	8	..	0.0	0.2		-39.4		60	6
Sao Tome Prn	2	..	11	9	10	11	0.0	0.1	0.1	9.8	6.2	1,040	58
East Africa	**1,009**	**1,776**	**2,573**	**2,710**	**3,056**	**3,275**	**20.1**	**22.8**	**18.8**	**12.8**	**7.1**	**405**	**12**
Burundi	3	1	1	1	1	1	0.1	0.0	0.0	55.9	25.0	10	0
Comoros	2	17	16	9	10	11	0.0	0.1	0.1	6.2	12.8	580	17
Djibouti	..	3	..	6	5	6			0.0	-10.7	4.3	190	12
Eritrea	..	44	39	65	59	53		0.3	0.3	-10.3	-9.6	635	11
Ethiopia	20	12	62	101	140	135	0.4	0.5	0.8	38.8	-3.3	595	2
Kenya	348	372	306	307	390	465	6.9	2.7	2.7	27.1	19.2	305	14
Madagascar	31	44	131	39	45	50	0.6	1.2	0.3	15.7	10.7	180	3
Malawi	13	13	28	21	19	19	0.2	0.2	0.1	-6.4	-0.1	45	2
Mauritius	192	329	587	615	686	700	3.8	5.2	4.0	11.4	2.2	920	569
Mozambique	..	..	80	86	77	104		0.7	0.6	-11.2	36.0	180	5
Reunion	..	216	320	365	360	355		2.8	2.0	-1.4	-1.3	870	457
Rwanda	8	2	5	23	35	39	0.2	0.0	0.2	53.8	11.3		5
Seychelles	99	99	151	151	138	154	2.0	1.3	0.9	-8.8	11.9	1,200	1,902
Tanzania	51	384	408	572	600	662	1.0	3.6	3.8	4.9	10.4	1,120	18
Uganda	8	60	179	163	206	306	0.2	1.6	1.8	26.5	48.8	655	11
Zambia	32	36	120	132	129	132	0.6	1.1	0.8	-1.7	1.8	195	12
Zimbabwe	47	111	135	54	156	80	0.9	1.2	0.5	188.8	-48.9	50	7
Southern Africa	**1,634**	**2,019**	**3,376**	**5,692**	**5,887**	**6,700**	**32.5**	**30.0**	**38.5**	**3.4**	**13.8**	**610**	**131**
Botswana	92	124	241	404	442	452	1.8	2.1	2.6	9.3	2.3	270	275
Lesotho	13	21	26	25	27	24	0.3	0.2	0.1	10.4	-11.8	80	12
Namibia	67	213	173	292	324	279	1.3	1.5	1.6	11.1	-13.8	360	138
South Africa	1,438	1,625	2,896	4,883	5,050	5,890	28.6	25.7	33.9	3.4	16.6	800	133
Swaziland	24	37	40	89	43	55	0.5	0.4	0.3	-51.4	27.8	65	49

Source: World Tourism Organization (UNWTO) ©

(Data as collected by UNWTO for TMT 2006 Edition)

World Tourism Organization ©

International Tourism Receipts by Country of Destination

	International Tourism Receipts (euro, million)						Market share in the region (%)			Change (%)		Receipts per arrival[1]	Receipts per capita[1]
	1990	1995	2000	2003	2004	2005*	1990	2000	2005*	04/03	05*/04		euro
Americas	*54,335*	*75,258*	*141,618*	*100,880*	*106,136*	*116,167*	*100*	*100*	*100*	*5.2*	*9.5*	*870*	*131*
North America	**43,090**	**59,243**	**109,864**	**74,484**	**78,956**	**86,060**	**79.3**	**77.6**	**74.1**	**6.0**	**9.0**	**955**	**198**
Canada	4,978	6,053	11,669	9,323	10,347	10,918	9.2	8.2	9.4	11.0	5.5	580	333
Mexico	4,339	4,724	8,980	8,276	8,679	9,488	8.0	6.3	8.2	4.9	9.3	435	89
United States	33,773	48,467	89,215	56,885	59,930	65,654	62.2	63.0	56.5	5.4	9.6	1,335	222
Caribbean	**6,784**	**9,354**	**18,573**	**15,773**	**15,509**	**16,409**	**12.5**	**13.1**	**14.1**	**-1.7**	**5.8**	**875**	**423**
Anguilla	27	38	61	53	56	69	0.1	0.0	0.1	4.9	24.7	1,115	5,234
Antigua,Barb	234	189	315	265	272	263	0.4	0.2	0.2	2.5	-3.3	1,070	3,825
Aruba	275	398	881	759	849	877	0.5	0.6	0.8	11.8	3.4	1,195	12,254
Bahamas	1,047	1,029	1,878	1,554	1,515	1,665	1.9	1.3	1.4	-2.5	9.9	1,035	5,518
Barbados	388	476	783	670	623	624	0.7	0.6	0.5	-6.9	0.1	1,140	2,237
Bermuda	385	373	467	308	342	346	0.7	0.3	0.3	11.3	0.9	1,280	5,287
Bonaire	14	28	64	75	67	68	0.0	0.0	0.1	-9.7	1.7	1,095	
Br.Virgin Is	104	161	374	302	316	351	0.2	0.3	0.3	4.5	11.2	1,040	15,515
Cayman Islands	185	301	605	458	417	284	0.3	0.4	0.2	-8.9	-32.0	1,690	6,409
Cuba	191	736	1,881	1,632	1,540	1,543	0.4	1.3	1.3	-5.7	0.2	680	136
Curaçao	94	134	205	197	179	192	0.2	0.1	0.2	-9.4	7.5	865	
Dominica	20	32	52	48	49	45	0.0	0.0	0.0	2.1	-7.2	570	655
Dominican Rp	642	1,201	3,097	2,765	2,534	2,828	1.2	2.2	2.4	-8.4	11.6	765	312
Grenada	30	58	101	92	67	57	0.1	0.1	0.0	-26.8	-14.4	585	642
Guadeloupe	155	350	453	..	..	198	0.3	0.3	0.2			530	441
Haiti	36	69	139	82	70	88	0.1	0.1	0.1	-14.9	26.4	790	11
Jamaica	581	817	1,443	1,198	1,156	1,242	1.1	1.0	1.1	-3.5	7.4	840	454
Martinique	188	294	327	218	234	225	0.3	0.2	0.2	7.1	-3.8	465	520
Montserrat	5	13	10	6	7	7	0.0	0.0	0.0	6.5	4.7	745	773
Puerto Rico	1,073	1,397	2,585	2,366	2,431	2,603	2.0	1.8	2.2	2.7	7.1	705	666
Saint Lucia	121	176	304	249	262	286	0.2	0.2	0.2	5.0	9.3	900	1,720
St.Kitts-Nev	46	48	63	66	83	86	0.1	0.0	0.1	24.9	4.1	680	2,213
St.Maarten	248	267	553	476	493	498	0.5	0.4	0.4	3.6	1.0	1,065	
St.Vincent,Grenadines	44	41	89	80	77	84	0.1	0.1	0.1	-4.1	9.4	885	718
Trinidad Tbg	75	59	231	220	274	364	0.1	0.2	0.3	24.5	32.8	785	339
Turks,Caicos	29	41	309	..	..	..	0.1	0.2					
US.Virgin Is	547	628	1,306	1,111	1,090	1,198	1.0	0.9	1.0	-1.9	9.9	2,060	11,024
Central America	**577**	**1,164**	**3,203**	**3,025**	**3,187**	**3,734**	**1.1**	**2.3**	**3.2**	**5.4**	**17.1**	**595**	**96**
Belize	35	60	120	104	107	172	0.1	0.1	0.1	3.2	60.7	725	611
Costa Rica	216	521	1,410	1,060	1,092	1,262	0.4	1.0	1.1	3.0	15.5	750	314
El Salvador	14	65	235	339	354	436	0.0	0.2	0.4	4.6	23.1	450	65
Guatemala	145	163	522	549	624	698	0.3	0.4	0.6	13.6	12.0	530	58
Honduras	23	82	281	314	332	373	0.0	0.2	0.3	5.7	12.1	555	52
Nicaragua	9	38	139	142	154	166	0.0	0.1	0.1	9.0	7.4	235	30
Panama	135	236	496	517	523	627	0.2	0.4	0.5	1.2	19.8	895	200
South America	**3,884**	**5,496**	**9,978**	**7,599**	**8,484**	**9,964**	**7.1**	**7.0**	**8.6**	**11.6**	**17.5**	**545**	**27**
Argentina	888	1,699	3,144	1,773	1,797	2,193	1.6	2.2	1.9	1.3	22.1	575	55
Bolivia	43	42	74	147	154	192	0.1	0.1	0.2	4.7	24.4	380	22
Brazil	1,172	743	1,960	2,191	2,590	3,104	2.2	1.4	2.7	18.2	19.8	580	17
Chile	424	696	887	781	880	891	0.8	0.6	0.8	12.7	1.3	440	56
Colombia	319	502	1,116	790	851	979	0.6	0.8	0.8	7.7	15.1	1,050	23
Ecuador	148	195	435	359	372	390	0.3	0.3	0.3	3.5	5.0	455	29
French Guiana	..	..	..	..	..	36			0.0			380	185
Guyana	21	25	81	23	22	28	0.0	0.1	0.0	-5.6	29.6	240	37
Paraguay	101	105	79	56	56	62	0.2	0.1	0.1	-0.4	11.5	185	10
Peru	170	327	906	851	918	1,052	0.3	0.6	0.9	7.8	14.5	710	38
Suriname	1	16	17	4	14	36	0.0	0.0	0.0	286.5	164.7	225	83
Uruguay	187	467	772	305	397	478	0.3	0.5	0.4	30.3	20.3	265	140
Venezuela	389	649	458	293	404	522	0.7	0.3	0.4	37.9	29.5	740	21

(Data as collected by UNWTO for TMT 2006 Edition)

International Tourism Receipts by Country of Destination

	International Tourism Receipts (euro, million)						Market share in the region (%)			Change (%)		Receipts per arrival[1]	Receipts per capita[1]
	1990	1995	2000	2003	2004	2005*	1990	2000	2005*	04/03	05*/04		euro
Asia and the Pacific	*32,305*	*58,048*	*92,272*	*82,687*	*99,606*	*108,090*	*100*	*100*	*100*	*20.5*	*8.5*	*695*	*29*
North-East Asia	**13,573**	**23,959**	**42,688**	**37,426**	**47,132**	**52,543**	**42.0**	**46.3**	**48.6**	**25.9**	**11.5**	**600**	**34**
China	1,742	6,674	17,573	15,387	20,692	23,548	5.4	19.0	21.8	34.5	13.8	505	18
Hong Kong (China)	3,677	5,932	6,395	6,309	7,234	8,273	11.4	6.9	7.7	14.7	14.4	560	1,199
Japan	2,810	2,465	3,652	7,794	9,059	5,329	8.7	4.0	4.9	16.2	-41.2	790	42
Korea, D P Rp	23	..	..	..	..	..	0.1						
Korea, Republic of	2,795	3,937	7,400	4,737	4,879	4,667	8.7	8.0	4.3	3.0	-4.4	775	96
Macao (China)	1,157	2,372	3,474	4,557	6,013	6,414	3.6	3.8	5.9	32.0	6.7	710	14,280
Mongolia	4	16	39	126	149	142	0.0	0.0	0.1	17.6	-4.4	420	51
Taiwan (pr. of China)	1,366	2,512	4,047	2,632	3,259	4,000	4.2	4.4	3.7	23.8	22.7	1,185	175
South-East Asia	**11,370**	**20,912**	**28,919**	**22,175**	**26,403**	**27,206**	**35.2**	**31.3**	**25.2**	**19.1**	**3.0**	**550**	**47**
Cambodia	..	41	329	344	485	675		0.4	0.6	41.1	39.2	475	50
Indonesia	1,653	3,998	5,386	3,569	3,857	3,634	5.1	5.8	3.4	8.1	-5.8	725	15
Lao P.D.R.	2	39	123	77	96	118	0.0	0.1	0.1	24.3	23.4	175	19
Malaysia	1,309	3,034	5,425	5,214	6,590	6,867	4.1	5.9	6.4	26.4	4.2	420	287
Myanmar	7	115	175	50	68	..	0.0	0.2		36.4		280	1
Philippines	1,026	868	2,334	1,365	1,622	1,821	3.2	2.5	1.7	18.8	12.3	695	21
Singapore	3,877	5,819	5,567	3,342	4,197	4,749	12.0	6.0	4.4	25.6	13.2	670	1,073
Thailand	3,397	6,146	8,085	6,920	8,066	7,709	10.5	8.8	7.1	16.6	-4.4	665	120
Vietnam	67	..	..	1,238	1,367	1,511	0.2		1.4	10.4	10.6	435	18
Oceania	**5,749**	**10,574**	**15,471**	**17,137**	**19,135**	**20,595**	**17.8**	**16.8**	**19.1**	**11.7**	**7.6**	**1,965**	**630**
American Samoa	8	..	..	..	..	..	0.0						
Australia	3,334	6,212	10,041	10,917	12,212	13,557	10.3	10.9	12.5	11.9	11.0	2,700	675
Cook Is	13	21	39	61	58	74	0.0	0.0	0.1	-5.1	27.8	835	3,457
Fiji	159	222	197	301	337	349	0.5	0.2	0.3	12.1	3.3	635	390
French Polynesia	134	249	..	424	420	419	0.4		0.4	-0.9	-0.3	2,015	1,550
Guam	735	..	..	..	..	..	2.3						
Kiribati	1	2	3	..	..	..	0.0	0.0					
Marshall Is	..	2	4	..	..	..		0.0					
Micronesia (Fed.St.of)	..	..	16	15	13	14		0.0	0.0	-10.1	3.6	725	127
N.Mariana Is	357	501	..	..	..	..	1.1						
New Caledonia	74	83	120	174	194	204	0.2	0.1	0.2	11.5	5.1	2,020	940
New Zealand	809	1,772	2,454	3,519	3,851	3,911	2.5	2.7	3.6	9.4	1.5	1,655	969
Niue	..	2	..	..	..	1			0.0			345	
Palau	..	..	57	67	78	78		0.1	0.1	16.6	0.3	905	3,849
Papua New Guinea	32	19	23	14	15	3	0.1	0.0	0.0	5.6	-80.3	40	1
Samoa	16	27	44	48	56	62	0.0	0.0	0.1	17.9	10.0	610	349
Solomon Is	5	12	4	1	3	1	0.0	0.0	0.0	106.8	-56.2	130	2
Tonga	7	8	8	12	12	9	0.0	0.0	0.0	-2.6	-26.7	210	79
Vanuatu	31	34	61	46	51	59	0.1	0.1	0.1	11.9	15.6	960	289
South Asia	**1,614**	**2,602**	**5,194**	**5,949**	**6,936**	**7,747**	**5.0**	**5.6**	**7.2**	**16.6**	**11.7**	**970**	**5**
Bangladesh	9	19	54	50	54	56	0.0	0.1	0.1	6.6	4.8	270	0
Bhutan	2	4	11	7	10	15	0.0	0.0	0.0	36.4	48.5	1,095	7
India	1,208	1,973	3,746	3,945	4,960	6,048	3.7	4.1	5.6	25.7	21.9	1,545	6
Iran	48	51	506	913	839	797	0.1	0.5	0.7	-8.1	-5.0	505	12
Maldives	70	161	347	355	328	230	0.2	0.4	0.2	-7.6	-29.7	585	660
Nepal	50	135	171	177	185	106	0.2	0.2	0.1	4.6	-42.7	280	4
Pakistan	123	84	88	108	144	145	0.4	0.1	0.1	33.4	1.1	180	1
Sri Lanka	104	173	269	390	412	345	0.3	0.3	0.3	5.8	-16.4	630	17

Source: World Tourism Organization (UNWTO) ©

(Data as collected by UNWTO for TMT 2006 Edition)

International Tourism Receipts by Country of Destination

	International Tourism Receipts (euro, million)						Market share in the region (%)			Change (%)		Receipts per arrival[1]	Receipts per capita[1]
	1990	1995	2000	2003	2004	2005*	1990	2000	2005*	04/03	05*/04	euro	euro
Europe	112,205	162,159	251,670	250,843	264,400	280,335	100	100	100	5.4	6.0	640	318
Northern Europe	20,627	25,930	38,910	36,597	39,614	43,317	18.4	15.5	15.5	8.2	9.3	850	487
Denmark	2,862	2,808	3,999	4,655	4,559	3,984	2.6	1.6	1.4	-2.1	-12.6	875	733
Finland	916	1,255	1,528	1,656	1,669	1,757	0.8	0.6	0.6	0.8	5.3	560	336
Iceland	119	142	247	283	299	329	0.1	0.1	0.1	5.7	10.0	375	1,108
Ireland	1,141	1,688	2,851	3,409	3,536	3,813	1.0	1.1	1.4	3.7	7.8	520	950
Norway	1,233	1,711	2,220	2,350	2,521	2,809	1.1	0.9	1.0	7.3	11.4	735	612
Sweden	2,282	2,654	4,400	4,682	4,981	5,969	2.0	1.7	2.1	6.4	19.9	1,905	663
United Kingdom	12,074	15,672	23,665	20,028	22,688	24,656	10.8	9.4	8.8	13.3	8.7	880	408
Western Europe	49,562	61,755	89,620	91,216	94,759	98,432	44.2	35.6	35.1	3.9	3.9	690	529
Austria	10,536	9,883	10,752	12,336	12,527	12,870	9.4	4.3	4.6	1.5	2.7	645	1,572
Belgium	..	3,477	7,137	7,241	7,423	7,932		2.8	2.8	2.5	6.9	1,175	765
Belgium/Luxembourg	2,907	..	..	..	..	..							
France	15,850	21,056	33,301	32,349	32,833	33,981	14.1	13.2	12.1	1.5	3.5	450	560
Germany	11,187	13,762	20,239	20,426	22,243	23,449	10.0	8.0	8.4	8.9	5.4	1,090	284
Luxembourg	..	1,316	1,956	2,646	2,940	2,906		0.8	1.0	11.1	-1.2	3,185	6,202
Netherlands	3,263	5,029	7,814	8,097	8,307	8,420	2.9	3.1	3.0	2.6	1.4	840	513
Switzerland	5,820	7,232	8,420	8,121	8,486	8,874	5.2	3.3	3.2	4.5	4.6	1,230	1,185
Central/Eastern Europe	1,647	15,010	22,032	21,258	23,257	26,079	1.5	8.8	9.3	9.4	12.1	300	68
Armenia	..	1	41	65	68	113		0.0	0.0	5.9	65.9	355	38
Azerbaijan	179	54	68	51	52	62	0.2	0.0	0.0	1.9	18.4	55	8
Belarus	..	18	101	236	217	203		0.0	0.1	-8.0	-6.3	2,240	20
Bulgaria	251	362	1,165	1,496	1,785	1,953	0.2	0.5	0.7	19.3	9.4	405	262
Czech Rep	329	2,202	3,219	3,144	3,354	3,752	0.3	1.3	1.3	6.7	11.9	590	366
Estonia	..	273	550	591	716	764		0.2	0.3	21.1	6.7	400	574
Georgia	..	..	105	130	142	194		0.0	0.1	9.2	36.7	345	41
Hungary	647	2,258	4,067	3,577	3,265	3,433	0.6	1.6	1.2	-8.7	5.1	340	343
Kazakhstan	..	93	386	499	577	563		0.2	0.2	15.7	-2.4	180	37
Kyrgyzstan	..	4	16	42	61	59		0.0	0.0	44.0	-4.0	185	11
Latvia	..	15	142	197	215	274		0.1	0.1	9.2	27.8	245	120
Lithuania	..	59	424	564	624	740		0.2	0.3	10.6	18.6	370	206
Poland	281	5,057	6,147	3,597	4,689	5,043	0.3	2.4	1.8	30.4	7.5	330	131
Rep Moldova	..	44	43	51	77	86		0.0	0.0	50.5	11.0	3,725	19
Romania	83	451	389	396	406	852	0.1	0.2	0.3	2.5	109.9	595	38
Russian Federation	..	3,297	3,713	3,980	4,200	4,472		1.5	1.6	5.6	6.5	225	31
Slovakia	55	476	469	765	724	972	0.0	0.2	0.3	-5.3	34.2	640	179
Tajikistan	..	..	..	2	1	2			0.0	-54.5	100.0		0
Ukraine	..	146	427	827	2,058	2,512		0.2	0.9		22.1	130	53
Uzbekistan	..	..	29	21	23	..		0.0		6.1		85	1
Southern/Mediter. Eu.	40,369	59,465	101,108	101,771	106,771	112,507	36.0	40.2	40.1	4.9	5.4	715	502
Albania	3	50	421	461	585	692	0.0	0.2	0.2	26.7	18.3	15,035	194
Bosnia & Herzg	..	..	252	332	388	413		0.1	0.1	16.8	6.4	1,900	93
Croatia	..	1,031	3,012	5,573	5,506	5,999		1.2	2.1	-1.2	9.0	710	1,334
Cyprus	988	1,375	2,102	1,848	1,811	1,874	0.9	0.8	0.7	-2.0	3.5	760	2,402
F.Yug.Rp.Macedonia	..	15	41	50	58	67		0.0	0.0	15.2	16.8	340	33
Greece	2,032	3,161	9,981	9,495	10,348	11,037	1.8	4.0	3.9	9.0	6.7	775	1,035
Israel	1,097	2,288	4,426	1,821	1,914	2,293	1.0	1.8	0.8	5.1	19.8	1,205	365
Italy	12,924	21,965	29,767	27,623	28,665	28,453	11.5	11.8	10.1	3.8	-0.7	780	490
Malta	389	500	639	638	622	610	0.3	0.3	0.2	-2.5	-1.9	520	1,530
Portugal	2,792	3,693	5,677	5,849	6,195	6,199	2.5	2.3	2.2	5.9	0.1	585	587
Serbia & Montenegro	..	32	32	178	..	..		0.0				370	16
Slovenia	..	827	1,045	1,184	1,310	1,447		0.4	0.5	10.6	10.5	930	720
Spain	14,515	19,306	32,446	35,047	36,376	38,558	12.9	12.9	13.8	3.8	6.0	690	956
Turkey	2,533	3,790	8,268	11,672	12,773	14,590	2.3	3.3	5.2	9.4	14.2	720	209
Yugoslav SFR	2,178	..	..	..	..	..	1.9						

Source: World Tourism Organization (UNWTO) ©

(Data as collected by UNWTO for TMT 2006 Edition)

International Tourism Receipts by Country of Destination

	International Tourism Receipts (euro, million)						Market share in the region (%)			Change (%)		Receipts per arrival[1]	Receipts per capita[1]
	1990	1995	2000	2003	2004	2005*	1990	2000	2005*	04/03	05*/04		euro
Middle East	*3,360*	*7,449*	*16,502*	*17,450*	*20,290*	*21,103*	*100*	*100*	*100*	*16.3*	*4.0*	*550*	*107*
Bahrain	106	189	620	636	695	739	3.2	3.8	3.5	9.1	6.5	190	1,074
Egypt	864	2,052	4,704	4,052	4,924	5,506	25.7	28.5	26.1	21.5	11.8	670	71
Iraq	136	14	2	..	..	..	4.1	0.0					
Jordan	402	505	783	939	1,069	1,158	12.0	4.7	5.5	13.9	8.3	390	201
Kuwait	104	93	106	104	142	132	3.1	0.6	0.6	36.6	-6.9	1,560	57
Lebanon	..	..	..	5,635	4,350	4,366			20.7	-22.8	0.4	3,830	1,141
Libyan Arab Jamahiriya	5	2	81	181	175	201	0.1	0.5	1.0	-3.3	14.7	1,175	35
Oman	54	..	239	340	332	387	1.6	1.5	1.8	-2.3	16.3	280	129
Palestine	..	195	306	95	45	..		1.9		-52.4		805	12
Qatar	..	..	138	326	400	611		0.8	2.9	22.8	52.7	670	708
Saudi Arabia	..	..	..	3,017	5,214	4,162			19.7	72.8	-20.2	520	158
Syrian Arab Republic	251	962	1,171	683	1,447	1,748	7.5	7.1	8.3	111.8	20.8	520	95
Untd Arab Emirates	247	483	1,151	1,272	1,281	1,768	7.4	7.0	8.4	0.7	38.0	215	690
Yemen	16	38	79	123	171	211	0.5	0.5	1.0	39.4	23.0	625	10

Source: World Tourism Organization (UNWTO) ©

(Data as collected by UNWTO for TMT 2006 Edition)

[1] Last year with data available

| : change of series.

3.   Methodological Notes

3.1   Concepts and Definitions

According to the UNWTO/United Nations *Recommendations on Tourism Statistics*, Tourism comprises *the activities of persons travelling to and staying in places outside their usual environment for not more than one consecutive year for leisure, business and other purposes.*

This concept can be applied to different forms of tourism. Depending upon whether a person is travelling to, from or within a certain country the following forms can be distinguished:

- **Inbound Tourism**, involving the non-residents received by a destination country from the point of view of that destination;
- **Outbound Tourism**, involving residents travelling to another country from the point of view of the country of origin;
- **Domestic tourism**, involving residents of a given country travelling within that country.

All types of travellers engaged in tourism are described as visitors. Visitors can be distinguished as same-day visitors or tourists (overnight visitors).

There are various units of measure to quantify the volume of tourism. An overview is set out below:

Unit of measurement			Comment
Visitors	*Arrivals*	*- at frontiers (VF)*	or at a specific place in case of domestic tourism
Tourists (overnight visitors)	*Arrivals*	*- at frontiers (TF)*	
		- at collective tourism establishments (e.g. hotels and other, such as campings, etc.) (TCE) *- at hotels and similar establishments (THS)*	- excludes tourism in private accommodation; - arrivals are counted in every new accommodation visited
	Nights	*- at collective tourism establishments (e.g. hotels and other) (NCE)* *- at hotels and similar establishments (NHS)*	

Inbound Tourism
Unless otherwise stated, this report concentrates on **International Tourism** as measured from an **Inbound Tourism** perspective, i.e. the tourism received by any given destination country (and in a few cases territories) from non-residents travelling to that destination.

The most common unit of measure used to quantify the volume of International Tourism for statistical purposes is the number of International Tourist Arrivals. For a proper understanding of this unit, two considerations should be taken into account:

- Data refer exclusively to tourists (overnight visitors): 'a visitor who stays at least one night in a collective or private accommodation in the country visited'. Same-day visitors are not included.
- Data refer to the number of arrivals and not to the number of persons. The same person who makes several trips to a given country during a given period will be counted as a

new arrival each time, as well as a person who travels through several countries on one trip is counted as a new arrival each time.

Figures on the volume of international tourism presented in the regional and subregional tables, preferably relate to the concept of *international tourist arrivals at frontiers*. However, as not all countries are collecting data according to this concept, another series may be used instead. In the tables, the series are indicated as follows:

TF: International tourist arrivals at frontiers (excluding same-day visitors);
VF: International visitor arrivals at frontiers (including tourists and same-day visitors);
TCE: International tourist arrivals at collective tourism establishments;
THS: International tourist arrivals at hotels and similar establishments.

With respect to the inbound tourism volume, if available, in the profile tables for individual countries in Chapter III, except for data on International Tourist Arrivals, furthermore, data is included on International Visitor Arrivals, Same-day Visitor Arrivals, Cruise passengers (considered as a special category of same-day visitors) and Nights spent in collective establishments and / or in hotels and similar establishments.

Outbound Tourism
Data on outbound tourism volume in this series of reports originate from two different sources and likewise relate to two dissimilar concepts:

- On one hand, many countries are reporting the number of outbound trips of their residents. Data availability and comparability, however, is still limited and it is often not clear whether the reported figures refer only to tourists or to visitors in general.
- On the other hand, data are synthesised from the data on inbound tourism to destination countries (an arrival received in a destination can also be taken as an arrival generated by the generating country). Data on arrivals to destinations broken down by region of origin are taken to estimate and aggregate the number of arrivals originating from each region. The unit of measurement is the number of international tourist arrivals generated by the region of origin concerned. For a proper understanding, it should be borne in mind that these figures do not correspond to the number of trips, as one trip taken might result in various arrivals in destinations.

Domestic Tourism
International comparable data on domestic tourism is unfortunately still rather scarce. If available for a certain country, this series is represented in the profile tables for countries in Chapter III of the regional volumes in the form of the number of nights spent by residents at hotels and similar establishments and / or at all collective tourism establishments.

Accommodation
As a measure for the capacity of accommodation, data is included on the number of rooms or the number of bed places in the country. When expressed in bed places, the number of rooms roughly will be half, as rooms on average count two bed places. The actual capacity of a country might eventually be larger, as some countries exclude hotels below a certain category or less than a certain size.

International Tourism Receipts and Expenditure
International Tourism Receipts are the receipts earned by a destination country from inbound tourism and cover all tourism receipts resulting from expenditure made by visitors from abroad, on for instance lodging, food and drinks, fuel, transport in the country, entertainment, shopping, etc. This concept includes receipts generated by overnight as well as by same-day trips, which can be substantial, as will be the case with countries where a lot of shopping for goods and services takes place by visitors from neighbouring countries. It

excludes, however, the receipts related to international transport contracted by residents of other countries (for instance ticket receipts from foreigners travelling with a national company). These receipts are covered in the separate category **International Fare Receipts**, which for most recent years is estimated at about 15-20% of total tourism and fare receipts.

International Tourism Expenditure is the expenditure on tourism outside their country of residence made by visitors (same-day visitors and tourists) from a given country of origin.

Data on receipts and expenditure related to international tourism are generally gathered in the framework of the Balance of Payments under the items 'Services, Travel, Credit and Debit' (International Tourism Receipts and Expenditure) and 'Transportation, Passenger Services, Credit and Debit' (International Fare Receipts and Expenditure). See the *Balance of Payments Statistics Yearbook, Part 2 and Part 3* of the International Monetary Fund (IMF) for details on methodologies, compilation practices and data sources.

The International Tourism Balance and International Fare Balance as included in the profile tables in Chapter III of the regional volumes correspond to the net receipts or expenditure of a given country on respectively international tourism or international fares, i.e. receipts less expenditure.

Further information
More detailed information on concepts, definitions, classifications, indicators, methods of compiling and units of measure can be obtained from:
- the *Basic References on Tourism Statistics* on the UNWTO website under the link <http://www.unwto.org/statistics/index.htm> setting out the main components that make up the System of Tourism Statistics (STS);

or from the following UNWTO publications:
- *Recommendations on tourism statistics* (1994),
- *Technical Manual No. 1: Concepts Definitions, and Classifications for Tourism Statistics* (1995);
- *Technical Manual No. 2: Collection for Tourism Expenditure Statistics* (1995);
- *Technical Manual No. 3: Collection of Domestic Tourism Statistics* (1995);
- *Technical Manual No. 4: Collection and Compilation of Tourism Statistics* (1995);
- *Data Collection & Analysis for Tourism Management, Marketing & Planning* (2000).

3.2   Sources, Data Treatment and Acknowledgement

General
Quantitative tourism-related data in this report is based on a selection of data included in the UNWTO database on World Tourism Statistics. This database contains a variety of series for over 200 countries and territories covering data for most countries from the 1980's on. The database is maintained by the UNWTO Secretariat and is updated on a continuous base.

Except where otherwise indicated, statistical data has been collected by the UNWTO Secretariat from the official institutions of the countries and territories (UNWTO member as well as non-member countries) or from other international bodies, e.g. the Caribbean Tourism Organization (CTO), the International Monetary Fund (IMF), etc.

The data for individual countries corresponding to 2005 are based on full year results, or projections, as communicated to the UNWTO Secretariat by the authorities of the countries and territories or disseminated through news releases, publications or on the Internet. For many countries, 2005 figures are still preliminary and subject to revision.

In the world and (sub)regional aggregates, estimates are included for countries and territories with data still missing based upon data available for a part of the year or the general trend for the region. In particular for the Middle East and Africa, the regional and subregional aggregates should be treated with caution as estimations are based on a relatively small number of countries and territories that supplied data for the entire year. In the tables, provisional figures are marked with an asterisk (*).

UNWTO tourism statistics generally refer to figures for a country as a whole. In the collection of statistics, however, except for independent states, there are also a number of dependencies or territories of special sovereignty included (for instance Hong Kong (China) or French Polynesia). These territories report tourism figures independently and are for the sake of tourism statistics considered as an entity in itself. Because of this, where reference is made to "countries" the term generally should be taken to mean "countries and territories". In a few other cases, dependencies are not separately listed but included in the total for the country they depend upon (for instance Guernsey, Jersey and the Isle of Man in United Kingdom).

In general, UNWTO does not collect data on the level of regions, states, provinces or specific destinations within a country (Hawaii is one of the few exceptions made because of its relevance for Asian outbound travel; in the overview tables, however, Hawaii is included in the United States figure). Most countries will have a further regional breakdown available as well as other series not included in the UNWTO database on World Tourism Statistics. Please refer to national sources for this data.

The regional country groupings are according to the UNWTO regional commissions. See the tables by country in the annex for the countries and territories included in the various regions and subregions.

The World Tourism Organization is aware of the limitations of the available statistical information on tourism. Despite the considerable progress made in recent decades, international tourism statistics are often not uniform, because definitions and methods of data collection tend to differ. Every user of this information should bear in mind that the international comparability of statistical data is still not optimal.

Tourism series in this report

The tourism data series in Chapter II and in the profile tables of countries in Chapter III correspond to the basic indicators included in the UNWTO *Compendium of Tourism Statistics*. Please refer to the latest publication for additional series, methodological references and notes on the series for specific countries.

A number of derived series are included relating tourism volume to the size of the population or tourism receipts and expenditure to tourism volume. In the profile tables in Chapter III, those series are marked with '-'. Ratios are based on simple divisions of the concept in question by the population or of the receipts or expenditure by the corresponding concepts:

$$\text{International Tourist Arrivals per 100 of inhabitants} = \frac{\text{International Tourist Arrivals}}{\text{Population}} * 100$$

$$\text{Trips abroad per 100 of inhabitants} = \frac{\text{Trips abroad}}{\text{Population}} * 100$$

$$\text{International Tourism Receipts per International Tourist Arrival} = \frac{\text{International Tourism Receipts}}{\text{International Tourist Arrivals}}$$

$$\text{International Tourism Receipts per International Visitor Arrival} = \frac{\text{International Tourism Receipts}}{\text{International Visitor Arrivals}}$$

$$\text{International Tourism Receipts per capita} = \frac{\text{International Tourism Receipts}}{\text{Population}}$$

$$\text{International Tourism Expenditure per trip abroad} = \frac{\text{International Tourism Expenditure}}{\text{Trips Abroad}}$$

$$\text{International Tourism Expenditure per capita} = \frac{\text{International Tourism Expenditure}}{\text{Population}}$$

Financial data is generally collected and kept in the UNWTO database in US dollars. In the cases where countries report in local currency, values are transferred by UNWTO into US dollars applying the average exchange rate for the corresponding year. However, part of the tables are also published in euros. These euro values are in general derived from the US dollar values using the corresponding average annual exchange rates for the two currencies. The following exchange rates have been applied:

Exchange rates US$ versus euro (ECU for the years before 1999) annual averages

	€/ECU per US$	Change (%)	US$ per €/ECU	Change (%)
1995	0.76452		1.30801	
1996	0.78756	3.0	1.26975	-2.9
1997	0.88180	12.0	1.13404	-10.7
1998	0.89199	1.2	1.12109	-1.1
1999	0.93828	5.2	1.06578	-4.9
2000	1.08270	15.4	0.92361	-13.3
2001	1.11653	3.1	0.89563	-3.0
2002	1.05756	-5.3	0.94557	5.6
2003	0.88402	-16.4	1.13120	19.6
2004	0.80392	-9.1	1.24390	10.0
2005	0.80379	0.0	1.24410	0.0

Source: Eurostat, European Central Bank (ECB)

As exchange rates fluctuate substantially over time, the evolution of International Tourism Receipts is estimated in (weighted) local currencies. For this, receipts in US dollars are recomputed in local currencies using an exchange rate table provided by IMF. In order to take care of inflation, receipts are calculated in constant prices using country data on inflation from IMF as deflator.

The data in the tables on international tourist or visitor arrivals and nights of international tourists by country of origin included in Chapter III correspond to the series as included in the UNWTO *Yearbook of Tourism Statistics*. Please refer to the latter publication for additional series, metrological references and notes on the series for specific countries.

Series from external sources

Information included, but not referring to tourism indicators, are in general taken from specialised international organizations and not collected by the UNWTO Secretariat from the individual countries and territories. Data are meant as indicators, providing a context for tourism performance and do not necessarily coincide fully with national data. The following series are included:

Population

Data refer to total midyear population as included in the International Database (IDB) of the International Programs Center (IPC) of the Population Division of the U.S. Bureau of the Census, <www.census.gov/ipc/www>. The IDB combines data from country sources (especially censuses and surveys) with IPC's estimates and projections to provide information dating back as far as 1950 and as far ahead as 2050. The IDB can be considered as a practically complete and consistent set of population data covering 227 countries and areas with 1998 populations of 5,000 or more.

Area

Data on the dimension of the area of countries and territories are taken from the Statistical database of the Food and Agriculture Organization of the United Nations (FAO) <www.fao.org> and refer to the total area of the country, including area under inland water bodies for the year 2000. In the case of Belgium and Luxembourg data is taken from national sources.

Economic Indicators

The series on Gross Domestic Product (GDP), Gross Domestic Product per capita and economic growth (annual per cent change of Real Gross Domestic Product) are based on the World Economic Outlook (WEO) of the International Monetary Fund (IMF). See <www.imf.org/external/pubs/ft/weo/weorepts.htm>.

4. Sources of Information

A. *UNWTO website <www.unwto.org>*

The UNWTO has a comprehensive website available with news and information on its programme activities, members, regional activities, publications, special projects, etc. in English, French and Spanish with a growing section in Russian, including:.

– A qualitative and quantitative overview of world tourism and selected statistical country data, available under the *Facts & Figures* link (see Tourism Indicators), including the most updated tourism trends and data in the *UNWTO World Tourism Barometer;*

– An overview of available publications and electronic products with detailed information on each item including contents and sample chapters can be found in the UNWTO Infoshop at <http://pub.unwto.org> or the WTOelibrary at <www.WTOelibrary.org>.

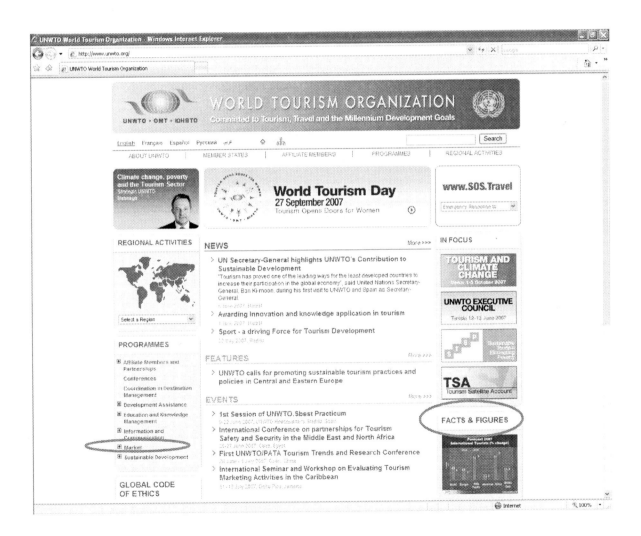

B. Related Publications of the World Tourism Organization

Inbound Tourism

This report is part of the *Tourism Market Trends, 2006 Edition* series consisting of 6 volumes:
- World Overview and Tourism Topics (in English, French and Spanish);
- Africa (in English and French);
- Americas (in English and Spanish);
- Asia and the Pacific (in English);
- Europe (in English and French);
- Middle East (in English).

Excerpts of this series are included in:
- *Tourism Highlights, 2006 Edition* (in English, French, Spanish and Russian). The electronic version can be downloaded free of charge from the Facts & Figures section of the UNWTO website at <http://www.unwto.org/facts/menu.html>.

- *Special report No 23:* Inbound Tourism to the Middle East and North Africa (2003; in English).

Outbound Tourism

- *Tourism Generating Markets: Overview and Country Profiles* (1999; in English, French and Spanish).
- Special Reports on specific markets:
    - No. 4: *Outbound Tourism of Korea* (2001; in English).
    - No. 5: *Outbound Tourism of Australia* (2001; in English).
    - No. 6: *Outbound Tourism of Japan* (2001; in English).
    - No. 7: *Outbound Tourism of Belgium* (2001; in English).
    - No. 8: *Outbound Tourism of Spain* (2001; in English and Spanish).
    - No. 9: *Outbound Tourism of Japan & Korea, Results 2000* (2001; in English).
    - No. 21: *Outbound Tourism of Scandinavia, Market Profile* (2002; in English).
- *Youth Outbound Travel of the Germans, the British & the French* (2002, in English, French and Spanish).
- *Chinese Outbound Tourism* (2003; in English).
- *Outbound Tourism from Saudi Arabia* (2003; in English).

Short-term Indicators

- *UNWTO World Tourism Barometer* (3 times a year since June 2003; in electronic format (PDF) and print, in English, French and Spanish).

The *UNWTO World Tourism Barometer* monitors the short-term evolution of tourism and aims at providing adequate and timely information on the state of the sector. The Barometer is published three times a year (January, June, and October). It contains an overview of short-term tourism data from destination countries and tourism sectors such as air transport, a retrospective and prospective evaluation of tourism performance by the UNWTO Panel of Tourism Experts and selected economic data relevant for tourism.

For more information see the "Facts & Figures" section of the UNWTO website www.unwto.org.

World Tourism Organization ©

Forecasting

UNWTO's long-term forecast *Tourism 2020 Vision* has been published in a series of 7 reports consisting of one summary volume and six regional volumes (2000, 2001):

- Global Forecasts and Profiles of Market Segments (in English, French and Spanish).
- Africa (in English and French).
- Americas (in English and Spanish).
- East Asia and the Pacific (in English).
- Europe (in English and French).
- Middle East (in English).
- South Asia (in English).

Tourism Products

- Tourism and Sport:
  - *Sport and Tourism. 1st World Conference* (in English, French and Spanish; forthcoming). Excerpts of the presentations and of the results of the World Conference on Sport and Tourism held February 2001 in Barcelona, Spain.
  - *Introductory Report on Sport & Tourism* (2001).
  - *Sport Activities during the outbound holidays of the Germans, the Dutch and the French* (2001, in English, French and Spanish).
  - *Deporte Y Turismo: Destino América Latina* (2003; in Spanish only).
- Ecotourism:
  - *Special report No. 10: The German Ecotourism Market* (2001).
  - *Special report No. 11: The British Ecotourism Market* (2001).
  - *Special report No. 12: The U.S. Ecotourism Market* (2002).
  - *Special report No. 13: The Italian Ecotourism Market* (2002).
  - *Special report No. 14: The Spanish Ecotourism Market* (2002).
  - *Special report No. 15: The Canadian Ecotourism Market* (2002).
  - *Special report No. 16: The French Ecotourism Market* (2002).
- MICE:
  - *MICE Outbound Tourism 2000* (2003;in English).
- Cruises:
  - *Worldwide Cruise Ship Activity* (2003; in English, French and Spanish).
- Cultural Tourism:
  - *City Tourism and Culture: The European Experience (*2005; in English, French and Spanish).

UNWTO Tourism Recovery Committee

- Special report No. 17: *The impact of the attacks in the United States on international tourism: An initial analysis* (included in the Annex of Special report No. 18, not available separately).
- Special report No. 18: *Tourism after 11 September 2001: Analysis, remedial actions and prospects* (2001; in English, French and Spanish).
- Special report No. 19: *Tourism Recovery Committee for the Mediterranean Region* (2002; in English, French and Spanish).
- Special report No. 20: *The impact of the September 11th attacks on tourism: The light at the end of the tunnel* (2002; in English, French and Spanish).
- Special report No. 21: *2002: Climbing Towards Recovery?* (2002; in English).
- Special report No. 22: *Fourth Meeting of the Tourism Recovery Committee - ITB Berlin 2003* (2003; in English).

Basic Statistical Reference

- *Compendium of Tourism Statistics* (2005; tri-lingual edition in English, French and Spanish and table descriptions in Arabic and Russian).
- *Yearbook of Tourism Statistics* (2005; tri-lingual edition in English, French and Spanish).

Statistical Methodology

- *Recommendations on Tourism Statistics* (1994; in English, French, Spanish, Russian, Arabic and Chinese).
- *Technical Manuals* (1995; in English, French, Spanish and Russian):
  - *No. 1: Concepts, Definitions and Classifications for Tourism Statistics.*
  - *No. 2: Collection of Tourism Expenditure Statistics.*
  - *No. 3: Collection of Domestic Tourism Statistics.*
  - *No. 4: Collection and Compilation of Tourism Statistics.*
- *Data Collection and Analysis for Tourism Management, Marketing and Planning* (2000; in English).

See for detailed information on concepts, definitions, classifications, indicators, methods of compiling and units of measure also the *Basic References on Tourism Statistics*, setting out the main components that make up the System of Tourism Statistics (STS), on the UNWTO website at: <http://www.unwto.org/statistics/index.htm>.

See for documentation on the Tourism Satellite Account methodology the UNWTO website at: <http://www.unwto.org/statistics/index.htm>.

Other

- *Tourism in the Age of Alliances, Mergers and Acquisitions* (2002, in English, French and Spanish).
- *Apuntes de la Metodología de la Investigación en Turismo* (2001, in Spanish only).
- *Marketing Papers No.1* (2002).
- *Evaluating NTO Marketing Activities* (2003; in English, French and Spanish).
- Special report No 26 - *The impact of rising oil prices on International Tourism* (2006; in English, French and Spanish).
- Structures and Budgets of National Tourism Organizations, 2004-2005 (2006; in English and Spanish)
- Handbook on Tourism Market Segmentation – Maximizing Marketing Effectiveness (2007, in English)

C.   References

International Organizations

- United Nations; <www.un.org>.
- United Nations Development Programme; <www.undp.org>.
- International Monetary Fund (IMF); <www.imf.org>.
- World Bank; <www.worldbank.org>.
- Organisation for Economic Cooperation and Development (OECD); <www.oecd.org>.
- World Trade Organization (WTO); <www.wto.org>.

Country Sources

References for information on the Internet of National Tourism Administrations (NTA), National Tourism Organisations (NTO) and / or web directions for research and data are included in the country contributions of Chapter III of the regional volumes of the *Tourism Market Trends, 2006* series.